Twayne's United States Authors Series

Sylvia E. Bowman, *Editor*

INDIANA UNIVERSITY

Henry Miller

HENRY MILLER

by **KINGSLEY WIDMER**

TUSAS 44

Twayne Publishers, Inc.   ::   New York

FOR THOSE IMPASSIONED FRIENDS,

PAST AND PRESENT

WHO WRYLY AND REBELLIOUSLY ARGUED

THROUGH MANY A DARK NIGHT.

Preface

THE TRUTH ABOUT Henry Miller is that he is neither "the greatest living author" and a "unique saint" nor the "foulest writer of meaningless nonsense" and a "madman." Between cops and cultists it is sometimes difficult to see the who and what. Miller, I shall argue, is a minor but intriguing writer whose best works are the rhetorical gestures of a rebel-buffoon. We must, of course, also recognize him as a significant American oddity and as a symptomatic figure of his time and place.

Miller's self-obsessed, fragmentary, and wandering prose runs to several million words. Discrimination—which is rarely applied to this chaos because Miller and his devotees oppose it and because his moralist and formalist denigrators lack responsiveness—seems worth attempting. A critic who refuses to play the roles of either moral magistrate or bumptious virgin in American culture always has a good bit of cutting to do. Not only must the sheep be separated from the goats, but considerable shearing must be done to get at the meat. Miller, fortunately, is also not fit literary flesh for bland methodologies or for genteel appreciation.

While it is my pleasure to practice criticism *as criticism*, I have no ideological or moral axe to sharpen on Miller's bald literary head. I am generally sympathetic to his libertarian views (pacifism, anarchism, extreme individualism), properly amused by his obscenity and wildness, and agreeably angry about America and much else; I have, therefore, no private battle to carry on over those. No doubt I lack full sympathy with his occultism and his cultish notions of the artist, as well as with his considerable bad writing and silly thinking, but I try to give them their due. Since I have defended Miller in public action and in the pass media against censorship, that dominant issue will be touched on only in passing. My purpose, then, is to put a responsive but sharp knife to Miller's conglomerate writings: to cut away the fat and to probe some of the major themes, meanings and qualities which give Miller significance for our literature and sensibility.

This study, so far as I know, is the first reasonably thorough one of Miller's published writings. (It would also seem to be one of the few extensive discussions by someone who does not know Miller personally.) The examination is biographical only to the small degree that biography seemed essential for an understanding of the literature. I have generally confined myself to the published material and have attempted to be reasonably thorough in going through the writings about Miller as well as through the books he has read. It has sometimes been too lengthy to cite all the sources for my generalizations, but this is not meant to excuse matters which are clearly opinion and interpretation. Another cautionary point: it is unavoidable in discussing Miller's work to call the central figure Henry Miller, as does Henry Miller, though this is not a claim that the experiences are literal fact. At some points, moreover, I have indicated that in all probability Miller's writings, about Miller are not true, in several senses.

A coherent commentary on the endlessly seamed fabric of Miller's multi-volumed confession-essay-letter poses difficult problems of organization. I have settled on a separate chapter for *Tropic of Cancer*, "The Apocalyptic Comedian," leavening the analysis of his first and major book with some background. The second chapter, "The American Abroad," carries the motifs of the first chapter into most of Miller's other writings about Europe. (For reasons of theme and comparison, some writings of this period have been discussed later and out of chronological order.) The third chapter, "The Brooklyn Passion," deals only with some of the more important representative motifs of the "autobiographical romances," from *Tropic of Capricorn* through *Nexus*. The fourth chapter, "The Outsider at Home" focuses on Miller's writings about America. The final chapter, "The Rebel-Buffoon," discusses some examples of Miller's views on literature, religion, and morals; it concludes with some suggested evaluations, a few comments on Miller's place in the American literary scene, and a broad interpretation. (The notes contain comments on some works not discussed in the body of the study.) Other matters are touched upon lightly or not at all: much more could well be said about Miller and surrealism; Miller's paintings are not discussed; many biographical problems have been ignored, including the "Miller circle" (Lawrence Durrell and others); and, of course, there is no space for most of the relevant history of our weird times.

Acknowledgments

This study is indebted to a number of past friends, all-American rebel-buffoons. They showed me how essential, amusing, and poignant a part of the American scene the Millerian gestures are. Several devoted students of Miller have been helpful with bibliography: Thomas Moore and Bern Porter. I was materially aided in obtaining a number of Miller items by the San Diego State College Foundation. George Wickes of Harvey Mudd College has generously provided me with copies of the Miller material he has been working on. The editor, Sylvia E. Bowman, has shown much patience and good will. More generally, for encouragement to think, teach, and write in my own way, I am indebted to several teachers (especially E. E. Bostetter), to an occasional rare colleague, to a scattering of wise-eccentric students, and to a few friends (especially Ken Moritz). One writer and longtime reader and defender of Henry Miller, Dr. Eleanor Widmer, has provided criticism, insight, and impassioned response —from which I sometimes perversely failed to profit—as well as that quality most praised by Miller: wisdom of the heart.

The following have kindly granted permission to quote from the works of Henry Miller:

Grove Press: *Tropic of Cancer*, Copyright © 1961 by Grove Press, Inc.; *Tropic of Capricorn*, Copyright © 1961 by Grove Press, Inc.; *Black Spring*, Copyright © 1963 by Grove Press.

New Directions: *The Wisdom of the Heart*, copyright 1941 by New Directions; *The Cosmological Eye*, copyright 1939 by New Directions; *The Colossus of Maroussi*, copyright 1941 by Henry Miller; *The Books in My Life*, all rights reserved; *The Air-Conditioned Nightmare*, copyright 1945 by New Directions; *Remember to Remember*, copyright 1947 by New Directions; *Sunday After the War*, copyright 1944 by Henry Miller; *The Time of the Assassins*, © 1956 by New Directions; *Stand Still Like the Hummingbird*, © 1962 by Henry Miller; *Big Sur and the Oranges of Hieronymous Bosch*, © 1957 by New Directions.

KINGSLEY WIDMER

La Jolla, California

Contents

Chronology

1891   Henry Valentine Miller born December 26 in New York City, the only son of a lower-middle-class German-American family. Father was a tailor, apparently genial, not very successful, and weak-charactered. Mother appears to have been extremely conventional, tidy, cold, and the source of considerable conflict with son.

1892   Family moved to Williamsburg section of Brooklyn.

1901   Family moved to Bushwick section of Brooklyn. Nostalgic descriptions of Brooklyn and boyhood friends appear in many of his works.

1905- Attended Eastern District High School in Brooklyn.
1909   Studied piano and read indiscriminately and widely. Formal education ended voluntarily after two months at City College of New York.

1910- Employed in clerical jobs. Traveled to West Coast and
1913   worked at odd jobs in southern California for a few months.

1914- Back in New York. Worked in father's tailor shop, then
1916   at a variety of menial jobs.

1917   Married Beatrice Wickens; daughter born in 1919; employed in various clerical and similar unsatisfying jobs during following years.

1920- Several months as messenger for Western Union, then
1924   three years as messenger employment manager. Started writing.

1924   Divorced first wife and married the Mona/Mara prototype of his later "autobiographical romances" (June Smith or Mansfield). Devoted himself, unsuccessfully, to commercial writing.

1925- Aspiring writer; occasionally employed as door-to-door
1928   salesman, as a clerk, in own "speak-easy," and as beggar. Wrote unpublished stories and novel and started painting water colors.

1928- A year as tourist in Europe with wife on money provided
1929 by her friend.

1930- Without wife or income, returned to Europe, living
1932 marginal existence in Paris with occasional jobs as proofreader and hackwriter. Taught for several months in
Dijon. Wrote *Tropic of Cancer*.

1933 Lived in Clichy with Alfred Perlès. Wrote *Black Spring*.
Toured Luxembourg.

1934 Returned to New York at end of year, after publication
of *Tropic of Cancer* in Paris (book denied entry into the
United States).

1935 Returned to Paris. Divorced from second wife. Wrote
miscellaneous periodical pieces and correspondence with
Michael Fraenkel (until 1938) later published as *Hamlet*.

1936 In New York first part of year. *Black Spring* published
(Paris).

1937- Living in Paris, except for brief visits to London and
1938 southern France, on writing income. Edited and wrote
burlesques for *Booster* (later *Delta*), essays for *Volontès*,
and published collection as *Max and the White Phagocytes*. Large circle of literary friends.

1939 *Tropic of Capricorn* completed and published in Paris.
Republished miscellaneous pieces in his first American
book, *The Cosmological Eye*. August through December
toured Greece.

1940 Returned to New York in January. Spent summer in
Virginia. Wrote essays and book on travels in Greece,
The Colossus of Maroussi (1941). In October started a
year auto tour of the United States.

1942 Settled in Los Angeles and painted water colors and wrote
essays.

1944 Third marriage, to Janina Lepska, and settled in Big Sur,
California.

1945 Daughter Valentine born. Completed *Sexus* and *Air-
Conditioned Nightmare*.

1946- Big Sur. Second volume of American sketches, *Remember*

1947 *to Remember.* Essays on Rimbaud and Wasserman. Entertained many devotees during years at Big Sur.

1948 Son Tony born. Wrote parodies of fairy tales. Visit of astrologer-friend Moricand later written up as *A Devil in Paradise* (1956). Writing *Plexus.* Painting many water colors at Big Sur.

1949- Big Sur. Now receiving substantial income from writing.
1952 Divorced from third wife (1952). Wrote *The Books in My Life.*

1953 Half-year touring Europe. Married Eve McClure.

1954- Mostly in Big Sur. Wrote casual sketches and recol-
1957 lections on Big Sur and on Paris days. Mother died (1956).

1958- Big Sur. Made several trips to Europe. Wrote and pub-
1960 lished *Nexus.*

1961 Separated from fourth wife. Visited Europe. *Tropic of Cancer* first published in the United States—best-seller and subject of dozens of local censorship cases.

1962- Intermittently living in southern California; wealthy,
1963 active, traveling celebrity. First American edition of *Tropic of Capricorn,* first play (*Just Wild About Harry*), collection of reviews and sermonic pieces (*Stand Still Like the Hummingbird*), and wide distribution of most of his writings.

CHAPTER *1*

The Apocalyptic Comedian

I *Tropic of Cancer*[1]

O N THE FIRST PAGE of his first published book, Miller writes: "This is not a book. This is libel, slander, defamation of character. This is not a book in the ordinary sense of the word. No, this is a prolonged insult, a gob of spit in the face of Art, a kick in the pants to God, Man, Destiny, Time, Love, Beauty . . . what you will. I am going to sing for you, a little off-key perhaps, but I will sing. I will sing while you croak, I will dance over your dirty corpse . . ." (1-2).

And sing he does, usually with some vivacious mixture of hyperbolic romantic abstractions and of Brooklyn street-corner invective. As Miller rightly warns, this libel on literature and this ecstatic dirge for much of conventional civilization should not be approached as a book in the usual ways. An intentionally eccentric work—with its fusion of anecdotes, rhapsodies, caricatures, philosophizings, and burlesques—the not-book of *Tropic of Cancer* (1934) best reveals Miller's hilarious and distinctive, though sometimes weird and tedious, wayward wisdom. Miller's peculiar talent consists less in dramatizing and transforming reality than in making fantastic gestures. For this literary *shaman,* the wild *logos* creates defiance, identity, and ecstasy against the world's blandness and destructiveness.

But before turning to those central gestures of *Tropic of Cancer,* we need part of the autobiographical context which Miller draws upon but also obscures in the book.[2] Forty years old, bald, near-sighted, he had been down and out in Paris for more than a year in the depths of the Depression—"no money, no resources, no hopes" (1). For nearly a decade he had hungered to be a writer. For half a dozen years he had played the role of "artist," living a marginal and bohemian existence while unsuccessfully attempting to produce commercial short stories and writing away at several autobiographical novels. Mostly self-educated after his graduation from a Brooklyn high school, his reading had been wide, erratic, and significantly marked by a taste for the late-romantics, idiosyncratic philosophy, and American and European naturalism and expressionism. By both personal need and literary conditioning, he viewed art in exaltedly therapeutic and salvational terms. Thus, to be an artist meant to Miller a rebellious freedom from a petty past and from society, an entrance into a magical larger world which justified everything; above all, it meant the definition, expression, and regeneration of a failing and fractured self.

For the most part, Miller's personal life seems to have been as pathetically unsuccessful as his artistic ambitions. The first dozen years of his adult life consisted of a dreary succession of ordinary jobs, menial and clerical, while his longest and major employment (hiring messengers) had been, he later reported, frenzied and sickening. His first galling marriage ended in divorce and the abandonment of his child; his second marriage to a passionately devoted but quite peculiar woman (by his accounts), who supported him and encouraged his faltering efforts as a writer, also disintegrated. By the end of the 1920's—after a visit to Europe had increased his sense of alienation from an America which he identified with his frustrations, and after his second marriage, his friends, his finances, and his literary ambitions had reached a low point—he desperately fled to a marginal existence in the capital of the overripe dreams of his youth: Paris.

The partly autobiographical *Tropic of Cancer* comes out of a bit more than a year of his Parisian experiences (1930-31), but its rage and longing emphatically derive from the failures of the previous decade of his life, failures which are implicit but never made quite clear in the book. An essential part of *Tropic of Cancer* may be viewed as the saga of an aging American failure who boot-straps himself into artistic success by writing *Tropic of Cancer*. While the book depicts scenes of defeat, desperation, and misery, the almost simultaneous writing about those experiences constitutes, for Miller, a joyous achievement. His way down becomes his way up, and we approach one of the pervasive oddities of all Miller's work—his fantastic ambivalences about suffering which allow him to reverse most usual senses of proportion and feeling.

Miller's failures as a man and as a writer were certainly extensive and genuine, though quite common, as were his alienation from America and himself. And his early circumstances in Paris, as the book shows, were certainly miserable enough; for much of his time was dominated by destitution and the anxieties of conniving for money or food and a place to sleep. However, Miller also simultaneously felt the exhilaration of the American outcast and the intense responses of a holiday among the ruins for the innocent abroad. It was by choice that he was severed from America, family, conventions, responsibilities, future, certitudes; he had, inside and out, the *luftmënsch* intoxication of the renegade from a restricted past. His chaos, aided by exotic newness, became positive. At the Parisian end of Whitman's Open Road, life was minimal and immediate; therefore, it was intensely itself and wide open for barbaric yawps.

Miller also carried some special talents into this chaos: a native appetite and zest; a rebellious improvidence about conventional amenities; an accomplished unscrupulousness and ability to beg, borrow, and steal; a loquacious personal charm which had always provided a circle of responsive, indulgent male companions; and a magical belief in himself as having the destiny of an artist and sage. He also had good American health: "When I say 'health,' I mean optimism, to be truthful. Incurably optimistic! Still have one foot in the 19th century. I'm a bit retarded, like most Americans" (45). Thus, again, the blows of suffering emphatically reverse on Miller, and he can carry out the major gestures of *Tropic of Cancer*, which consist of artfully inverting failure, misery, and the sense of a doomed civilization into individual ecstasy. More simply, he was prepared to give an exuberantly uninhibited report of a literary man's underground life.

Because Miller went to Paris in 1930, following the much publicized expatriation of the previous decade, *Cancer* has too often been viewed merely as posthumous literary Americana of the 1920's.[3] Also, while some of the book's scenes and characters can be translated out of their hyperbole and "slander" into documentary material on marginal bohemian life in Paris in the 1930's, such works as George Orwell's *Down and Out in Paris and London* or Eliot Paul's *The Last Time I Saw Paris* provide more useful social docmentation without Miller's prose peculiarities and gestures.[4] Deeper patterns than social-moralist reporting and expatriate celebration can be recognized in this compatriot of Emerson and Whitman.[5] As a twentieth-century urban Thoreau, Miller takes the stance of answering, in similar metaphoric, wry, and iconoclastic terms, the problem of where and how the poet is to live; and he, too, is fully prepared to publish to the world the meanness of life, if such he finds. Miller's enchantment with the forest of European culture, and his detailed (and sometimes overelaborated) fascination with the flora and fauna of the Parisian streets, belong to our main literary tradition of the American individualist, as does the loose form of his autobiography-essay-poem about a year's self-discovery. The sex, the incongruities, the miseries, and the grotesquerie were just the weather on the twentieth-century side of Walden Pond. The many and fundamental parallels between the curious books of the two American Henrys—libertarian egotists declaiming in elaborate prose their defiant quests for individualistic regeneration—should not be obscured by the historical change of scene from rural Puritanism to megalopolitan amoralism, nor by the equally prevalent switch of nature metaphors from forest to phallus.

Tropic of Cancer consists of fifteen loosely connected, unnumbered and untitled, anecdotal chapters. What unity the book has must be discovered mostly in its metaphors. Its shape is that of a merging flow of description, fantasy, and rumination which emphasizes, at any cost, the subjectivity of the narrating author. Acceptance of the unprincipled flux of life remains dominant, from the Emersonian epigraph, which insists on the importance of autobiography, to the final scene of affirmation of the outcast's present.[6] In that final scene, for example, Miller watches the Seine flow by on a fine spring day. Having just decided not to go back to the frenzy represented by New York, he drinks a *demi* in "golden peace" and feels the organic flow of the river in him. He accepts his alienation, which has become his identity as the self-discovered outsider responding to the absurd flow of life. The endless run of Miller's garrulous prose confirms the theme.

Miller is given to long passages of philosophizing on metaphors—many of the anecdotes simply provide an incongruous scaffolding for these verbal pyrotechnics—which may be char-

acterized as *apocalyptic essays.* In one of the longest of these
pieces (220ff.) he quotes a fragment (apparently from James
Joyce): "I love everything that flows." He then catalogues:

> rivers, sewers, lava, semen, blood, bile, words . . . everything
> that flows, everything that has time in it and becoming, that
> brings us back to the beginning where there is never end: the
> violence of the prophets, the obscenity that is ecstasy, . . .
> all that is fluid, melting, dissolute, dissolvent, . . . that makes
> the great circuit towards death and dissolution (232).

These metaphors of "flow" pervade the book. For Miller, this
process philosophy provides the fundamental antithesis to the
authoritarian, abstract, mechanical, and anti-human rigidities
of the modern world.

In this apocalyptic essay Miller starts, as he often does,
with the grossly specific—with certain physiological details
of a prostitute—which he turns into elaborate poetic prose.
By such rhetorical antithesis he attempts to fuse the sub-
lime and the grotesque. His "bloody shout of joy" requires
that mean physical fact shall turn into rich metaphysical possibility. (This extreme gesture, which is an attempt to unite the
disparities of experience, is often a literary mannerism—"the
bloated *pages* of ecstasy slimed with excrement" [229, my
italics].) His cosmic rebellion insists that all existing values
must be overthrown so that "out of nothingness rises the sign
of infinity" (227), and out of a neo-Nietzschean destructive
process, value arises *ex nihilo* and subsists entirely in responsiveness to the incongruous flux of reality: "Do anything, but
let it produce joy" (227). Or, in Miller's characteristic philosophical style, those alive to the flux of life demand a "world
that produces ecstasy and not dry farts" (231).

Now living at the bottom of society, Miller exploits the
literary possibilities of what is down under—including the
gynecological and excremental details. Rebellion against decorous convention, American male iconoclasm about the obscured
crudity of life, esthetic and moral enlargement of literary style
and subject (via Joyce and Lawrence), and considerable
bravado and whimsicality—these provide much of the ground
for Miller's famous "obscenity." When the narrator lavishly
and wryly describes scenes of disgust, as in his visit to an

impoverished Russian emigré to mooch a meal, the vermin, the filth, the odors, and a detailed view of the excrement sump soon put him to flight.[7] From the handling of such scenes, as well as from other sources, it seems clear that Miller, contrary to popular misunderstanding, is essentially fastidious. Thus, indeed, he shows an obsessive concern—like the compulsive cleanliness of his mother that he describes elsewhere— with mess and muck, to which his shouting, flight, and disgust are exaggerated responses.[8]

More important than the scenes of wryly "naturalistic" reporting with their inverted obsession are Miller's *excremental visions.* Two major burlesque anecdotes, one early and one late in the narrative, will indicate how Miller turns the mucky flux into a metaphysical flux in an ebullient defiance which provides much of the shape of *Tropic of Cancer.* In the first, according to his account, he served for a short period in Paris as the servant to a Hindu pearl merchant, Nanatatee, whom Miller had heard boast in New York of his fine life in Paris. Now Miller, always righteous about hypocrisy, finds the dirt behind the rhetoric as he does errands, cleans the toilet, and plays sycophant in the shabby room of the penurious, crippled Hindu. An indication of Miller's private feelings, rather than those of his semi-fictionalized picaresque self-hero, comes in his aside, "I'll have a great laugh over it when I am out of his clutches, but just now I'm . . . an untouchable . . ." (73). The portrait of Nanatatee achieves the amusing nasty-grotesque in catching his mixed piety and obscenity, mannerliness and meanness— the tea with the rose leaf and the smugly emitted flatus.

Such incongruities, both for their own and for his art's sake, provide the essence of Miller's style and revelation. Equally characteristic is his indifference to his ostensible subject: the collector of pearls and of moldy bread quickly disappears from the account to be replaced briefly by several other hastily sketched figures who then disappear in a long apocalyptic essay.

Miller has been hired to guide a young follower of Ghandi through Parisian night life. The hypocritically "gay disciple" soon reveals himself as naïvely pompous and vain, decked out with "a beret, a cane, a Windsor tie . . . two fountain pens, a kodak . . . some fancy underwear" (83), and with childishly self-righteous opinions. To Miller's iconoclastic eye, the would-be saint shows less fraudulence in his simple-minded lust and avarice than in his mixture of Ghandianism and "the cheap idealism of the Americans"—his Y. M. C. A. moral blather of "a contaminated saint who talks in one breath of love, brotherhood, bath-tubs, sanitation, efficiency, etc." (86). Miller briefly gives two comic episodes of visits to whorehouses with the Ghandian. In the first there is a rather sniggeringly presented comic uproar because the religious devotee shocks the Madame and the girls by defecating in the *bidet*. For the second visit, the Ghandian demands a cheaper place where he can afford a covey of prostitutes. While he dances with a fat-creased naked blonde, Miller drops the episode and the character for an apocalyptic essay on the excremental vision.

In doing this, Miller displays his peculiar and recurrent method of achieving a self-delighting reverie. By withdrawing in mind from the immediate scene while yet physically partaking of it, he reaches an "epileptic" clarity of dissociation in which memory and reverie so obliterate present time that he has a feeling of "hair-trigger eternity" in which "everything was justified, supremely justified" (88). In prose re-creation this quasi-religious state, a kind of self-induced hypnosis which Miller repeatedly searches for, comes out as a swirling rhetoric around an incongruously elaborated image. Miller rages, once again, about the disparity between gross physical fact and man's ideal aspirations—roses in the dung, cockroach priests and phantom hosts, and bilious ideas obscuring the horrendous truth:

> And so I think what a miracle it would be if this miracle which man attends eternally should turn out to be nothing more than these two enormous turds which the faithful disciple dropped in the bidet. What if at the last moment, when the banquet table is set and cymbals clash, there should appear suddenly . . . a silver platter on which even the blind could see that there is nothing more, and nothing less, than two enormous lumps of shit . . . (89).

A naturalistic narrative fact has been carried into an inverted metaphysical vision, a reverse miracle appealing to Miller's comic iconoclasm; he feels that he is the only man who "could imagine the possibility" (89). The excremental visionary displays the perceptive awareness, overlooked by pietists, that once one posits ideal realms anything at all is possible. He also displays the usual egotism of the violent prophet.

Miller draws a large moral from the excremental vision:

> Somehow the realization that nothing was to be hoped for had a salutary effect upon me. . . . all my life I had been looking forward to something happening, some extrinsic event that would alter my life, and now suddenly, inspired by the absolute hopelessness of everything, I felt relieved. . . . Walking down Montparnasse I decided to let myself drift with the tide, to make not the least resistance to fate, no matter in what form it presented itself. . . . nothing had been destroyed except my illusions. . . . I would hold on to nothing. . . . By what he calls the better part of his nature, man has been betrayed, that is all. At the extreme limits of his spiritual being man finds himself again naked as a savage. When he finds God . . . he is a skeleton. One must burrow into life again in order to put on flesh. . . . I have been trying to save my precious hide, trying to preserve the pieces of meat that hid my bones. I am done with that. I have reached the limits. . . . As far as history goes I am dead. If there is something beyond I shall have to bounce back. I have found God, but he is insufficient. I am only spiritually dead. Physically I am alive. Morally I am free. The world which I have departed is a menagerie. The dawn is breaking on a new world in which the lean spirits roam with sharp claws. If I am a hyena I am a lean and hungry one: I go forth to fatten myself (89-90).

The anti-miracle kills off illusions, history, morals, and all the false claims of purpose that obscure immediate reality. In this spiritual—rather than literal—primitivism, self-definition and exhilaration come from moving with the "tide" of life and from seeing horrendous and hilarious reality in absurd images. The excremental vision becomes comic nihilism; our ideas are so far from our realities that the free and alien spirits can rejoice in the refuse of our jungle life, and laughingly live.

Here, I believe, appears the most essential gesture of the early Miller; it is a powerful one, obscure only to those who live in a morally constipated universe. The form of the grotesque, multiple anecdote with its comic-apocalyptic ending also seems to be the essential art of Miller. In exuberantly inverted didacticism, he demands a personal revelation which turns the casual and the incongruous into self-conscious art and affirmation. Responsiveness is all.

But this amoral affirmation provides only one side of the excremental vision; a later episode shows that what was only imagined becomes the actual condition of life. Miller spent a few months in the winter as a tutor of English in a lycée in Dijon. The first part of this piece shows an apt, almost Dickensian, narrative flow about his room with the crooked stove pipe, the slimy nineteenth-century stone school, his puppet-like colleagues, and the dreary mustard capital in the winter. But Miller's art never stays long with narrative because of his obsessive concern with his own revelations and responses—most of which, in Dijon, are violent. The characteristic teacher is that "cipher who forms the nucleus of a respectable and lamentable citizenry" (246)—a trimmer in the vestibule of Hell. Humanistic ideology reveals "something obscene in this love of the past which ends in bread-lines and dug-outs," and so "every man with a bellyful of the classics is an enemy of the human race" (248). Teaching is "grinding grist for that paradise which is alway a wet dream"—for his own teaching he discusses the sex life of elephants because he is "a plenipotentiary from the realm of free spirits" (248, 252). The cafés of the orderly dead city (the music "as if old Euclid had . . . swallowed Prussic acid") and the whole of provincial bourgeois life epitomize northern Europe's bitter, white winter of Christianity with its icy moral geometry.[9] Miller's rage, often effectively turned by his style of overstatement and verbal playfulness, achieves its insights more by enlarged responses than by careful representation.

The capping response depends on the exacting gross imagery in which the bad food, dead spirits, and miserable winter "put the whole penitentiary into a state of constipation"; then the plumbing freezes, human dung accumulates and spreads, and fecal matter pervades the "whole stinking civilized world . . ." (256). For contrast, Miller develops an ornately sentimental description of the symbolic night watchman; his very drinking of wine is a pouring of rubies. This outcast and nobody, though Miller hardly knows him, stands for the human dimension, for hidden Mediterranean warmth, and for all the associated virtues of the heart smiling above the frozen order, restraint, and general spiritual muckiness.[10]

Miller seems defeated by the sordidness of the place, the futility of teaching, the loneliness of the displaced bohemian among the pedants, and even by a childish fear of the dark and the foreign. His exuberance falters; he recognizes "a fear of living separate, of staying born" (258). Though the message throughout *Cancer* turns on the acceptance, even embracement, of the flowing chaos of life, here the "constant flux" brings the shipwrecked sailor of the American voyage to "dead center, and there you slowly rot" (259). Unable to accept the flux in its ordinary round of misery or to continue shouting King of the Hill from the top of the quite unmiraculous pile of everyday excrement, Miller abruptly flees Dijon and goes back to Paris where he can play the artist as burlesque and apocalyptic confidence man.[11] The meaningless world can best be accepted in romantic and rebellious terms, as an artistic-religious vision, and not as the ordinary substance of life. Perhaps partly in spite of himself, Miller makes a striking confession in this episode which just precedes the final chapter of the book and which helps explain his culminating refusal to return to ordinary American life: the excremental absurdity of life demands that one have a rebellious role as the outsider abroad.

The book's title provides other reverberating metaphors. For Miller, to devise a title is almost an end in itself: "We're all dead, or dying, or about to die. We need good titles" (36).[12] Reflecting on Paris as seen in one of his many walks, he notes his attraction to the "leperous streets," to the malevolent spirit of place, and to the vision of the city as "a huge organism diseased in every part" (37). The recurrent images of cancer, syphilis, plague, decay, and corruption make Paris—the most symbolic megalopolis of modern culture—an encompassing malignancy reflecting the Spenglerian malaise of the Western world. The "tropic" of the title refers to apocalyptic geography—"the meridian that separates the hemispheres of life and death" (241)—and the meta-temporal weather which "will continue bad" because the "cancer of time is eating us away" (1).[13] Medicine? It is homeopathic. As one of Miller's women appropriately tells him, "You're cancer and delirium" (53). Disease and cure are one and the same; the therapy for the self-devouring civilization and self consists of cancerous gestures with apocalyptic heat.

It will not do, however, to overemphasize the book's unity since fragmentation is central to Miller's art. He aptly speaks of his responses as "schizophrenic"; his fractured sensibility provides many of his distinctive insights and properly reflects his twentieth-century world. Disparate conjunctions provide his affirmations, as, indeed, they do in most of the "modernist" styles of poetry and painting. If the discrete fragments, as in the first two chapters of *Tropic of Cancer,* seem beyond order, then the very disorder, by imitative form, gives the quality of his "anecdotal life." If his misery threatens to become meaningless, then meaninglessness becomes the one meaning—and both a subject matter and a point of view. If there seems to be no end to his suffering on Parisian streets, then suffering becomes an almost smug form of success. He plays with his fragmentation, writing in front of a cracked mirror, exalting in his contradictions and confusions, intensifying the schizophrenia by the disjunctions of surreal rhetoric. Powerless to change actuality, he can call it different names and elaborate personal chaos into cosmic proportions ("I want the whole world to be out of whack"). He purges the anomie from despair by a whimsical and mannered embracement. Such gestures provide, as Miller says of Van Gogh and similar artists, "the triumph of the individual over art" (10), which really means the desperate assertion of individual artfulness over a grim and messy reality.

In a role denuded of the usual pretenses at wholeness, Miller's hyperbolic acceptance includes a desperate voraciousness and a missionary braggadocio in "the recording of all that which is omitted in books" (10). Thus Miller's burlesque description of his longing for a friend's wife—"I will bite into your clitoris and spit out two franc pieces . . ."—fuses with the antithetically heightened description of the Paris spring, "indigo sky swept clear of fleecy clouds, gaunt trees . . . gesticulating like a sleep walker" (5). Experiences no longer fit together? Good, for they then become intensified and expressionistically overwhelming discrete moments. The romantic and anti-romantic become simultaneous states—"the splendour of those miserable days"—in which, in conjoined sentences, he is "going mad with the beauty" of the Seine and "getting an erection looking at the dumb statues in the park" (14). The Baudelaire-cum-Whitman atmosphere constantly reveals "misfortune, ennui, grief, suicide" which he yet finds "exhilarating." Because everything has gone

smash, Miller can only yearn for the heightening of what is—
"for more and more disasters, for bigger calamities, for grander
failures" (11)—as an affirmation of a perverse reality.

Miller's use of prostitutes throughout *Cancer* also illustrates
this leap.[14] A cheap and genial prostitute like Germaine, who
cannot possibly be related to love or passion—a "good heart"
but "without reference to any fixed point within" (41)—thus
comes to represent genuine being: "She was a whore all the way
through—and that was her virtue!" The affirmative alienation
goes even further, and Miller rhapsodizes over the saleable
part of Germaine's anatomy just because it becomes uniquely
dissociated from all other meaning: "she spoke of it as if it were
some extraneous object which she had acquired at great cost
. . . a magic, potent treasure . . ." (39); and Miller glories in
such self-alienation. While the sentimentality of the masculine
legend of the golden-hearted whore—it runs through much of
American folk mythology, as we can see in the "Western"—
may well have directed Miller's choice of subject and encouraged his entranced description, his literary strategy results
in heightening degradation as a perverse gesture for authenticity. The genuine prostitute provides a standard in a world
of ingenious prostitutes. Perhaps, too, the absence of love creates
a distinctively passionate assertion!

In a later, and low-keyed, episode (188ff.) Miller describes picking up a woman on the street who wheedles fifty
francs out of him by nothing more than a flattering sentimental
appeal. Later that night, a second prostitute mixes equal pathos
with too obvious lies and avarice for services rather hurriedly
rendered for a hundred francs. When she leaves the room (to
check on her sick mother, she says), Miller swipes the hundred
francs from her purse and flees. The fifty-franc sentimentality
for the first woman has been cathartically reversed to a hun-
dred-franc cynicism. Some readers, who apparently respond
with shock to Miller's lack of moral concern here, attempt to
explain away such behavior by reference to his marginal
circumstances, or to *epater lé bourgeoise,* or to the author's
immorality. While these characteristics may have some general
applicability to Miller, they lack specific relevance because they
quite miss the bemused amoralism in his presentation of the
perverse logic of the heart—especially of his own heart. While
Miller's cancerous world reveals no moral law, there is the

amoral rhythm of response, the alternating flow of sentimentality and cynicism, of acquiescence and revolt.[15]

Miller's affirmation of whatever *is* comes at the price of isolating his insights from additional responses and from efforts toward continuity and communion. Thus no matter what themes and metaphors shape the whole of *Tropic of Cancer*, its anecdotes and persons must remain discrete and the narrator's responses fragmentary. While it may not be surprising that the half-dozen prostitutes make isolated appearances, the same discontinuity applies to the other *personae* as well. The artists *manqué* who provide most of the figures in this ragged tapestry generally lack past, future, and depth. Boris, with whom Miller lives as the narrative opens, simply provides a silhouette target for a bit of mockery of labyrinthine Jewish intellectuals.[16] Moldorf appears only long enough to be the object of a surreal fantasy of dismemberment which illustrates Miller's savage contempt for ordinary familial *Weltschmerz*. Sylvester, apparently a dramatist and one of Miller's weekly meal patrons, receives only the burlesque invective imbedded in the narrating rogue's violent interior monologue against a husband who doesn't seem to understand "how a change of semen can make a woman [his wife] bloom" (54). Krueger, "sick saint" occultist painter, appears only long enough to illustrate Miller's sycophancy, comically ending with Miller's being thrown out.[17] Collins—genially gusty American sailor-adventurer, apparently drinking and whoring himself to death—may intrigue the reader, but Miller presents only the passing details of what he does for Miller. Marlowe, scholarly drunk and editor of the review which significantly first published Miller (as we know from outside sources), appears only in a few lugubrious strokes which show Miller's insouciant bohemian opportunism.[18] Borowski simply remains a disembodied name for a writer with insufficient mad obsession to be a true Millerian artist.

Several painters who demonstrate that art depends more on hatred than love, the caged teachers at Dijon, and a number of other figures, only exist as the locus for a hyperbolic metaphor or two. These fragmentary caricatures seem to be more a result of Miller's sensibility than of the actual-life prototypes on whom he had a continuous, though hostile, dependency. While the kaleidoscopic treatment of people in *Tropic of Cancer* provides some of the distinctive torrential whirl of the book, it also becomes a solipsism that often leaves the art—and the reader—awkwardly dangling. Miller's amoral quest for personal identity affirms the most fundamental and genuine alienation.

The mosaic opening chapter of *Cancer* gives scattered details and aphorisms about marginal life, culminating in an anecdote about a dark, passionate woman, Mona, who, from other sources, we know to be the narrator's image of his second wife.[19] Some scattered assertions suggest that she be understood as the Dark Goddess of the city of despair. Her image, midway in one of Miller's journeys through the infernal streets, suggests to him the Paris of Dante and Strindberg and the sojourn in the depths for "the tortured, the hallucinated, the maniacs of love" (163). But Miller quickly turns to apocalyptic essay—Paris as the all-too-human universal charnel house of failure, regret, and loneliness. Mona, as either presence or metaphor, fades away; for Miller only achieves maniacal love in a comic perspective, and no agon of the heart can dominate his chaotic city.

A more picaresque spirit than that of fumbled *femme fatale* controls the longer sections of the narrative. In one of his most intermittently sustained descriptions (91ff.), Miller presents Van Norden, a Millerian *alter ego* and grotesque with whom the author has a parasitic relationship (including some of the appropriate mixture of malicious observation and sly sycophancy). Along with Carl, another refugee, Van Norden is a would-be writer working on an American newspaper in Paris. I take the key to the Miller-Carl-Van Norden episodes to be in an early Miller aside: the three men call each other "Joe" because "it's easier that way. It is also a pleasant reminder not to take yourself too seriously" (93). The three male companions have taken on the anonymous identity of the "American Joe."[20] As with the archetypal Joe of American naturalistic fiction, the "good Joe" of American folk speech, and the pervasive later "GI Joe" of World War II, we have the typically innocent footloose boys on the town and out of the settled world; they curse, drink, whore, and gripe in that odd mixture of rebellion and accommodation that characterizes the netherworld of American maledom. It is the comic fraternal order, rather than forced images of romantic passion, which provides the appropriate tangible world for the all-American boy *in extremis,* Henry Miller.

In contrast to the surreal fantasies and the apocalyptic essays, Miller's handling of the picaresque episodes with his male companions shows an artful, if sometimes too lengthy, naturalistic reporting—a largely external and "deadpan" recording of monologues. The section centering around Van Norden probably contains the highest proportion of "four-letter words" in the book. To set off the weather, room, woman, book, job, idea, soul, and most major nouns, with the most commonly used of obscenities, points not to Miller's nasty mind but to his accurate ear. Such diction is standard style in many marginal and discontented social groups, including some quite literate ones. Then, too, punctuating with obscenity has long been a form of blasphemous decorum. More important, the high-low fusion of vulgar and intellectual language expresses the intimate relation of the obscene and the exalted. In some of his most obscene lines, Miller achieves a holistic poetry.

Ostensibly burdened with the usual American artistic ambitions (a novel which "tells all') and with metaphysical despair (everything is no f——ing good), Van Norden, the egotistical and neurasthenic newspaperman, can only pursue his two compulsions—complaining and seduction. This devotee of Goethe displays the petty Faustian sundering of knowledge and meaning. He has, with his solipsistic disillusionment, explored the female microcosm in quantity and even, quite literally, with a flashlight:

> "When you look at it [the pudendum] that way, sort of detached like, you get funny notions in your head. All that mystery about sex and then you discover that it's nothing—just a blank. Wouldn't it be funny if you found a harmonica inside . . . or a calendar? But there's nothing there. . . . It's disgusting. It almost drove me mad . . ." (126-27).

Miller, whose own verbal elaborations on the naked world show a similarity to this longing to find some mystery in the empty thing, commented earlier on Van Norden's Don Juan pathos:

> His one fear is to be left alone, and this fear is so deep and so persistent that even when he is on top of a woman, even when he has welded himself to her, he cannot escape the prison

which he has created for himself. "I try all sorts of things," he explains to me. "I even count sometimes, or I begin to think of a problem in philosophy, but it doesn't work. It's like I'm two people, and one of them is watching me all the time. I get so god-damned mad at myself that I could kill myself . . . and in a way, that's what I do everytime I have an orgasm!" (118).

This American abroad has breached the last Puritan frontier only to find the fatality of desperate self-consciousness.[21]

One of the amusing Van Norden anecdotes consists of an artfully mean twice told tale.[22] Carl, though only shadowily developed up to this point, tells Miller, in fulsome and agonized detail, of his faltering efforts to align himself with a rich and aging woman who, after a long barrage of plagiarized love letters put together with Miller's aid, apparently wanted to be seduced. But on the crucial evening Carl needed to go to the toilet, was too embarrassed, and was upset by the lady's skinny, aging arms. Nothing happened to the reluctant seducer. Then comes the double play: Van Norden enviously reports to Miller the version of that evening which Carl, with boastful and lavish malice, had told him; in it everything imaginable had happened. The tongue-in-cheek preciseness of Miller's account reveals would-be artists playing would-be rogues; but, as with the genially sad masculine world of the American street-corner and tavern, nothing but longing talk occurs. Miller's sly zeal and flowing colloquial prose present men as they are in their pyrrhic camaraderie. The effectiveness partly derives from Miller's lack of pretensions to those universal conceptions of heroic man, love, beauty, goodness, and all the other admirable falsifications which make books—and which he announced he was done with on the first page of *Tropic of Cancer*.

A more portentous significance of Van Norden's satyriasis—and the whole schizoid quality of modern life—comes out in another grotesque anecdote which Miller turns into an apocalyptic essay. In a café Van Norden finishes lecturing Miller on his disgust and despair about sex; then he sees a whore, a hungry, gentle, and sad creature; and he grimly gets her agreement to double services for the bargain rate of fifteen francs. No one shows the least bit of passion. Miller's fragmented sensibility can sympathize with the pathetic girl, partake of her services, and bemusedly watch Van Norden's compulsions.[23]

He compares his friend's sexual gyrations to a machine slipping
its cogs, for when the "spark of passion is missing there is no
human significance in the performance" (130). Or rather, as
Bergson argued in *Laughter,* the human then becomes a comic
mechanism. But at the edge of laughter lies outrage, and Miller
thinks of the sexual mechanism as comparable to modern
business processes or to modern war in which the machine goes
on and on in its nightmarish logic simply because the mechanism
has started, though it satisfies no one's real desires. Only the
rebellious human refusal, the completion of alienation, the
apocalyptic overreaching of mad logic, could stop the mechanism from going on forever.

The same devastating perception of modern systematic dehumanization applies to Miller's ruminations on his non-sexual
activities. In the job Van Norden helps him get as a newspaper
proofreader, the fantastic mechanism insists that he scrupulously
place semicolons between calamities. No human response is
relevant. The only allowable reaction to the mixture of horror
and trivia constituting a newspaper—he presents some of it
in a burlesque verbal equivalent of postdadaist collage—must
be determined by his job and the existing rules of orthography
and punctuation. The same "negative reality" in making a
living also applies to his other marginal occupations as tutor,
cicerone, hack, ghost writer, etc. Miller, with his usual angry
asides for America, which point up much of the significance of
his role abroad, claims that in Paris, at least, the viciousness of
what is called "making a living" lacks the hypocritical American
claims of opportunity and freedom.

He is profoundly aware of our basic corruption. His personal response to his part in the work-mechanism illustrates
the same principle of fractured feeling as when, early in the
narrative, he reports casually seducing a pathetic woman:
"Somehow I feel sorry as hell for her and yet I don't give a
damn" (22). The art of such insouciance becomes the Millerian
ideology; his message to Carl, Van Norden, the world—and
himself—is that one must accept, like a "new religion," the paradoxical need to live in "a world without hope" and yet "never
despair" (136): "No sorrow, no regrets. No past, no future."
"Today! *Le bel aujour'hui!*" (46). Partly, of course, this becomes
literary gesture to cauterize outraged feeling and personal

failure, but the acceptance of the absurd also releases human comedy and vitality.

The price of such affirmation includes fundamental discontinuity. Though Van Norden receives elaborate detail in a group of anecdotes, Miller's treatment extends into neither his past nor future, and lacks much of human concern. Van Norden simply drops out of the narrative, except for a briefly contemptuous summary in the final section that the Don Juan has given up women for a fancifully elaborate form of onanism—an appropriate fillip. He is replaced, in narrative focus, by another Millerian alter ego and more genial "Joe," Fillmore, who dominates many of the remaining anecdotes and becomes the narrator's, double. A somewhat more usual 1920's expatriate, Fillmore, a young graduate of an Eastern college who is still getting money from home and is not very seriously fooling with art, pursues a bohemian good time.[24] Miller shrewdly, and contemptuously, cultivates what he considers to be this American bore. Fillmore-Collins-Miller repeat the earlier boys-on-the-town of Van Norden-Carl-Miller, including a drunken and brawling weekend in Le Havre which is awkwardly handled and has very little point —though its pointlessness may be taken as the point.[25] That episode does have an effective wry comment at the end as Miller mocks the sentimental longing for home and the manly dream of America as "a big patriotic open space with cows and sheep and tender-hearted men ready to bugger everything in sight, man, woman or beast. It doesn't exist, America. It's a name you give to an abstract idea" (187).

Ostensibly having dismissed the American Dream, Miller will soon dismiss the American dreamer and that part of himself represented by Fillmore. But, in the meantime, the genial American moves Miller into his apartment so that he has a place to write, gives him a daily allowance, and shares his liquor, literary conversations, and whores. Several hilarious anecdotes follow the sly dead-pan manner of the Van Norden episodes, the most extended one being about Macha, an apparently striking, down-and-out, completely erratic Russian emigrée "Princess" who moves in on them. Fillmore's purpose is seduction; the Princess wishes to exploit without paying the expected compensation—so, in a partly different sense, does Miller, for he is writing this book and needs both material support and the material for his aslant gestures. With a dry touch of resentment, he reports fragments of the battle between Fillmore and the "Princess." She dramatically delays the obvious seduction, makes prolonged claims of menstruation, then, at a crucial moment, confesses to gonorrhea. When Fillmore decides to risk even that, physiological obstacles stop him from completing the act with the sex-titillating and sex-hating poseuse. However, good-natured Fillmore also puts her up and supplies a second daily allowance. The "Princess," who wants to be a movie star, recounts her outrageous and contradictory history while, amidst fastidious denunciations of crude Americans, she wanders around with a bloody venereal towel between her legs. Renouncing sexuality, she mixes neurasthenic elaborations on her own delicacy with gross stories of her past sexual exploits, both male and female. Finally finding Fillmore's apartment too chilly and his threatening "candlestick" too warm, the anti-sexual, modern-love Princess moves in with a "castrated" sculptor.

While such grotesque material justifies itself as comedy—particularly by way of Miller's shrewd eye for disparities—two other points about this and similar material should also be noted. The description of the outrageous ménage in Fillmore's apartment, like earlier descriptions of the manners of pimps and prostitutes in a café, shows an implicit satiric edge in which these extreme cases provide devastating parodies of more conventional appearing domestic arrangements.

Then, too, we should note the pervasive inverted romanticism of Miller's treatment. When he first moved into Fillmore's apartment, he commented on the scene viewed from the window: "The neighborhood appealed to me, particularly at night when the full squalor and lugubriousness of it made itself felt" (200). The sordid, the sinister, and the richly repulsive become objects for aesthetic contemplation. So, too, do the "Princess," Van Norden, the prostitutes, the older Parisian streets—indeed, all of cancerous Paris and, more generally, the whole sick ambience of the years of miserable Depression filling the gap between two horrendous wars. Miller also views from that window the "lunatic" activities going on in an adjacent military barracks yard which, in his cosmic detachment, seem like "something going on on another planet." We can hardly overemphasize the early Miller role as ultimate angry man, and *Cancer* insistently, and sometimes irrelevantly, turns to negative images of the Depression, of war, and of the death of the old abstractions (God, Love, Beauty, etc.). But in a world, from Miller's down-under perspective, so little open to remedial illusions, disinterested contemplation—and the resultant stylistic effulgence—tends to be the dominant reaction. Far enough down and outside to be immune to the popular reformist and revolutionary hopes of the 1930's, Miller only reacts with mocking gesture, art-fantasy, and the ultimate defiance of apocalyptic faith.

Yet, of course, the insistence and ebullience of his refusal either to commit himself to the common fraud or to take a moral stance depends on a rebellion against the usual institutional values. Thus when he and Fillmore wander, seedy and full of champagne, into the Eglise Ste. Clotilde during Mass on Christmas Day, Miller precisely perceives a dismal, cold tomb filled with a weird dirge and mumbling faces like "cauliflowers" sticking out of shrouds—a dumbshow in a "crepuscular glow" directed by an "epicene caterwauling" from what must be an altar. The American outsider, staring at the "dementia" of an ancient and irrelevant vestigial ritual (which "no longer contains a shred of meaning"), scorns it for equally blessing babies and battleships, high explosives and lowly misery, with the "mumbojumbo" of Christendom. Is that a "dinner bell or atomizer" (236) in the priest's hand? And this is the product of two thousand years of civilization? "Marvelous."

The American iconoclast abroad in the fraud of traditional moral culture sympathizes a bit with the long-skirted, "ridiculous" lackey who gets "sore as hell" and drives the laughing protestants out. After recalling to mind a similar "ludicrous incident" with an uncharitable priest in the 1920's in Florida, Miller swings into a Whitmanian catalogue and apocalyptic essay:

> The same story everywhere. If you want bread you've got to get in harness, get in lock-step. . . . Production! More nuts and bolts, more barbed wire, more dog biscuits, more lawn-mowers, more ballbearings, more high-explosives . . . more tooth-paste, more newspapers, more education, more churches . . . (240).

A strange assortment, from Paris to Florida, from barbed-wire to churches—or is it so strange? Miller's flowing invective does reflect our One World in which all is part of the same decorously demented productivity. So he responds with the Parisianized gesture of the boy from Brooklyn:

Salut au monde! Salute of twenty-one guns bombinating from
the rectum. "I wear my hat as I please" . . . said Walt. To get
a hat that fits now you have to walk to the electric chair. They
give you a skull cap. . . . [then mocking even his hero Whitman]
The Democratic soul! Flood-tide! Holy Mother of God, what
does this crap mean? . . . *Forward!* More gonococci! More
streptococci! More bombing machines! More and more of it—
until the whole f——ing works is blown to smithereens. . . (241).

As he repeatedly insists, no allegiance is due such a world—
"I am proud to say that I am *inhuman,* that I belong not to men
and governments, that I have nothing to do with creeds and
principles" (229). While the middle class "rot in comfort" (217)
in their fenced-off world, compassion for the rest of suffering
mankind becomes a joke—"at the bottom of every heart there
is a drop or two of love—just enough to feed the birds" (219).
Thus, says Miller, making a metaphor from a topical issue of
the time, we have gone off "the gold standard in ideas," art,
love (219). And as he drinks a vermouth in a cheap café, he
reflects that it has the bitter taste of "the lees of our great Western
civilization, rotting now like the toe-nails of the saints" (221).
Miller's well-turned rage, with its sharp colloquial immediacy—
as we view it through three decades of mass-murder and war
misery, technological fragmentation and dementia, and vestigial
and counterfeit values—has not lost its relevance.

But a more mundane world remains, and when we return
to the narrative of the final chapter, we have the roguish comedy
which serves as correlative to the violent elegy for our civilization. Fillmore, Miller finds on returning from the Dijon disaster,
has been locked up in a hospital, apparently suffering from
alcoholic poisoning, venereal disease, and a guilty conscience
about one of his French girl friends. When it comes to narrative
fact in *Tropic of Cancer,* we have less of a doomed world than
a messy one. From the sly Miller perspective, Fillmore isn't
"exactly nuts"; he is just going through a "typical Anglo-Saxon
crisis. An eruption of morals" (265). Since Miller doesn't suffer
from that malady, he plays Fillmore along and blandly reports
to others the anecdotes of Fillmore's tribulations. When shattered Fillmore is released, Ginette, wayward daughter of a
stolid French rural family, terrorizes him to marry her and
settle down to shopkeeping. Miller records, with considerable
bemusement, the raging squabbles between the mercurial,

grasping French girl and the groggy American tourist with his New England fraternity-boy conscience. Convinced that what Fillmore really wants now is to go home, Miller encourages and finally pushes him on his way back to the States. Or is that his motive? Miller comes out 2,800 francs ahead—the money was supposed to be Fillmore's sop of conscience to the French girl he was cruelly deserting—and with Miller's amazingly unencumbered candor, he neither hides nor rationalizes his despicable motives but, with topsy-turvy charm, makes the most of them. Straight vice hath its virtues.

We may also detect in Miller's mixture of sympathy and contempt, the double image of the narrator once again displaying the heart's rhythm of sentimentality and cynicism. In a sense, Miller worked hard to ship back to America the absurdly innocent and morally decent part of himself. Midway in the episode, Fillmore, previously the insistent Francophile (as Miller was later to become), goes into a diatribe about French selfishness, rigidity, petty respectability, and lack of enthusiasm and feeling.[26] To himself, Miller harshly notes that the tourist has discovered that the circus is an arena; Americans, he says, are senile children with optimistic dime-store conceptions, and so they foam into confusion and violence when they come up against harsh reality (277).

At the end, with a pocket full of money for once, Miller asks himself if he wants to return to America, to the Manhattan of which Whitman once sang but which Miller has earlier visualized as fantastic prisons over a void surrounded by mechanized crowds "who walk along like blind geese and the searchlights spray their empty faces" (62). His only answer is to accept the spring day beside the flowing Seine and hope that "for a little while I would be able to look around me" (287). As the episodes have shown, life is only an immediate and expedient process, so he is apocalyptically and roguishly detached from all abstract loyalties and from most actual men (up close they "appear ugly and malicious"). His alienation affirms not only his individuality but also his role abroad in life.

As Miller glared and chortled his way through the underground life,[27] he sometimes revealed confusions as to whether his quest was an exalted or a burlesque transformation. The apocalyptic essays often lack convincing relation to the comic anecdotes of marginal existence.[28] And while *Tropic of Cancer* supposedly provides the apotheosis of his alienation, he has treated the act of recording his gestures both as the comedy of writing an anti-book (24) and as the naïvely sententious salvation which will change the world if he dares tell "truly his truth" (225). Similarly, Miller makes much of his moral righteousness about "the discrepancy . . . between ideas and living" in Western civilization (219); yet he himself repeatedly exemplifies its most "schizophrenic" (223) dissociation and fragmentation.[29]

This fissure runs far and deep: his apocalyptic essays often mix burlesque humor and earnest indignation, which tend to cancel out; his caricatures show both detached perception and drastic short-circuiting by a blatant egotism in which the figures do not exist in their own right but only because they collide with Henry Miller; his fine verbal gusto of irreverence often includes a self-indulgent and tiresome play of exotic words, as may be found in reading almost any complete episode;[30] his excremental visions and gynecological poetry have the obvious brilliance of incongruous insight but often tend toward prolix and mannered fusions of the Whitman catalogue and surrealist disjunctions. The bravado of believing that "art consists in going the full length" (70) produces not only some unique prose gestures but also considerable fanciful noise when egotistical whimsy takes over. The brilliance of the American outsider's confrontation with a harsh reality—best developed in his burlesque and his invective, his sardonic reporting and his rebellious stance—is marred by the equally American pretentiousness about self-expressive art.

But *Tropic of Cancer*, despite its muddle and artiness and basic fragmentation of sensibility, is rather more than a document of its times or a record of a buffoonish-romantic would-be American genius.[31] Miller did achieve a frequently vivacious prose, significant gestures of defiance, and an enlargement of feeling probably incompatible with the moral structures of bourgeois fiction and the decorous strictures of any more coherently controlled style and method. While some of this is derivative—Thoreau and Whitman, Joyce and Lawrence[32]—Miller's fusion is sufficiently distinctive and intense to give the book a valuable place, both for itself and for the literary and human directions it points. Miller also discovered, within the intense pressures of an experienced man's first book, and perhaps in spite of his fanciful slogans and confessional bravado, some wayward wisdom: the fundamental disorder and absurdity of our world and the usual claims made about it; and the intensely amoral rhythms of sentimentality-cynicism, incongruity-beauty, and misery-ecstasy. At the perverse bedrock of his life he makes profound discoveries beyond reason, convention, art, morals, and perhaps even beyond himself. That is the merit of such testimony.

For while this is drastically ragged work, it has sufficient energy, style, and truth to stand above the ordinary run of literature and with the lively anti-books of American individualism. Which is to say, although appearing harshly negative—America and Europe, customs and honor, morals and society, work and ideas, culture and religion, friendship and love, are badly trounced—Miller made a brilliant, if inevitably egotistical and fractured, discovery. All collapsed in a dehumanized world, the beginning of everything remains—the gayly responsive self. That was the point of Miller's quest, and the odd by-product, *Tropic of Cancer*, is, I think, thus one of the most outrageously affirmative books in American literature. Exuberant defiance provides the delight and the enlargement of felt experience, and the intriguing perspective of apocalyptic comedy.

CHAPTER 2

The American Abroad

I *Black Spring*

THE INITIATION of the American into the European and the transformation of the outcast into the artist, which were the results of writing *Tropic of Cancer,* inevitably changed the direction of Miller's work. Considering himself to have an identity now as a capital-A artist, and justification as a unique personality, he no longer had the underlying subject matter or point of view of his first work. Only occasionally does Miller's later writing show the early desperate confrontation with absurdity and extremity. The wild and sly gesture directed at a grotesque, fragmented, hopeless reality does not fit so well into a self-important, continuing world in which he has an exalted role. Postures tend to replace perceptions when the outsider finds a spiritual home. The artist as an alien must pay the price of staying outside, or lose his one talent, his energetic defiance.

Black Spring (1936),[1] his second published book, seems to to have been written partly before and partly after the delayed publication of *Cancer.* Miller repeatedly refers to the post-*Cancer* period as "euphoric," "ultra-happy,"[2] and the title of *Black Spring* may be translated as "rebirth into ecstatic despair." Less at war with the world, his energy turns to artistic images and to nostalgic memories. The self-made epigraph for the first section—"What is not in the open street is false, derived, that is to say, *literature*" (9)—suggests *Cancer,* as do a number of flourishes in the ten autonomous sketches; but the street leads down memory to his early Brooklyn days ("The 14th Ward") and is far less of any actual street than in his first book. That is to say, its poetic-prose rambles are largely "literature."

Even when Miller deals in *Black Spring* with the present and Paris, as in its third piece, "A Saturday Afternoon," he plays the literary man at ease rather than the anguished stranger. The epigraph is "This is better than reading Virgil" (43). What is better? The genial physical sense of Paris—bicycling on a spring afternoon, looking at the Seine, eating in a sidewalk café, taking a tourist's delight in a French urinal, and free-associating. The piece is a pleasantly effusive literary appendix to *Tropic of Cancer*.[3] Miller briefly mocks Carl and Van Norden —major figures in the earlier book but otherwise unclear here— for their difficulty in writing. They should let go like true surreal madmen, follow Whitman and "accept Time absolutely" (47), and leap to the hyperbolically eternal present moment; they should make the grotesque comic gesture, such as eating wormy cheese and being "Miguel Feodor Francois Wolfgang Valentine Miller" (48); they should, like the Seine, let all things freely flow into exotic images and ruminations. The longest section of flowing association comes when Miller uses a street urinal ("To relieve a full bladder is one of the great human joys" [52]). Thus to live in the immediate means being a Robinson Crusoe; moral: "everyman his own civilized desert" (54). But the classic refugees from the cancerous plague of modern life, such as Gauguin and Lawrence, did not take enough pleasure in their alienation. So down with Virgil and classic literary restraint and up with Rabelais and all the "fine, lusty genuine spirits" (57). The ruminations—Parisian spring, moldy cheese, urinals, and self-satisfaction notwithstanding—turn into literary commentaries. This prose-poem sparkles with some burlesque gestures and amusing slogans, but it also tends toward drifting wordiness without the very agonal and joyous concentration on the intense moment which it advocates.

Trapped in an obsessive and fragmented self, Miller's escape most often takes the form of exploiting his weaknesses, of flight *into* rather than *away from* his failings. One of the most literal accounts appears in the next sketch, entitled "The Angel Is My Water-Mark!"[4] Unlike many of the other ruminations, this has a definable subject, the "genesis of a masterpiece"— Miller's art. He starts out describing, more or less, how he writes. As should be evident from the results, Miller is a pack-rat collector of odd phrases, images, and notions. These he uses to set off reminiscences and ruminations; then he compulsively annotates his annotations. Moved by obscure hungers, he nurtures a flow of verbal frenzy, and pours out a swirl of words linked to a phrase or image. This self-hypnotic process of art he calls "dictation" (70), though not specifying whether the dictator is the surrealist's unconscious or the sage's cosmos— or just slyly obsessed Henry Miller hungering to be a unique artist.

Gratuitousness and pose play a considerable part. A pamphlet, he tells us, about the art of lunatics sets him off on a painting, water colors being his alternate therapy to writing. His description of his atttempt to draw a horse—it threatens to turn into a "liverwurst" and a good many other things—is amusing, but at times the performance simply becomes "cute." At least according to his description, his art shows an odd mixture of sophistication and naïvete—primitivistic surrealism—in which he bemusedly combines fragments of fantasy and accidents. Chance and association provide the only teleology, culminating in the gratuitous image of an angel which catches his fancy. Memories of earlier anti-painting (such as stamping on pictures) and of things he has seen in museums combine with his "simulating" madness and with his destructiveness (blotting out and scrubbing off) in frenzied attempts to make art reach "infinity" (85). But Miller remains too "literary"—too concerned with his personality and his verbal and imagistic associations—to reach what the abstractionists were later to call "pure" or "absolute" painting. After having blotted out the horse and put the water color under the faucet, Miller sees more rather than less associations in the blob. There also remain apt imagistic pieces representing the dual Miller—a horse's ass and the angel in the corner—and the magical sense of that gratuitous angel as being unremovable in a grandiloquent affirmation of Miller.[5]

What he did with water colors, he also attempts with words, as in one of his least interesting pieces, "Jabberwhorl Cronstadt." This wordy burlesque of a Paris friend blots out much of the image of that apparently eccentric figure in heavy wordplay: "Jabberwhorl glausels with gleerious glitter, his awbrous orbs atwit and twitter" (157). Miller drags in his usual catalogue of exotic names and miscellaneous tidbits of information (frequently spurious), and his joking delight in scientific jargon: "the great vertiginous vertebration . . . the zoospores and the leucocytes . . . the wamroths and the holenlindens . . . everyone's a poem" (159). But the long jumbled images of Cronstadt drunk equally on alcohol and on Miller's jabbering whorl, and including a swan song about sinks and time running out, have insufficient thought or satiric direction to pipe the playfulness. Though the flow may have seemed magical a generation ago, following the tiresome later work of James Joyce and the *transition* school, the flush of words washes out experience and any revealing perspective.[6]

In another literary experiment, "Into the Night Life . . . ," subtitled "A Coney Island of the Mind," Miller develops his version of the surrealist nightmare, or rather, a dozen nightmares lumped together. This work shows the to-be-expected frenzied journeys, horrendous transformations, snakes coming out of female organs, disintegrating bodies, mechanized desert landscapes, and threatening menageries of night life. Perhaps the material would be of some interest in providing psychogenetic patterns for a biographer of Miller: the "poor, desperate father" (holding a rusty razor) with whom the son can't communicate (177); the injured girl-child (his sister or his daughter?) whom he can't save; the recurring images of surgery and dismemberment; the agonized stumbling into childhood scenes next to cemeteries and the recurrent nostalgia for the "street of early sorrows"; the horrifying reappearances of the "witch mother" (166, 194); the images of sexuality always turning into grotesque mechanisms (including wives); and the italicization of personal guilt (his customs declaration: "*I want to declare that I am a traitor to the human race*" [168]).

But Miller's hyperbolic language and literary fantasizing of guilty dream material do not seem adequate to give this over-extended prose-poem incisiveness or shape. Listening to another person's dreams, even when told with Miller's verbal lushness, is a bore. The more significant public themes, such as the trail of guilt or the "coney island of the mind" motif, symbolizing the pasteboard and neon quality of modern life (173), never develop. The spatial-temporal displacements of dream life may provide vivid material for paintings or cinema; but more than thirty pages of such prose seem merely mannerism or private therapy. Reality, I think, may be significantly explored by borrowing from the nightmare, but the nightmare itself cannot provide adequate reality.

Why these derangements of sense, syntax, and reality? Miller gives varied names and titles to his purpose, but they all resolve themselves into the wild rhetoric of the search for identity, finally achieved only by self-apotheosis. In one of those pieces that I have characterized as an apocalyptic essay, entitled "Third or Fourth Day of Spring," Miller simply states his two gestures of escape: "You have the dream for night time and the horse laugh for day time" (30). But they are not really separate for Miller, and the laugh is emphatically nightmarish and diseased. Each great period, he suggestively notes, is followed by its characterizing malaise: the Crusades—Black Death; Columbus—syphilis; nineteenth century—schizophrenia. The twentieth century laugh thus tends toward hysteria, toward cackling at catastrophe.

However, Miller also claims a different stance of "gay, hard wisdom" (33). He would like to possess the sardonic delight of Petronius (whose Trimalchio's "piss warm and drink cold" provides the epigraph here), of Rabelais and his pan-human hyperbole, and of Whitman's embracing song. But, as a point of fact, he more often sees "only catastrophes," and his longings are messianic. He claims to be on the way, with his escape from the "black curse" of America and with his awareness of millennial circumstances ("I am dazzled by the glorious collapse of the world" [32]). More crudely, he accepts himself deified: his life is of great "importance" and "significance"; his writing provides "a history of our time—a history of all time" (31); his words become "divine stuttering." His megalomania raises up an image greater than Christ or God Almighty, "*MYSELF*." He is the "new *reality*" in the "Universe of Death." True, Miller shrewdly qualifies his schizophrenic pretensions by comic hyperbole, as in his burlesque horoscope:

I am Chancre, the crab, which moves sideways and backwards and forwards at will. I move in strange tropics and deal in high explosives, embalming fluid, jasper, myrrh, smaragd, fluted snot and porcupines' toes. Because of Uranus which crosses my longitudinal I am inordinately fond of c——, hot chitterlings and water bottles. . . . I am volatile, quixotic, unreliable, independent, and evanescent. Also quarrelsome. With a hot pad under my ass I can play the braggart or the buffoon as good as any man. . . . This is a self-portrait which yields only the missing parts—an anchor, a dinner bell, the remains of a bird, the hind part of a cow. In short, I am an idle fellow who pisses his time away. I have absolutely nothing to show for my labors but my genius (37).

Burlesque or not, then, he does have a destiny, his role as artist; his gestures are confined to sitting before the typewriter; and the wild images ("missing parts") may cover the longing to be more than the comedian he essentially is. He ends this apocalyptic essay by using the strategy of extremes, insisting that the choice is between song and listerine, "Fourth Eclogue or 13th Arrondissement!" (41). But, on the basis of the rest of the collection, to which this seems the displaced prologue, he has not chosen either, though convinced of his transformation and that his gestures of nihilism will at least save him from the more usual "lesser, muddier annihilations" (40). And perhaps he was right, though the art would have been better if he had stuck to eclogue or, more likely, to the streets of Paris—if he had been able to follow through pure extremity as mad saint or, much better, as buffoon. As is, we have an occasionally provocative and amusing, but often pretentious and messy, burlesque confession.

So far, we have discussed half the pieces in *Black Spring*. Most of the remaining ones, while not separate from these gestures, turn self-definition to a flight from the present into Miller's own history prior to his self-discovery as an artist. These rhapsodical memories of his Brooklyn-New York life start with the much worked first piece, entitled "The 14th Ward." With a "patriotic" love of its streets, though not of the neighborhood's Lutheran morality, Miller joys over his boy-heroes and the lost richness of the time when "foam was on the lager and people stopped to chat" (13). No doubt the pre-World War I, German-American neighborhood did have a sense of community no longer to be found; but this is not really Miller's interest since most of his nice concrete details and rhetorical flourishes point to the sense of mystery in the good old days of beer, burlesque, and boys. The simple American male ethos, which underlies so much of Miller's work and response, holds him in the "clutching brilliance" of memory. The insistence on returning to the world of memory reveals a longing for the time when his life, bounded by a simple masculine code, seemed "whole"; and therefore the ways of the 14th Ward become holistic. One of the curious forces driving all through Miller's work is a sense of Edenic loss which he can never quite pin down. Maturity he sees, accurately for himself, as a "great fragmentation" (18). The awesomeness of youthful vision with its awareness of mystery in common things, and, probably later, of literary discoveries not as ideas but as rituals, had a brightness which now belongs only to dream and longing. He ends with an apostrophe to a lost world which seems to have doomed all other worlds since they cannot match the innocent eye of poignant memory.

The longest piece in *Black Spring* is "The Tailor Shop," with Miller's own pathetic-clown epigraph: "I've got a motter: *always merry and bright!*" (89). This genre piece about the days when he worked in his father's tailor shop (his early twenties, before and during World War I) reveals nostalgia going bitter. The first part consists of a series of character sketches—with broad sentiment but shrewdly sardonic detail—of cursing Irish bartenders, earnest Jewish cutters, irascible well-to-do customers, loquacious and drunken drummers, and several pathetic imposters. As he later notes, "the men who passed through my father's shop reeked with love" (133); more exactly, they were endearing failures, and Miller's recognition of that bedrock type provides a solid American motif of the pathetic role of sensitivity in our society.

In the first part of this narrative, Miller subordinates the elaborate verbal play of his other sketches to an only slightly exaggerated account. Only in his dallying with sex—the too easy seduction of the too-beautiful widow of one of his father's customers—does reality get lost, and we have a presentation suitable to one of the "old cronies" in the shop. But as the piece progresses, customers die off, the narrator fights with his wife, and outrage grows. While Miller—again claiming the example of Rabelais (115)—insists on boisterous gaiety, the misery twists the humor. He turns from the tailor shop—never able to maintain dramatically intense narrative—to the reunions of the "freaks who made up the family tree" (116), and he catalogues the heavy food and heavy troubles of his jolly Germanic tribe. Tante Melia, who went "completely off her nut" (121) and had to be taken to the asylum by Miller, focuses the horror; the "too good"—the "half-witted angel" types—are, he says, always destroyed. He thus laments the lost innocence of Henry Miller.

As a narrative, "The Tailor Shop" now disintegrates. Hyper-awareness becomes verbal hyperbole, with fragments of events (apparently drawn from various years) obscurely linked in an enlarging and often surreal rhetoric. His claimed artistic gropings (dream-writing in his head a vast ancestral book, of which only the title—*The Island of Incest*—exists) attempt to counter the decline of his actual world.[7] The disordered prose insists on an anguish whose cause remains unspecific and disproportionate to the obvious problems of reaching manhood which the situation suggests. The pyrotechnical fragments would seem to mark, in Miller's consciousness, the simultaneous decline of his father's tailor shop, the prewar world, and a whole way of life. Decay, death, madness, and suffering—Miller does want to accept them, and so shores fragments of memory against the loss which threatens to become his one reality.

Miller's wasteland is less cultural and more personal than most of those which mark the second decade of the twentieth century, and it is treated as a cry of the heart rather than as a mythic theme. The touched-on pieces of experience—erotic (the painful liaison with a much older woman), familial (the complaining, unforgiving Protestant mother), literary (the admiration for Nietzsche)—become most effective when most simply direct. But Miller's narrative impatience seems to express a more obscure anguish and pervasive sense of guilt. Maturity and the twentieth century both came hard, though the emphasis on desperation and rage and outcast state goes beyond such causes. The long sketch concludes with an hysterical apostrophe: "Now I am lost, *lost*, do you hear? You don't hear? I'm yowling and screaming—don't you hear me?" (142). The shouting, smashing, and self-exhibition insist that someone must hear, someone must understand, that the "always merry and bright" gestures won't work. This, I suspect, is not just the anguish of the loss of American innocence—though certainly that—but the terror that there may never have been anything at all, and that life, truly seen, must always have been dreary, miserable, and ordinary. And this Miller can't accept.

Miller writes, as D. H. Lawrence once said of himself, not for art's sake but for his own sake. Midway in one of his burlesque pieces, entitled "Burlesk," Miller sloganizes: "THE GREAT ARTIST IS HE WHO CONQUERS THE ROMANTIC IN HIMSELF" (245). But his own means of conquest turns out to be violent surrender. To overcome his past and his obsessions, he makes them his one subject; to cure himself of overstatement, he exaggerates and shouts. A weird and rather forced line of associations leads from the Paris of the present to the New York of his past. The mania for titles becomes the heavy repetition of capitalized signs and shouts: *"Don't Spit on the Floor"* and "AMEN! GLORY! GLORY! HALLELUJAH!" (233). These incongruities come from a store-front gospel tabernacle in New York. Then, by natural antilogic, we move to Cleo, the queen of a burlesque show.[8] The style sometimes turns from shouts and violent yokings into just bad verse: "The night is cold and men are walking in lockstep. The night is cold but the queen is naked save for a jock-strap" (239). The nuclear experience underneath these verbal gestures—"the grotesque and the void, with the heart-breaking loneliness" (242)—intermittently comes through the mannerisms, sometimes with vivid detail.

The cathartic process, rather than any narrative sequence or logical coherence, apparently provides the rationale for a group of brief anecdotes. These include a sadistic-obscene one of a friend punishing his frigid and unfaithful wife, which is told with amoral relish (one of the few "obscene" bits in *Black Spring*). Of the sketchy sordid-fantastic anecdotes from his youth, Miller says, "I am speaking of things that brought me relief in the beginning" (246). But better therapy for his longings appears in the super-romantic conceit of writing a "beautiful book" which "will contain the absolute truth" of his life (246) and will be of religious significance. To obscure the crude naïveté of this confession, Miller switches to parody of academic explication, supposedly of the frontispiece of his projected holy writ. The burlesque concludes with an apocalyptic longing for "a new heaven and a new earth" (250), a plea for the absolution of his own disorder and disappointments.

There are some lively bits here, but the gusto is really hysteria. Miller is struggling to accept himself and his world, which he is of but not in. He can only glue the fragments with the "opiums of dream" (202) and the gestures, but not the full substance, of art. Thus, in "Walking Up and Down in China," he makes the magic flourish of calling his alienation "China"—a favorite and repeated "symbol"—in the attempt to give shape to the shapeless by the transcendentalism of the exotic word. In his reflections on America, and on his "obsessional walks" in the streets of Paris, he attempts to subsume both worlds into the dream of art. Fragments of the city scene—street whores, horrors, and a series of burbling clichés about Paris (208)—and some further recollections of childhood do

bring bits of reality into these poetic musings. But, as *Black Spring* evidences all through, the heightened concentration on the absurd immediacy of *Cancer* will not do. To put together his "countless egos" (202) Miller turns away from the actual and praises "those who have the courage to close their eyes . . . , whose permanent absence from the condition known as reality can affect our fate" (209). Thus mystery, memory, and art increasingly replace the actual.

Part of "Walking Up and Down in China" is a series of violent and sometimes perceptive gestures against America— a rejection of that all-too-powerful actuality with its "half-celluloid" beings and with the forced geniality of the *"smile that never comes off!"* (205). For Miller, America appears to be the center of isolation. Yet Paris really comes off no better, as we see in an elaborate near-paranoid fantasy of death in Paris fused with a catalogue of American place names, in each of which he left his dead body. This hyperbole of fear makes all actual places impossible. The tumbling rush of possessed memory also results in several pages of incantation of American proper names, from American Can through Carter's Little Liver Pills to the Banks of the Wabash. Thus alternating pathetic confession with wry burlesque, he also brings in several episodes from his Brooklyn childhood, centering again on such surrogate figures as the crazy, suffering ones he knew. The concluding set of images comes from a pleasant bohemian evening with a friend, with contrasting images of his lost childhood friends, and ending with the insistence that the whole world is lost. An apocalyptic passage prophetically suggests atomic holocaust. All the magic words, then, only exorcise his mixed fears and longings.

The brief conclusion to *Black Spring* has the acute title of "Megalopolitan Maniac."[9] The self-made epigraph does equally well: "Imagine having nothing in your hands but your destiny. You sit on the doorstep of your mother's womb and you kill time— or time kills you. You sit there chanting the doxology of things beyond your grasp. Outside. Forever outside" (251). Outsideness is the quality of the city with its glittering desert streets and sardine people, for whom he writes a sardonic paean to the vulcanized loneliness for God. Mixing sharp mechanical tropes with swelling romantic rhetoric, he hyperbolically insists on the intensity of living the apocalyptic last moments until all is "blotted in final annihilation" (257). God and the *Song of Love*, of course, have become a stinking fraud, but they point by their absence to a new and greater dynamo of love ten thousand years hence. Waiting on a Nietzschean mountain top for the new revelation, he meanwhile wishes to contemplate "a lone individual, a man without name or country, a man whom I respect because he has absolutly nothing in common with you —MYSELF" (259).

Such I-am-ism of an outraged Whitman abroad must do for divinity, short of the new world. This carefully written gesturing and polished invective could well have been the epilogue to *Tropic of Cancer*, or the foreword, rather than the conclusion, to *Black Spring*. For the book which it ends had already turned away from the actuality of the city, relatively little of which (either of Paris or New York) appears in it, to self-contemplation and verbal posturing.[10] His powerful subject of megalopolitan man has been increasingly obliterated by the indulgent manias of Miller. The difference between his first and his second book is, of course, only partial; but the rebirth into artist has reduced the actuality which gave tension to the comic and apocalyptic gestures of the earlier work. While the mixture of eloquence and grandiloquence may be the essential Miller, its artiness too often reveals the lack of artistic mastery of his obsessions. Only the most discrete bits—such as titles, epigraphs, some of the "Tailor Shop" details and the epilogue— achieve the polished raw material of art, without adequate context. The over-all product thus falls somewhere between document and literature, and it is a provocatively suggestive but only weakly satisfying anthology of rhetorical gestures.

II *"Max," and Other Grotesques*

A dozen portraits and literary experiments of the early period will suggest other perspectives on Miller, at both his best and worst.[11] Miller's first publication in Paris—and thus his first significant publication—was a portrait sketch, "Mademoiselle Claude."[12] The ostensible subject is a whore, and the opening gesture displays the usual iconoclasm in which the prostitute is superior to other women. But self-portraiture of course takes over, with Miller as Claude's patron and then as her "pimp." In this inverted self-aggrandizement, sentimentality and cynicism again fuse. Miller almost playfully alternates between the two, portraying Claude as both common street whore and "angel," and the narrating author as both hard-boiled and shuddering innocent.

Miller, according to this portrait, exploits Claude, taking cheap advantage of her credulity with a letter of gross flattery that includes passages lifted from Valéry (he makes a sentimental point of her natural good taste in preferring the Valéry parts). He becomes so entranced with the paradoxical notion of having a *"faithful whore"* that his fantasy runs wild. Drawing on the male sentimentality which defies puritanic sexual virtue by insisting that whores make better mates than other women, he fantasizes going off to live in some mythically sunny clime with Claude.

This inverted dream of connubial bliss with a prostitute also draws upon a recurrent obsession of Miller's with the positive side of sexual degradation: a whore has "the whole damned current of life flowing . . . through her. . . . Give me a whore always, all the time!" (146). Apparently the vicarious love, plus the good, practical care Claude provides her *maquereau,* induces a "mystic feeling" of "the unity of life" (147). But he rather neatly undercuts this semened beatitude by being unfaithful to his faithful whore, and he ends by giving her gonorrhea. No wonder the Paris of *Cancer* looks so diseased! Moreover, he deceitfully blames the illness on Claude's other clients, though bizarrely admitting to himself that his saintly fascination with whores was to blame. He concludes with images of Claude as an angel and of himself as less than a man, and with a guilty longing to take her away to live "in the sunshine . . . birds, flowers, life streaming by, just she and me . . ." (151).

Through a series of gestures—iconoclastic, sentimental, amoral, cynical, guilty, mythical—turning about a poor genteel street whore, he provides not only a pathetic-grotesque confession but a paradigmatic suggestion of man's relation to woman. That Miller must place his insight—the mixture of sentiment and degradation, of romanticism and exploitation, which so often characterize erotic love—in the extreme form of the prostitute's round rather than the suburban home, should not be allowed to obscure his perception and its rather apt, if base, art.

Some of the same perspective would seem necessary for a much longer and somewhat more digressive portrait, "Max," written a few years later (apparently in 1935).[13] Max, a Polish-American Jew and middle-aged pants presser stranded in Paris without job, money, friends, or hope, provides a study of the suffering Jew and of Miller's mixed responses. The anecdotal piece shows Miller cauterizing his emotions, in part, by mocking the lumbering and lamenting Jew, whom Miller finds repugnant; his suffering is too emphasized—as if by "a sort of holy, unctuous light . . . stolen from the synagogue" (9). But the image enlarges until Max becomes the quintessence of misery—"suffering itself"—and the epitome, like the cripple in Nathanael West's *Miss Lonelyhearts*, of all the anonymous victims of unemployment, defeat, and despair. Misery, of course, wears its repulsive truth like a distorted mask, which Miller occasionally catches in some apt surreal images—"the look of absolute disgust which hung about his face like a rotten halo" (13). The portrait also catches bits of the pathetic-sardonic quality of Jewish humor. One of Max's great laments is that, when most miserable, he has officially been reclassified as an American tourist. He has also been given a suit that looks too prosperous for a beggar, and Max groans, "If only I shouldn't look so well" (15).

The self-irony of Jewish lamentation may cut both ways on a gentile tongue. For Miller displays hyperconsciousness of Max not just as the sufferer but as the suffering Jew. Miller takes Max to a friend, a more cerebrally refined sufferer, a well-to-do neurasthenic American Jewish intellectual, so as to observe sardonically the double image of the suffering Jew. The guilty detachment of the Jewish intellectual, however, sets Miller to righteously imagining himself as the suffering Jew, and in his hostile sympathy he comments: "If I were a Jew [in the 1930's] I would tie a rope around my neck and throw myself overboard" (31). Misery is almost as degrading for the observer as for the sufferer, but Miller, as imaginary Jew, counters his own hostility by gestures of compassion and by some New Testament sermonizing on the need for tangible brotherly love.[14]

Miller intermittently treats Max well, giving him a suit (which doesn't fit Miller anyway), a bath, a meal, and a good many lectures on Miller's own seriocomic role as suffering artist. With shrewd candor, he capitalizes on his own egotism. Max is literary material for the writer, who says to himself while feeding Max, "Today I'm going to listen to you, you bugger . . .

listen to every nuance. I'll extract the last drop of juice—and then, *overboard you go!*" (18). But within the mixed games-manship of repulsion and sympathy for the suffering Jew, Miller makes several discoveries. Why is the former down-and-outer of *Tropic of Cancer* not, finally, as desperate as the suffering Jew? It is not just luck, Miller decides, but born "innocence" which saves him from the black luck of Max; it is his egotistical energy, his optimistic practicality, and his untragic sense of destiny of traditional American innocence. Miller, in short, never fully suffers.

The grotesque portrait, however, does not end with Miller but with Max; and this focus helps make it one of Miller's better pieces, cutting deeper than innocent egotism. The assorted Parisian scenes, shrewd bits of dialogue, and apostrophes of love-hate come to focus on Max's deepest suffering. Charity— a bath, a suit, a meal—doesn't cure Max's plight but simply opens to view the unresolvable suffering, the devastating alone-ness and bitter fears of the aging outcast in an impersonal world. Max, overwhelmed with anxiety, obsessed with possible mad-ness and death, ends the piece with a semi-literate letter to Miller, begging for help. The hopeless case, the archetypal lugubrious Jew, finally emerges simply as suffering man, gro-tesquely without end or solace or dignity, which one can only accept as the absurd nature of the world.

Now much of the power of a grotesque portrait like Max comes not only from the acute effort to confront agonized reality but also from the drama of Miller's mixed feelings. When Miller lacks that agonal edge, he makes more purely literary gestures, and writes badly. Another portrait of that period, "Benno, the Wild Man from Borneo," shows Miller as an accomplished, and empty, verbal manipulator.[15] The piece— all effusive praise of some vaguely identified artist friend— quite lacks conflict, time, and place. As a substitute for any sort of reality Miller provides a harum-scarum bag of fanciful al-lusions and rococo comparisons. The last three sentences—they could just as easily be the first three—give us as much, and as little, as we are to get of the man turned into Miller's whimsical version of surrealist tropes, mythological longings, and stock antitheses: "He is of the old line of Pelagians, the ridgerunners who traveled over the sunken Andes to found a Mexican world. He is as tough as an old turkey, but warm-hearted and inhumanly tender. A sort of wild man from Borneo with central heating, spring mattress, castors and a boomerang in his left hand" (18).

These self-portraits, whether as mannered rhetorician, imaginary suffering Jew, or American tourist as Parisian pimp, partly indicate Miller's search for a literary role. He usually succeeds least in this when he is being most elaborate. In "Scenario (A Film With Sound)"[16] Miller, a movie buff during his Parisian years, takes over such cinematic principles as the multiple montage, the surreality of visual splicing, and odd-angle perspectives.[17] Mistranslating these directly into prose descriptions, he gives nine loosely linked visual scenes of mechanical and heavy lesbian melodrama—and kills even the limited qualities of his literary source, Anais Nin's *House of Incest*.

In other literary experiments in the mid-1930's, Miller plays more comic roles. In *Money and How It Gets That Way*,[18] a pamphlet apparently written in 1936, he does a parody of an economic monograph, with fanciful learned allusions, surreal free associations on gold, wisecracks at businessmen, and ornate puns. He calls for new efforts at "economic disorder" (19), for improved "Marxian diuretic," and for one sure approach to money—"*spend* it" (62). But he tiresomely overelaborates a mild joke.[19] Money is, perhaps to Miller's credit, simply too abstract for him to deal with. He does a trifle better as economist and writer when he returns to his role as belligerent beggar in another pamphlet, *What Are You Going To Do About Alf?* (1935).[20] Part joke, part appeal for money for his friend Alfred Perlès (probably really for Miller), part justification of the artist as beggar, in this "open letter" Miller insists—quite consciously against the leftist socio-economic thinking of his contemporary writers—that plans and systems don't meet his individual needs. He and his kind are not writing "proletarian" literature but the purely personal art of "our happy life of shame" (10), so "to hell with your superior economic order" (19) which has no relevance to those who want today to eat, drink, smoke—and especially to write. The ultimate justification appears as apocalyptic rebellion: "Things are so bad, we say, that it's useless to pretend any more. Get what you can by hook or crook. Lie, beg, steal, wheedle, cajole, threaten, calumniate, whimper, wail, dance, scream, stand on your head—*anything*, *but don't surrender!"* (20). But what Miller really justifies is such behavior for "artists," He carries to its extreme the romantic "logic" of the uniqueness of the "creative" man and his separation from all merely human standards—except the economic!

Miller, we see, takes his role as *homme de lettres* with amusing, fantastic, and often wearying literalness—and writes, and publishes, endless letters. Apparently always a compulsive letter writer, he may have produced tens of thousands of long rambling missives.[21] In 1935, this *blagueur* man of letters engaged in an elaborate quasi-joke with Michael Fraenkel: the two of them were to write one thousand pages of letters on the metaphysical problem of our age, "Hamletic man." By 1938 they had, and the results were eventually published in two volumes entitled *Hamlet.*[22] Somewhat more indirectly, Miller carried out similar letter programs with other writers. Probably the major motive of that vast verbiage of letters, and its major weakness, comes from Miller's addressing his letters less to human beings than to readers, posterity, and a bloated self-image.[23] Most often his subject is God, alias Henry Miller.

Though the *Hamlet* letters have occasional curious passages of description and rumination, and a few good Miller apothegms, they certainly will not go down among the great letters of either literature or documentation. Actually not letters at all but loose essays, they are, Miller admits with his usual candor, a "pompous monologue" (I, 166). The fault of eliminating a sense of dialogue is in good part Miller's, for he takes advantage of the agreement (including, apparently, Fraenkel's promise of publication) to write loose sermons on whatever pleases him. His subjects rarely include the despised Shakespeare, Hamlet, or the Faustian death theme which obsesses Fraenkel; but they do include Henry Miller, D. H. Lawrence, Henry Miller, and a variety of miscellaneous preoccupations of Miller as sage, writer, and moralist. Fraenkel, a bit more reluctantly, retaliates by writing his own essays.

The countergamesmanship reaches its exhausting apogee in Miller's final "letter" of a hundred published pages (II, 366-465) which, if nothing else, demonstrates Miller's ultimate aesthetic: "Writing is a compulsive, and delectable thing. Writing is its own reward" (II 315; also I, 348). Consequently, no limits apply, though at one point Miller effectively argues that all other men (but Miller) need drastic limits (I, 99ff.), including consistency, accuracy, and decency. A rather mean side of Miller comes out in his repeated vicious attacks on Fraenkel, and also on a dead friend (II, 224). Fraenkel, reasonably enough, accuses Miller of incomprehension, inconsistency, bad motives, and, harshest accuracy of all, posing ("you are only stringing words, making literature" [II, 237]). Yet there is an odd method in Miller's badness; for, as he writes of the archetypal sages, "Lack of integrity can become a virtue when raised to the highest degree" (II, 296).

Miller's strategy of excess, in his writing in general as well as in his letters, uses egomania to overcome personal failure and chaos. When these polarities are most evident, Miller is most successful, I think, in making egotism into comic-pathetic drama. His buffoon-tourist role produces better art and wisdom than his artist-sage role. "Via Dieppe-Newhaven,"[24] a long autobiographical tourist piece, mostly in his plain style, provides an appropriate pathetic self-dramatization. The first half-dozen pages are poor—an insufficient and irrelevant account of money and emotional tribulations with his second wife in Paris. The main substance, which comes from Miller's trip from Dieppe to Newhaven and back (apparently in late 1933), shows some acute observations of the world around, a nice sense of laconic dialogue, and a wry image of himself.

Out of a job and ambivalent about his wife and Paris, Miller wants to flee to London. He goes with only a few francs in his pocket for what he claims will be a short visit, though, since he takes a trunk of manuscripts, that is uncertain. He sardonically observes the English on the boat over, shrewdly noting their firm independence of character and, especially, their irritating social-class mannerisms (". . . all this yes sir and no sir. *Sir my ass*, I say under my breath" [206]). But with the superior and suspicious English customs officials, Miller reveals himself as the uncertain fool in a scene of comic dialogue in which the bureaucrats shortly turn up his lack of respectable order, job, money—and then cancel his visa. He is taken over by the polite and decent constable assigned to watch him in the "hoosegow," until he can be shipped back to France the next morning. The constable watches him even in the W.C.; this, Miller says with his usual excremental impetus, inspires him to write his account.

In noting the weirdness of Anglo-Saxon law and morality—
"on the one hand they manhandle you, and on the other they
nurse you like a baby" (218)—he succinctly catches the genteel
authoritarianism which, I think, is one of the most basic qualities
of British civilization. Miller becomes sentimental about his
constable, and even comes out with praise for "civilized" England. However, as he leaves England on the boat back to Dieppe,
he feels joy in rejecting "that man-made muck which we
glorify with the word civilization" (221), and which has re-
jected him. Having been timorous all the way through, he can
now, to himself, make the hyperbolic gesture of verbally just-
ifying even crime against that civilization. The contradictory
view of civilization typifies Miller, but the double-response of
praise and revolt also has its own validity, for modern "civilization" really demands a contradictory response.

Miller, as the episode with the customs officials emphasized,
acts inept in a mildly rebellious way. Anxiety overwhelms him
on the trip back: what if the French authorities reject him,
too? Then he would have to return to the States: "Better a
beggar in Paris than a millionaire in New York" (222). But
the less efficient French bureaucracy admits him again, and
he burbles in emotional release from his anxiety, ending with
a comic-apocalyptic paean to the "sense of voyage." Just how
self-conscious Miller may be in playing the fool here—grand-
iloquently philosophizing on a ferry trip and alternating rhetorical swagger with practical cringing—must remain uncertain.
The casual but lucid presentation of a shrewd fool is amusingly
effective. Such a self-portrait of the grotesque tourist lacks the
anguished awareness of "Max," but it goes beyond the literary
posturing Miller so eagerly turns to in his inchoate desires to be
something other than his perceptive rebel-buffoon American
self.

III *Colossus of Maroussi*

The 1930's and Henry Miller's decade-long tour of Europe
ended with World War II. Miller had long announced that
doom, but with characteristic quick-footedness he found several
ways to escape his own violent apocalypse. On one level this
was by appropriately leaving France just before the war broke
out for a few months' tour of Greece (August, 1939, to early
January, 1940). And in Greece he escaped doom at a more

elaborate level by self-induced revelations before quitting Europe entirely for America.

The series of illuminations, given loose form in *The Colossus of Maroussi*[25] (written the following year in New York), shine on Greece, art, friendship, and religion, and cast shadows on American and French civilization. The light also is turned towards a new saintly Miller, shadowing the *enfant terrible* and the wise clown dominant in his best works. *Colossus* draws to a close with a rather effective catalogue of his images of his Greek tour, and then concludes:

> The Greek earth opens before me like the Book of Revelation. I never knew that the earth contains so much; I had walked blindfolded, with faltering, hesitant steps; I was proud and arrogant, content to live the false, restricted life of the city man. The light of Greece opened my eyes, penetrated my pores, expanded my whole being. . . . I refuse categorically to become anything less the citizen of the world which I silently declared myself to be when I stood on Agamemnon's tomb. From that day forth my life was dedicated to the recovery of the divinity of man. Peace to all men, I say, and life more abundant (241).

The natural world and ethical revelation often seem intricately, if contradictorily, linked in the American imagination. Of course, the light of the Miller gospel derives less from the Greek sunshine than from antithesis to the darkness of World War II. He declares his benign lack of allegiance in flight, geographical and spiritual, from the war world. While the alienation is not new, some of the benignity is.

The Greek experience, at least in memory, was "a veritable re-birth" (237) for Miller; but, we recall, each of his experiences is credited with redemptive power. Here the motif seems to be the "blinding, joyous illumination" of the Greek landscape which soon takes on a "transcendental quality . . . something holy" (45). In good part we must understand this as humanized transcendence—not in the academic sense of humanistic but as man writ large, as in the entitling figure of the book, the colossal Katsimbalis, Greek poet, monologist, cicerone, egotist, drinker, self-dramatizer, and warm-hearted friend to Miller. We are told more about the entrancing effect on Miller of this favorite Miller type than about the man himself (28-32 and 73-75). Miller, as we have previously noted, rarely writes concretely and well of people except from disgust or malice.

Katsimbalis serves as cicerone for the touring Miller in part of the first and last episodes of the book, and Miller seems to project onto him his own magical responses to such places as Poros, Epidaurus, and Hydra. Miller, as we know from his earlier obsessive gynecological imagery, always looks for a return to the warm womb world. The entrance to Poros harbor comes to seem "the joy of passing through the neck of the womb" (53). The genial Greeks and their confined world give Miller a sense of scene far more manageable than the frightening vastness of the purposeless cosmos, or of impersonal America.

Miller's repeated moral insists on the "human kingdom" which lies between the natural and the divine (77), and here is to be found "the peace which passeth all understanding." His more tangible values are the simplicity and individuality of a Mediterranean Thoreau. Intensity, not moderation, is the moral key. The Greek emphasis on the human, he shrewdly notes, takes its tone from the belief "that *genius* is the norm, not mediocrity" (83). The anarchic lucidity of the Greek scene, the enthusiasm and passion of the Greek temper, the dense continuity and limitation of the Greek world, contrast for Miller with the antagonism and emptiness, the machines and money, of America. And not only America, for France now seems to him unfriendly, destructively skeptical, arbitrary, and petty (32ff.). At Agamemnon's tomb Miller achieves the supporting revelation:

> The earth is flamy with spirit as if it were an invisible compass we are treading and only the needles quivering luminously as it catches a flash of solar radiance. We are veering towards Agamemnon's tomb. . . . Stop before the heart glows through. Stop to pick a flower. Shards everywhere and sheep droppings. The clock has stopped. The earth sways for a fraction of a second, waiting to resume its eternal beat.
>
> I have not yet crossed the threshold. I am outside, between the cyclopean blocks which flank the entrance to the shaft, I am still the man I might have become, assuming every benefit of civilization to be showered upon me with regal indulgence. I am gathering all of this potential civilized muck into a hard, tiny knot of understanding. I am blown to the maximum, like a great bowl of molten glass hanging from the stem of a glass-

blower. Make me into any fantastic shape, use all your art, exhaust your lung power—still I shall only be a thing fabricated, at the best a beautiful cultured soul. I know this, I despise it. I stand outside full-blown. . . . I am going to put my foot over the threshold—*now*. I do so, I hear nothing. I am not even there to hear myself shattering into a billion splintered smithereens. Only Agamemnon is there . . . he fills the still beehive: he spills out into the open, floods the fields, lifts the sky a little higher. The shepherd walks and talks with him by day and by night. Shepherds are crazy folk. So am I. I am done with civilization and its spawn of cultured souls. I gave myself up when I entered the tomb. From now on I am a nomad, a spiritual nobody (92-93).

This revelation, which he returns to as the crux of his Greek experience in the final pages of the book, seems to be the same one Miller is always having of direct acceptance and responsiveness. He has come prepared to find the Greek myths vibrantly alive—in contrast to any learned niggling by a "full-fledged chimpanzee" of a professor—and he ends "knowing" Agamemnon's crime and the answer to it, in a simple faith separate from all "cultural rigamarole" (95).

So much for the first part of *The Colossus of Maroussi*, which consists of such arguments, surrounded by fragmentary descriptions of touring Greece, miscellaneous personal details, and a sermon on his revelations (76-86)—all without much significant order or sequence. Though Part Two, which centers on Miller's solitary stay in Crete, carries on many of the same motifs, somewhat more art and order appear. The first preliminary incident to the Crete trip, for example, provides one of the few topical perspectives. Along with a Greek audience, Miller applauds the American film *Jaurez* with its denunciation of the "tragic plight" of Mexico under Maximilian's dictatorship, so analogous to the Greek dictatorship of the 1930's.[26] For Miller, this suggests an almost favorable view of what America represents (102). It is an appropriate, if cursory, perspective, for Miller never really loses, no matter how loudly he shouts, his sense of being "thoroughly American" (222).

The second preliminary incident, which he gives in his surrealist-burlesque style, shows his American cosmic iconoclasm and exuberance. Miller and Lawrence Durrell visit an astronomical observatory in Athens. They do not respond to the "prison of logic" of the science nor to the "feeble-minded" game of its mathematical tools but to their own ecstatic visions of the cosmos. For Miller, a view through the telescope revealed "an effulgent rose window shattered by a hand grenade," an "eternity of beauty" and "cosmic violation," the wisdom of Hermes Trismegistus, and the power of imagination over mere fact. He counters his own portentous romanticism with the usual rhetorical violence—several pages of free-swinging malediction on the symbolic significance of Saturn (104-6). The catalogue of associations includes "tripe, dead gray matter, . . . rheum, ectoplasm . . . constipation . . . feeble novels . . . red tape . . . Y.M.C.A.'s . . . spiritist seances . . . T. S. Eliot . . . Chamberlin"; also germane are the "double mastoid" of "the soul," "senseless fatality," "the diabolical sweat of learning for its own sake," and "those evil looking shreds which one hawks up in the morning." Much more of modern life belongs in the polemical house of this mock-astrological chart, this "lymphatic globe of doubt and ennui," as Miller employs comic verbal play and shrewd incongruities in a rhetorical assault on the melancholic and devitalized.

After yet a third preliminary anecdote and poetical flight—this one employing rather sentimental praise of Greek gamins and peasant women for an epode on Greek beauty—he finally gets to Crete and then to his description of a trip to Phaetos (156-66). This includes a forceful account of that harsh countryside which provides counterpoint for the benign revelations that follow. Miller exalts over the view from the car of a brutalized earth "wherein God abdicated" and nature set "in a frozen vomit of hate" the destructive "absolute" which forces all meaning to be purely human (158).

The Minoan palace ruins provide the Edenic antithesis. Walking the final stage of his pilgrimage, Miller is overcome with reverential bliss. A persuasive Greek tourist guide greets him by announcing that God has sent Miller to the Minoan monument (gross flattery always charms Miller). When the guide also picks him a flower, cleans his shoes, serves lunch with a good wine, and continues to flatter him, Miller becomes ponderously benign: "I had reached the apogee, I wanted to give, to give prodigally and indiscriminately of all I possessed" (161).

Miller does not really describe the scene apart from the sycophanti sensitivity of the tourist guide, but he insists on his own regal reactions. Apparently, part of his lavish feeling derives from his fancies of the beauty of mysteriously ancient civilizations. The fancy provides the experience, and encourages the fortuitous priestliness in which he wants to "send out a benediction in every direction" (161) and to feel "united with the whole world" (162). His twenty-year dream of seeing such a place (112, 153), and his primitivistic romanticism combined with creaturely well-being on that particular day, produced a foregone unitary revelation of the standard sort. The magical reverence for life provides, at the end of Part Two, a moral fulcrum for hurling angry condemnations at the Western world for doing little about the Smyrna slaughter of 1922, and at all the similar outrages that make "civilization . . . a wordy phantom suspended like a mirage above a swelling sea of murdered carcasses" (173).

Miller, of course, had been a violent pacifist and righteous condemner of the barbarism of civilization for at least a decade, so the Cretan "illumination" has little particular relevance, and it is not effectively presented. More common-sense perceptions show more art and verve. His stay in Herakleion, presented with a sharp eye for the visual and anomalous, shows an equally wry awareness. With several local literary figures, Miller plays the American artist, mocking a pompous Greek's "cataract of flowery horse shit" (119). He scorns the local literati's worship of things American, their belief in the United States' cultural renascence and role as "the hope of the world" (141). With usual hyperbole, he insists that America is more impoverished than Greece, and that America's one virtue is that men have faith in their "own powers" and not in America (133-34).

France, now that Miller is out of it, becomes the subject of a diabolical parody of its pervasive *petit bourgeois* virtues of parsimony, insularity, and self-righteousness. The French proprietress of a Cretan souvenir shop, who comments scornfully on Crete's lack of civilization, provides the focus. In joyous reaction against Franco-American culture, Miller writes a burlesque directed against the petty and nasty civilization represented by such a woman. He sentimentally exalts in "the great Negro race which alone keeps America from falling apart" (138), and its super-civilized aristocracy of Duke Ellington,

Count Basie, and other true descendants of Isidore Ducasse and "the great and only Rimbaud." He elaborates this surrealist conceit into a long "barbaric passacaglia" (138-45) directed at the proprietress of petty civilization. The mélange consists of jazz terms and song titles of the 1930's, figures from Greek mythology fused with his Whitmanesque delight in American names, and burlesque puns and denunciations. Miller fuses the glory that was Greece—its violently lucid mythologies—with another impassioned cultural form, American jazz mythology, to mock a pseudo-civilization represented by the souvenir shop mentality and the culture of mechanized murder. Miller rightly insists here that he, not the proprietress and all her kind, furthers true civilization.

Also practicing that major, though now generally vestigial, lively art of meditatively walking the streets, Miller contrasts Paris, New York, and Herakleion. He perceives, I believe, several of the most essential qualities of civilization. In the Mediterranean light, each thing stands out lucid, finite, specific, with "nothing . . . perpetuated beyond its natural time," nothing the product of "iron will" or of grandiose assertion. "By comparison Park Avenue seems insane and no doubt is insane. The oldest building in Herakleion will outlive the newest building in America. Organisms die; the cell lives on. Life is at the roots, embedded in simplicity, asserting itself uniquely" (146-47). Miller is one of those longing Americans who is questing for *the* civilization, the mythological roots. He also idealizes Knossus where "before the dawn of that blight called Christianity" there was produced a richly superior style of life (154). Whether this is actually true or not, Miller thus cries for the dead gods, for the fullness of life realized in a tangible and immediate life order, for his American dream of the lost primal civilization.

The third and final part of *The Colossus of Maroussi* draws on Miller's last weeks in Greece as he waits to leave the war-threatened country. Most of that time centers on Athens, with a few side "excursions" (Delphi, Eleusis, Sparta). The account is miscellaneous, generally good-humored, occasionally pompous. For those who assume Henry Miller to be mortal, the silliest section is his earnest description of his visit to an Armenian "soothsayer" (201-7). This astrologer common-sensically notes that Miller is "schizophrenic"; the rest consists of flattery and fantasy which Miller ponderously reports and seems to take seriously. Miller asks if his writings will make him "immortal," and the charlatan goes one better and insists that Miller will literally "never die" and that he has "all the signs of divinity" (203). Miller insists, without giving examples, that all the astrologer's predictions were amazingly true (one of the few concrete ones—that Miller would never have money—has long been patently false). The writer was "profoundly impressed" by the interview, which seemed to confirm his childish image of himself as a great artist and sage; he has become his own colossus.

Part of Miller's charm is that his egomania and silliness are so gross, so simple-minded, and so uncensored as to be poignant. His quaintness also comes out in his love of shabby hotels and just as shabby people—an easy exoticism for anything which has "an aroma of the past" (177). His reactions to Thebes (177), Delphi (195), and Sparta (221) are gratuitous subjective connections with quaint memories of his own past or with magical word associations. The responsiveness of the free-floating psyche flows both ways: back to the child's amorphous dreams of the classical world but also in revolt against his real childhood. The mythic view of Greece and the scorn for America provide continual counterpoint. Miller mocks the Americanized Greeks he encounters for their worship of American success; back in New York, he praises two Greek-Americans for their intelligent failures as a lavatory attendant and a night-elevator operator in a hotel (235). While Miller's rage against things American has a lack of discrimination which suggests inchoate rebellion against his own lack of success, he also reveals an inverted snobbery—the traditional American folk delight in finding the "humble" better than the successful. Given what many successful people in rootless America are, the inversion has considerable truth. Unfortunately, however, Miller simply asserts the merit of the lowly rather than demonstrating it, perhaps because of his own righteous conceit.

Miller went to Greece, as to Paris, to affirm himself and his myth. In Greece he finds his image of himself simply and joyously reflected in his literary friends who were "open, frank, natural, spontaneous, warm-hearted" (210). His American individualist's vision of a small, communal, vital, fully humanized world shines in the actual Greek light (236-37). An American innocent, carrying within an exuberant freshness of the legendary past, he went prepared for the revelations of a colossal land of the heart's desire; and, of course, he found them in moments of illumination in the obvious, fabled places. Self-created ecstasies found a congenial place in the Greek ambience. Since Miller was a responsive, if often indiscriminate tourist, coming upon the legendary scenes with literary "familiarity" and a priori "intense adoration" (209-10), the ordinariness had little effect. And even with the ordinary, Miller was so unabashedly ready to find reflections of Henry Miller's memories and desires in slums, women, ruins, scenery, and friends that they all took on subjective wonderfulness. With such childlike, and sometimes childish, willingness to be awed and confirmed, he readily discovered the great Greek heritage with its gods of a "vision" of light in a "man-sized world."

The art of *The Colossus of Maroussi,* as has been noted, is frequently defective—often vague, strident, silly and sentimental.[27] Rhetorical assertions repeatedly override any sense of time and place, thus undercutting its own *raison* as a "travel book." The experiences in which Miller discovers his post-Parisian doctrine of a peace which passeth into bland truisms and egotistical projections are only partly balanced by comic defiance, in the satiric asides on false culture and authority and the burlesques on science and on American, English, and French ersatz civilization. The rather dubious mystagoguery on peace and unity may well be less an authentic reaction to Greece than to the World War which only peripherally comes into the book in his apocalyptic asides. For, in point of fact, Greece, the entitling figure, and the ostensible revelations are not very substantially presented. But this aslant quality and irregularity also provide the book's limited virtues of distinctive voice and individual responsiveness.[28]

Several years after writing *The Colossus of Maroussi* Miller wrote an exceptionally tiresome coda, as it were, to his Greek book, "To-day, Yesterday and Tomorrow."[29] In this sermonic essay on the Greek resistance to the Nazi invasion, Miller forgets his pacifist revelations and shouts in praise of Greek heroism. His main thesis appears to be that fifth-century Greek values—all abstractly super-human—inhere in modern Greece. The careless supporting examples all come from non-personal and learned materials. Miller always goes bearing gifts—the literary man's legacy. Miller's conclusion from his ten-year tour of Europe—and its significance—is more characterized by culture-mongering than by distinctive personal experience; in Europe he found and affirmed the literary life.

But the most powerful gesture of the American abroad is a lively disaffiliation. As Miller wrote in *Tropic of Cancer*: "I haven't any allegiance, any responsibilities, any hatred, any worries, any prejudices, any passion. I'm neither for nor against. I'm a neutral" (138). This expresses, I believe, the most essential American role when confronted with the European burden; the American separates himself and asserts a positive nihilism, a mocking individuality, and a joyous isolation in refusing to play the traditional "civilized" game. Certainly the gestures arising out of that limited but stoic-sensual-skeptical American male ethos have been repeated often enough—especially in Americans abroad such as Hemingway's Frederick Henry and Donleavy's Sebastian Dangerfield—so that we should recognize them in Henry Miller's Henry Miller. In this stance of the outsider is the "new man," the "true American"—as much as there ever will be one—whom D. H. Lawrence demanded in *Studies in Classic American Literature*. Lawrence, however, insisted that all he could see was "a sort of recreant European." And he was considerably right. That American separateness, as we see in Miller's decade in Europe, increasingly reveals the counterfeit Good European.

Miller's most distinctive qualities are the iconoclasm, exuberance, hyperbole, directness, physicality, amoralism, alienation, and utopianism of the true American, especially when confronted with the cultural religiosity of the recreant European. That confrontation provides some of Miller's best writing—the dramatization of the gay renegade.[30] But as Miller takes himself with increasing seriousness as a man of letters, a defender of the European heritage, and as a sage of the traditional unitary vision, his own unique qualities are obfuscated. As a buffoonish outsider, Miller has something to tell us; as a propagandist for art and religion, almost nothing. The afterglow of his conversion to the European light reveals his posturings as artist and saint, and these weaken the apt gestures of the rebellious American abroad, in Europe and in life.

CHAPTER 3

The Brooklyn Passion

I *The Dark Lady*

MILLER'S MAJOR OBSESSION as a writer, after his first works, is the life that led up to his identification as an "artist," and henceforth his literature becomes the endless re-creation of the myth of his own history. Of this, we can no longer discuss specific works, only the motifs running through thousands of additive pages of episodic, garrulous ruminations and fanciful poeticizations of his Brooklyn past and self. The American alien in Europe flees his vivacious outcast role to find a home and an identity in willed acts of memory-fantasy. In the two decades (1940-60) following the one spent in Europe, Miller had several ways of sustaining his role as artist-sage, but his perplexed and nostalgic account of how he became *the* Henry Miller dominates them all. For a writer whose most congenial modes were burlesque, caricature, invective, buffoon poses, and apocalyptic flights, the overweening ambition to re-create time and place, development and destiny, seems grotesque. At his best a sardonic and ecstatic maker of rebel gestures, and at his worst a diffuse and bombastic rhetorician, Miller at all times writes in egotistical, fragmented, exaggerated ways. When these characteristics are directed towards complex people, a life-pattern, and mythologies of romance and salvation, the results can only be a weird mélange.

The several thousand published pages which comprise Miller's "autobiographical romance" about the artist as topsy-turvy Horatio Alger had an ostensible master plan. In a chronological summary, Miller put down as one of the key entries for 1927: "Compiled notes for complete autobiographical cycle of novels in twenty-four hours."[1] Elsewhere, he several times restated this plan, perhaps most significantly in *Nexus*.[2] According to that source, the day Lindbergh completed his "Homeric feat," Miller planned one of his own, "My Doomsday Book" (199). Writing much of the night, he sketched out page after page of his "tragedy," he says, which would run from the time he met his second wife (apparently 1923) to that day in 1927. According to *Nexus*, he informs his wife that she will be "immortalized" in the long work which will tell the truth about their life. When an interior voice asks if it will qualify as literature, Miller answers: "Then to hell with literature! *The book of life*, that's what I would write." And when the mocking inner intelligence asks whose book it will be, Miller replies, "*The Creator's*" (262).

Miller's attempt to give his life cosmic shape, or at least to re-create with an imitation of divine plenitude, becomes a megalomania. A decade later, he partly presents that plan in *Tropic of Capricorn*.[3] After he returned to America, he apparently shifted focus, style, and plan; he then retells the story in a multivolumed series under the general title of *The Rosy Crucifixion*: *Sexus* (two volumes), *Plexus* (two volumes), *Nexus* (one volume). The end is not yet visible in Miller's seventy-first year, for he has vaguely announced several more volumes.[4] While the more than two thousand pages of autobiographical romance center on the 1923-27 period, they extend beyond it at both ends and incorporate (frequently by loose association) much material drawn from all periods of Miller's life. Where Miller's earliest books attempted to defy "literature," these half-dozen volumes attempt to turn dreary, perplexing reality into a purely literary life.

Several portentous themes very loosely connect these six volumes of fantasy and autobiography. The metaphor of "The Rosy Crucifixion," for example, suggests joy through suffering or, if we judge by the results, a burlesque messianic role.[5] A more tangible form of this odd suffering comes out in the misery and inspiration connected with the Dark Lady of passion. She is partly the *femme fatale* of the romantic, an inverted traditional muse of the artist, the Eve-Lilith of primordial knowledge, a witch-goddess of sexuality and power, and, according to Miller's insistence, his second wife. Under the names of Mona and Mara, she haunts most of Miller's work; and she appears, at least briefly, in almost every book he has written. In *Tropic of Cancer* she briefly appears as the sensual woman of the first chapter who wakes with lice in her beautiful tresses—a characteristic undeveloped image of inverted romantic passion (17). Later, she becomes a Strindbergian metaphor, a destructive dream-woman in a dance of death (163) as the narrator wanders the Parisian streets. He says that for seven years he was more faithful to her than the Christian to his God— "even when I was deceiving her" (160)—and that she is the source of both his anguish and his power.

With this Dark Lady, the literal woman quickly turns into a metaphor. In *Quiet Days in Clichy*, Miller, in anecdotal reflections about his post-*Cancer* Parisian period, writes of the wife who visited him in Paris in 1933: "my life seems to have been one long search for *the* Mara who would devour all others and give them significant reality."[6] In sharp contrast we get a present tense, more prosaic-pathetic view of the irresponsible wife he can't live with in the opening pages of "Via Dieppe-Newhaven."[7] But two decades later, she has become pretentiously literary. Miller discusses "Her" in relation to H. Rider Haggard's "She" (the heroine of *She*, Haggard's crude late-Victorian exotic-fantasy romance which Miller eulogizes):

> I dedicated the cornerstone of my autobiography [*Tropic of Capricorn*] to "Her"! . . . "Her" also strove desperately to give me life, beauty, power, and dominion over others, even if only through the magic of words . . . if "Her" dealt me death in the Place of Life, was it not also in blind passion, out of fear and jealousy? What was the secret of her terrible beauty, Her fearful power over others, Her contempt for her slavish minions, if not the desire to expiate Her crime? *The crime?* That she had robbed me of my identity at the very moment when I was about to recover it . . . having dedicated myself to the task of immortalizing Her, I convinced myself that I was giving Her Life in return for Death. I thought I could resurrect the past, thought I could make it live again. . . . All I accomplished was to reopen the wound. . . . I see the meaning of the long Odyssey I made; I recognize *all* the Circes who held me in their thrall . . . immeasurably more: I found at last that all is one.[8]

The Dark Lady, Mona/Mara, "Her," has become the "She" of murky Circe-myth in which personal failure is not understood, explained, or presented but simply heightened into the unitary vision. Some sly personal mystification, and literary-occult "oneness," subsumes a bad marriage under the guise of eternity.

Midway in the mythicizing of his muddled love and identity comes a curious document, "Letter to Anais Nin Regarding One of Her Books," in which Miller discusses Mona as she appears as a character in one of Nin's books. Alternately quoting and commenting upon Nin's portrayal, he characterizes Mona as the "insatiable one," and he approvingly quotes the description of her as " copulating with cosmic furies and demons." He says that Nin caught the essential qualities of "the nymphomaniac in her, the aura of drugs, the sadism, the necrophilia, the infantilism, the regressions, the Stavrogin complex." These heavy accusations suggest the author's reactive rage more than the characteristics of an actual person. Miller goes on, quite contrary to the image of himself he encourages in the sexual scenes in his books, to express his horror at her excessive sexuality. But, leaving aside the biographical peculiarities, the real literary key appears to be in another comment—my "deepest feelings about her: that I had *invented* her qualities!"[9] For whatever the facts about Miller's second wife (and whatever other women he draws upon), the Mona/Mara we meet in the quasi-autobiographical passion emerges as a mythic female monster who serves as schizophrenic muse to the boy from Brooklyn. And the real pathos, as we shall see, is the inadequacy of that literary invention.

Tropic of Capricorn, dedicated "To Her," and with an epigraph from Abelard, ostensibly centers on the story of his castrating passion. Actually, she remains peripheral in *Capricorn* as well as *Cancer.* The narrating author of *Capricorn* briefly mentions meeting her in a Broadway taxi-dance hall (80),[10] but he develops nothing more until two-thirds through the book when he identifies himself as the product of a "wound," and names the Dark Lady as the cause (238). To transcend his perplexity he enlarges the passion to religious dimensions: "In the tomb which is my memory I see buried now, the one I loved better than all else, better than the world, better than God . . ." (239). But it was a demonic passion, a "black" love in which he "penetrated to the very altar and found—nothing" (240). He so insists on the demonic enigma of Mara that the whole description clots around the claustrophobic "blackness" of his own response, and the woman remains an indefinite force of narcissistic and nymphomaniacal sexual diabolism. The descriptions expand the metaphors rather than the character: "She dressed in black almost exclusively, except for patches of purple now and then. She wore no underclothes, just a simple sheet of black velvet saturated with diabolical perfume" (241). Their life? "We lived in black holes with drawn curtains, we ate from black plates, we read from black books. We looked out of the black hole of our life into the black world" (241). It was, in short, the "long dark night of the soul" (241).

Mythically Mona belongs under the aegis of a black star, the "dead black sun," and is surrounded by an emblematic imagery of snakes, predatory birds and animals, violent monsters and machines, and appropriate demons for "the conjugal orgy in the Black Hole of Calcutta" (244). The dark images seem compulsively repetitious, though occasionally the prose breaks through with metaphoric verve (she had "an acetylene torch in her womb"). Miller asserts that the enigma belongs to her in large part, for she seemed a witch of shifting identities: "a bag of lies, of inventions, of imaginings, of obsessions and desires" (249). We are told, but not shown, that she alternately treats Miller as a dope fiend, a god, a madman, and as an extension of herself. But he also admits he can neither present nor understand her because he remembers "too much" (242), and too closely identifies himself with her shifting image. Miller, I should say, falls between the literary desire to present that Dark Lady of our traditional myths of passion, and the autobiographical need to exorcise (even to revenge perhaps) a confusing personal experience. Thus he produces mostly a prose of clogged anguish.

At the end of this episode, Miller simply breaks off, reminded of other sexual matters in other times and lands of fantasy. A hundred pages later in *Capricorn* the associations bring him back to Mara and to their first meeting in the dance hall. A few tangible details slip through the swirling prose, but the treatment tends to be summarized literary talk of Strindberg's evil women. It also becomes the myth of, as well as on, Broadway, U. S. A.:

> She is America on foot, winged and sexed. She is the lubet, the abominate and the sublimate—with a dash of hydrochloric acid, nitroglycerine, laudanum and powdered onyx. Opulence she has, and magnificence. . . . For the first time in my life the whole continent hits me full force. . . . America the emery

wheel of hope and disillusionment. Whatever made America made her, bone, blood, muscle, eyeball, gait, rhythm; poise; confidence; brass and hollow gut" (356).

Actually, Miller uses Mara to condense the major theme of *Capricorn*—the American horror (which we shall return to in a later chapter)—and not for the earlier theme of the Dark Lady who serves as muse and witch. At least implicit in his surreal metaphors and the leap to the outrageous analogy is his rhetorical extension of the Dark Lady into the machined American love goddess.

Miller does suggest that Mara's power derives from her very lack of identity and reality, although the overstatement of mythic rhetoric confuses that analysis. She who came "disguised as Venus" turns out to be "Lilith" (361). In perplexity at the cosmic shape he has given her—or at the shifting American reality?—he chooses to submit to this "destroyer of the soul" (362). *Tropic of Capricorn* ends here, with the incomplete act of exorcism. He hopes for rebirth by accepting the flow of destruction—even more, by burrowing into the horrendous womb of blackness.

The story of Mara/Mona and his regenerative suffering Miller both tells and doesn't tell again in the volumes of *The Rosy Crucifixion*. While Mona/Mara provides the ostensible focus of the five volumes, only a small part of them actually centers on her. A novelist with any feminine identification might have done much with the Dark Lady, but Miller is no novelist, or even an apt storyteller, and he also totally lacks the skill to project into the feminine sensibility. Thus we never get his heroine's thoughts, feelings, motives, or sense of existence. Amusingly enough, one of Miller's very few excursions into feminine empathy occurs in *Tropic of Cancer;* his is bored listening to Debussy and his mind wanders: "I find myself wondering what it feels like, during intercourse, to be a woman—whether the pleasure is keener, etc. Try to imagine something penetrating my groin, but have only a vague sensation of pain" (69). And so, too, with the Dark Lady; the reports of the narrator mostly come out as painfully vague masculine sensations.

Another difficulty appears in the grandiloquent role Miller unfortunately gives himself at the start of his history: "I was approaching my thirty-third year, the age of Christ crucified" (*Sexus*, 9).[11] With his messianic destiny, no wonder that he must plaintively insist all through the account of these years that she never understood him (21). His commitment alternates between rhetoric and indifference: she was the "one woman in the world whom I can't live without" (20); but he has hardly announced his deep love for Mara to his best friend when he is already backing another woman, just met, against the bathroom door. And he oddly refuses to be upset or jealous when he learns of Mara's relation with a wealthy old man (66). Later, in *Plexus*, he is more than cooperative in not inquiring into his wife's meetings with a series of elderly male admirers. Miller's and Mara's passion has hardly been consummated when we are teasingly presented with a scene in which he wishes to exchange her for another girl with a friend. Similarly, after his guilty break with his first wife for the "great adventure" (212) of a new life with Mona (she changed her name), he is planning to visit another woman (235) and is regularly making sexual visits to the wife whom he claims to find repulsive. When living with Mona, he rather gratuitously elaborates on his sexual visits to his first wife (273-88), despite Mona's jealous suicide attempt. Further such scenes with his first wife, including an elaborately implausible three-way orgy with a neighbor girl (477-88), give a gross comic tone to what we are told is a romantic saga.[12] Such confusions of material and tone are pervasive and turn the "romance" into an uncertain parody.

In order to maintain the mystification about Mona, the narrator must remain absurdly obtuse while slyly explaining how Mona got her dance hall job, obtained money from elderly men both before and after her marriage to Miller, and how she maintained her schizophrenic role-playing. Whether he be willful mystifier or dupe, Miller certainly lacks artistic intelligence in his presentation of the Dark Lady. Actually, romantic passion appears to be uncongenial to Miller—as does internal understanding of other persons. More to his taste is the elaborately detailed story of how Mona had been brutally, though rather willingly, raped. Miller's natural cast of mind constantly dredges up materials antithetical to his announced theme.

For example, Miller and Mona mark their nuptials by going to a burlesque theater—a congenial and favorite subject for this Brooklyn boy—to celebrate "the rites of spring with rubber emotions" (605). (Miller is both tediously fascinated and sarcastically critical with his own gross sensibility.) Part of the author's implicit theme seems to be the polymorphous perversity of passion. As we know from the tradition of the romance, passion roots itself in adulterous ambiguities of feeling and violent reversals of emotion not susceptible to moralistic treatment.[13] But Miller's confused and amoral gusto, as we have seen in his earlier fascinated treatment of whores and similar material, belongs to quite a different kind of perversity. His sensibility is altogether too crude to present the labyrinthine ways of romantic passion, and so, when he becomes concrete, he turns to gross sexual contradictions, interspersed with the camouflage of sentimental avowals, which simply confuse the myth of his demonic Dark Lady.

Perhaps the garbled art rests on a deeper confusion. Miller takes on the romantic mantle of a prophet of love, and his passion for Mona, apparently, aims to provide an education of the heart. But the pathos of whatever personal trauma he draws upon runs contrary to the artifice of his later intelligence. Thus, early in *Sexus* Miller inserted a pompous self-analysis, made by a mysterious woman melodramatically introduced for this sole purpose. This woman of occult characteristics says of Miller: "Because the woman can never give you what you want you make yourself out to be a martyr. A woman wants love and you're incapable of giving love" (54).[14] His work generally confirms these two statements, though they undercut the murky, suffering love-romance which follows them. While his version of the Dark Lady myth aims to show Miller as the victim of love, he really presents himself as the victim of his own lovelessness.

That Miller generally accepts, despite some nagging irritations, the role of quasi-panderer for his wife may thus be seen as something other than his vaunted "acceptance" of life. "Why was it that I always got a thrill when I thought of someone making love to her?" Answer: "The more lovers she garnered the greater my own personal triumph" (326). She, who "had offered herself to hundreds and perhaps thousands of others" now gives that accumulation of feeling to loveless Miller.[15] "I had become worshipful." Often religious feelings of love are the mark of inability at actual human love. With his Dark Lady Miller

has the same cult of vicarious love that made whores—like
Claude and Germaine—objects of veneration. "I had asked for
a woman and I had been given a queen" (541). Promiscuity
creates her royal power, and his as consort. The debased re-
ceptacle of "love," by a peculiar synecdoche, gives all love.
Second-hand love provides one way to get, or at least to get
near, the love of mankind. And the bad boy retelling his
confused longings in *The Rosy Crucifixion* hopes to immortalize
his inchoate lovelessness and thus garner the indulgent love
of that part of mankind which reads books.

Miller's exaltation of such consubstantial love, as represented
by the prostitutes and Mona, seems to draw on the male fascination with the despoiled woman, and thus glorifies the despoil-
ing. The degraded sexuality of *Sexus* may be the inverted worship of female power as well as part of the revenge on women
which pervades this son of a puritanic mother. The repeated
rhetorical calls for "love" reveal some curious foundations.
Miller talks incessantly of love-ecstasy and so, of course,
lacks it. The physical acts of love in his writings invariably emphasize detachment and dehumanization—often hilariously so.
Even early in his supposedly exalted passion with Mona he
describes part of himself as feeling "as if it were made of
old rubber bands . . . it was like pushing a piece of stiff suet
down a drain pipe" (180). With bemused self-alienation, he
also views that part of his anatomy as "disgustingly like a cheap
gadget from the five and ten cent store, like a bright colored
piece of fishing tackle minus the bait" (181). The arresting
candor of such perception, totally severed from all other values,
also applies to Mona who is viewed not as a person but as
"just a mass of undefinable contours wriggling and squirming
like a piece of fresh bait seen upside down through a convex
mirror in a rough sea." Such news from down under—we all
live there part of the time—has authentic freshness and evokes
the poet in Miller. Like his anti-heroes Van Norden (in *Tropic
of Cancer*) and MacGregor, Miller reveals himself as the self-
alienated man, who is significant as a writer in his ability to
report such extreme fractured sensibility. But what has this
to do with Miller's ostensible story of a romantic passion for a
Dark Lady? That manifest content becomes a tedious sentimental masquerade for the pathetic portrayal of a dehumanized
character named Miller. The "masquerade" (434) which he

attributes to Mona seems pure displacement. The distrust of the female principle—one of his basic themes—receives more adequate, and grossly comic, treatment when Miller forgets his dubious love-romance.

Mona receives some small development, mostly additive, in *Plexus* and *Nexus*, where we read casual detailings of her fluctuations in identity and jobs of taxi-dancer, actress, candy salesman, proprietress of a speak-easy, village waitress and predator on wealthy men and lesbians. Much of these volumes centers on other characters, and her peregrinations in bohemia and her weird friends remain flat and disconnected.[16] Miller wrote that "People have had enough of plot and character. Plot and character don't make life" (*Sexus*, 47).[17] Certainly the traditional novel's interior analysis, climactic sequence, and verbal and character patterns show arbitrariness; but one cannot so readily dismiss plot and character and analysis *if* he is doing exactly what they were developed for, as Miller intermittently attempts to do in the Dark Lady story. For example, when Miller presents what should be a crucial scene, Mona's turning to lesbianism (*Plexus*, 625ff.), it is sandwiched between a chapter of deadpan reportage on a crude genre scene in an Irish bar and the concluding chapter of *Plexus*, Miller's long essay about the effect on him of Oswald Spengler's *Decline of the West*. The chopped up, willful, egotistically indifferent presentation of Mona does not even achieve minimal character analysis or dramatic coherence.

Nexus, a somewhat better volume than *Plexus*, shows a more conscious effort to explain and interweave, with its fulsome discussion of Anastasia, Mona's lesbian friend, and with the repetition of motifs in *Sexus* and of the Strindbergian metaphors of *Cancer* and *Capricorn*. The lesbian material of *Nexus* may receive somewhat more incisive handling because of Miller's detachment from it.[18] The passing revelation of his inability to love, made in *Sexus*, is picked up again as he thinks back over more than three decades: "How simple and clear it all seems now! . . . *I had lost the power to love*" (44). What a nice, pat, italicized confession—an innocent and all-encompassing explaining away! Miller has a platitudinous way, in and out of his autobiographical romances, of repeatedly making that same discovery. His absence of love becomes his great mystery and even his one passion—his motive not only for telling his history but for becoming a writer.

More interesting is the revelation that rises out of his "underground life" (*Plexus*, 417). Miller lives in a dark basement with Mona and her girl friend while he is ecstatically reading Dostoyevsky and sinking "deeper and deeper into the pit. Hysteria became the norm. The snow never melted" (*Nexus*, 53). The "hero of love," as he oddly calls himself, finally gets an underground man's courage, after years of inexplicable dallying, to look into Mona's past. Briefly coming out into the ordinary day, he visits Mona's mother and brother and learns—unkindest cut of all—that Mona is merely pathetic (*Nexus*, 172-79). Mona's background shows "nothing unusual or remarkable" (177): she is the wayward and self-romanticizing daughter of a perfectly ordinary Jewish family. After this discovery he cannot, he says, relate his black passion to the pedestrian girl of commonplace fact. Thus, "Neither of them existed any more. Nor did I perhaps" (179). The pathetic revelation, then, is that Mona as the Dark Lady of passion did not exist except as the product of Miller's own naïveté and fantasy.

While Miller, with his absence of dramatic narrative, does not directly relate the collapse of his Dostoyevskian underground anguish and passionate "love" to the usurpation of the ordinary, that seems to be the heart of it. He soon finagles an ordinary job in a park department office, and Mona and her girl friend run off to Europe. It is during this period that Miller reputedly plans the work we are discussing. It might be viewed as an obvious compensation for the anguish of being betrayed by two girls; better, it can be seen as a pathetic effort to give his love a shape which reality seems to have denied it. In either case, art provides a desperate refuge from the power of ordinary fact—and this becomes the major esthetic of Miller's later writings.

Then the ordinary takes over on all levels; Anastasia runs away from Mona with a man;[19] Mona stays on with some other men but soon drifts back to Miller. Now her real function as practical muse to a would-be writer becomes clearer, and she establishes Miller, with money she obtains from another man, in lavish circumstances while he attempts to write a novel. Miller, not concerned with Mona but with his role as "artist," says that how she obtained the money "in no way disturbed the smooth relationship we had established" (224). Their life of about a year is summarized, with Miller devoting himself to the arts of good eating, self-gratifying whimsies, ruminative walks, and other hobbies in his retirement from ordinariness. Mona's "other man" gives her sufficient money so that she can indulge Miller in another of his dreams of comfortable culture—a year's tour of Europe. Here the first volume of *Nexus* breaks off with a wry Whitmanesque catalogue of good-bys, mostly addressed to the folk heroes who provide the mythic boys' America Miller can accept. But what happened to the passion for the demonic Dark Lady? She merely turned into an ordinary woman to be exploited—the somewhat erratic female who indulged, supported, and encouraged Miller in his ambitions to lead an "artistic" life in Brooklyn. The rhetorical, romantic mythology of the Brooklyn boy who finally found the literary life to be the be-all and end-all of a perplexing reality turns out to be a buffoonish fantasy.

An apparently crucial scene with the Dark Lady is the one, placed out of chronological order, which concluded the first double-volume, *Sexus,* as if Miller were insisting that this confession must be blurted out regardless of what happened to the rest of the story. Curiously, Miller's most confessional episodes, such as this, are the least direct. During the wedding celebration at the burlesque theater, Miller slips into a parabolic fantasy about a synthetic assassin-*flaneur,* Osmanli, who wills his own death because he does not love.[20] The episode apparently represents the "immeasurable emptiness" (614) of the mind carrying the fantasy—Miller's. Another horror-fable follows, this one apparently relating to the *ménage a trois* developed more literally in *Nexus.* The narrator presents himself as confused, petulantly destructive, and unable either to stop or to flee his wife's lesbian and adulterous relationships. He repeatedly imagines himself a brutalized and whimpering dog. In the concluding episode, he is a dog on exhibit; the beloved woman takes a knuckle-bone he wants, which is encircled by a wedding ring, sucks out the marrow, and places it over the metaphorically appropriate part of the dog's anatomy. But the bone and the wedding ring fall to the ground, and the inadequate dog-Miller ends with a plaintive "Woof, woof, woof!" (634). This bitter image of self-degradation seems to be an elaboration of colloquial adages about a husband in the doghouse—given a bone by the powerful wife, his marrow and manliness are sucked out and his degradation is complete. Despite some of the usual fragmented lapses of tone and order, it is an intense, and perhaps intensely self-pitying, episode.

Separated from the narrative to which it belongs, and climactically concluding the volume, it becomes a nuclear confession. Explicitly fused to the nuptial celebration—and to the hallucinatory figure of burlesque-queen Cleo with her rubber contortions and emotions, and to the paradigmatic empty husband, Osmanli, who becomes an assassin-*flaneur* and suicide —it is a devastating bit of marital debasement and confession. We might "explain" at several levels the causes of this hallucinatory bitterness: by the diabolically elusive Mara/Mona, by Miller's self-defeating dependence on and resentment of women (which harks back to his cold-hearted mother), or, more generally, by the destructive pattern of the ersatz Amercan love-goddess and the hollow, boneless, modern man in his role of doggy American innocent. Miller's explanation may be that the suffering was part of his fate which led to the benign rebirth as saintly artist—the "rosy crucifixion" of the general title. Or, as he puts it in *Nexus*, in his greatest misery he discovers he was emotionally defeated and dead because he had "striven so vainly and ignominiously to protect his miserable little heart." A "guardian angel" has restored his heart after this pseudo-suffering; he can now accept and pass his benediction on to all mankind—"Take heart, O brothers and sisters. Take heart!" (213-14)

Self-forgiven and self-canonized, the narrator leaves us perplexed about the obscure candor of his confession. The murky and mechanical dallying with Mona/Mara does not allow her much significance as a fictional character or as a coherent image of reality, but as a figure out of rhetorical mythology she is demolished by the irrelevant messages of the narrator. The rest of the context of the narrator's life in Brooklyn, which we shall discuss next, also destroys her appropriateness and meaning. What we end up with is a dragged-out and unadmitted parody of the Dark Lady of passion. As actual confession, the work is tedious; as artifice, it is pointless. Miller acknowledges that the burden of "suffering," which he endlessly manipulates and inflates, only provides a "pseudo-tragedy," and in detail the suffering generally lacks authenticity as applied to the self-indulgent, obtuse, and frequently indifferent narrator. The work, then, must be an exposé of a fraudulent lover, an ersatz artist, and a bumbling and fragmented human being. But to what end? Within and without the work, Miller claims, after all, that we are dealing with the self-discovery of a passionate lover, a unique artist, and even a near-saint. The ambiguous candor of undercutting his own claims remains the one large and genuine confession of *The Rosy Crucifixion*. His most ambitious work of art and quest for identity reveals pathetic buffoonery. Saddest jape of all, an occasionally talented prose writer spends decades of obsession and thousands of often dreary pages to produce a monument which contains only a few bits of literature—and a weirdly murky confession of art as an escape from life.[21]

II *The Brooklyn Boys*

To discuss the confused dark passion of Miller's autobiographical romance may suggest a concentration which the half-dozen volumes do not have. In Miller's free-associative ragout, the Dark Lady provides the bone, but that hardly defines the meal. As with most of Miller's work, loose narrative sequences alternate in a casual way with comedy and fantasy episodes; and these often culminate in ruminative or apocalyptic essays on Miller as philosopher, Miller as genius, or Miller as occultist. Among the characteristic Milleriana are the sometimes deadpan, sometimes rhetorically sentimental, vignettes of his buddies over thirty-odd years. In these, at least, Miller achieves a kind of semi-artistic social documentation of a significant, if limited, hunk of American reality.

None of the portraits in the half-dozen volumes on his Brooklyn days achieves the sardonic immediacy of Van Norden in *Tropic of Cancer*. One reason may be sentimentality. When he describes a taciturn Irish cop, O'Rourke, who appears as a detective for the "Cosmodemonic Telegraph Company" in *Tropic of Capricorn* and as a friend in *Sexus*, the author blandly informs us that he knew "absolutely nothing" about the man's private life (*Sexus*, 368); and he does not imagine one for him, except for the mawkish assumption that O'Rourke may have suffered from a "frustrated love." A kind of functional father-figure for Miller, this quietly persevering and kindly-cynical detective receives Miller's highest accolade as "a unique being" (367) who "symbolized" an "inscrutable cosmic law." The inscrutability of both cosmos and cop partly comes from a lack of detailed dramatization.

With some of his characters, as with Mona, Miller insists on presenting portraits almost solely in terms of his feelings. In this solipsism, the characters achieve hardly any existence outside of their relation to the narrating Miller, and thus they become simply metaphors in his peculair mind. However, in *The Rosy Crucifixion* there does seem to be some conscious but crude effort to fill in some of the figures. The musician he calls Arthur Raymond may serve as an example. First presented (397ff.) as an intense romantic artist of diverse talents in the 1920's when Miller and Mona lived with him, we are informed, by leaping out of the narrative, that he later became a Communist, and finally a middle-aged failure—just how and why remains quite vague. Miller, meeting him on the street for a moment many years later, finds his talk "effusive gush" and his hopes for his son "pitiful" (407). Miller flatly rejects the man for all time. He moralizes his contempt: "If he [Raymond] had stopped anywhere along the line and fought his way through, life would have been worth while" (408). This playing the Norman Vincent Peale of bohemia is one of the less attractive sides of the later Miller, but it has some unintentional humor.[22]

Miller does better when dealing with considerably lesser and more Miller-like types in his rambling, episodic caricatures that mix sentimentality and malice with sly, sharp-eared observation. MacGregor, in many ways a parallel to the Van Norden of *Cancer*, must have more than a hundred pages devoted to him in *Capricorn* and in the later volumes. We first see Mac, an old Miller friend now in his early thirties, telling the gross but observant story of his seduction of a pious Catholic girl (*Capricorn*, 96-97). Miller wryly comments that the pudendum "was always the opening theme, and the closing theme" of Mac's conversation since it "was his way of saying *futility*" (98). Mac also endlessly laments his own weakness and failure, as he compulsively pursues another female (109ff.), or reports past seductions and crudities. Miller dryly presents much of this in the apt dialogue of the American male, but he also shrewdly summarizes the basic characteristics of all the American MacGregors: tough-guy manners masking weakness and outrageous sentimentality; the compulsive "dirty story" telling which indicates the "limited horizon"; "the contempt for the rich, the hobnobbing with politicians, the curiosity about worthless things, the respect for learning, the fascination with the dance hall, the saloon, the burlesque" (281-82). A blurred mixture of inchoate longings and gripings and sentiments and fears, this eternal boy seems one of the "lovable failures" who represent the heart of America.[23]

The pool-hall philosopher, cursing and timid, genially talkative and desperately lonely, reveals a smattering of ideas and information completely split to accord with his cynical accommodation to his petty job and with his earnest fantasies of something different. Miller clearly perceives the type and—wittingly or unwittingly—himself; for this lower-class American male, with his unformed rebellion and frustrated sensibility, provides Miller's basic gestures—and, I suspect, the type of Miller's basic audience. The very qualities that Miller identifies as his own appetite, curiosity, geniality, malleability, and dreams (291) make him simply a spokesman for the MacGregor world.

In the various volumes of *The Rosy Crucifixion* MacGregor again appears in Miller's deadpan reportage style, though in a somewhat debased ventriloquistic function. In a long episode in *Sexus* (150-78), MacGregor discusses Miller's great potentialities as an artist and—in an only slightly vulgarized version of what Miller writes in his essays—expounds Miller's views of art. While the portrait of the aging, cigar-chewing Brooklyn bull-artist is obviously satiric, the Millerian similarities override the mockery. MacGregor, like Miller, makes much of the artist's mistreatment by society, though he finally inverts Miller's view: "F—— you, Jack. You're not putting anything over on *me!* You ain't making me starve to prove that I'm an artist. No siree. . ." (174). Miller, of course, made the hungry leap into Parisian semi-starvation, as if to prove to a world of MacGregors that he was an artist.

The long friendship, the similarities, however parodied, and the good tangible sense of MacGregor which we get in Miller's suitable dialogue, give a poignancy to the final confrontation of the Brooklyn boys in *Nexus*. MacGregor tracks down Miller, who has been avoiding him for some time while playing the superior artist, and he complains of his rejection by his buddy and alter ego. Miller scorns him, and adds that they "haven't a thing in common" (348) because MacGregor, though apparently the same as ever, now appears "tame" to Miller and inside the usual social "straight-jacket." They also argue, rather improbably, about a much later interest of Miller's—oriental religion. For inexplicable reasons, Mac gives in—even humbly begs Miller to repeat one of his pseudo-profundities (the purpose of life is "to drink of its undying essence" [352])—but the sycophantism doesn't work, and Miller righteously sends his oldest friend away.

The narrating Miller, a man in his late thirties, wants to grow up. But he carries his own MacGregor; his longing to escape his Brooklyn identity and to find exotic horizons belongs to that same limited masculine ethos. The MacGregor world—a large part of the autobiographical materials belongs within it—generally appears, despite Miller's loving prolixity, as tedious, callow, nasty, and pathetic; yet that mean life is of major importance in American experience. Miller does, in *The Rosy Crucifixion*, partly weaken the independent reality of that material by rather fatuously trying to prove that he was a genius who broke out of the Brooklyn boy's world.

So much of Miller depends on the elaboration of the Brooklyn-boy sensibility of two generations ago, of the lower and lower-middle-class American male ethos, that it can hardly be overemphasized. Here, at least, two other extensions of it should be touched upon: sex and humor. Much of the traditional American male sexual bravado shows an iconoclastic, self-conscious, stark sexual aggression, which must be the reactive and desensitized product of our Puritan heritage and the emotionally atomizing side of our individualism. Miller artistically exploited this sexual bravado in *Tropic of Cancer*. *Tropic of Capricorn* appears to go "one better": it contains scenes of aggrandizing sexuality which, regardless of what they may or may not be based on, are handled as unadmitted fantasy. The first volume of *Sexus* attempts to out-do *Capricorn*. *Plexus* and *Nexus* and most of Miller's remaining work, except for some nostalgic and casual fantasy-type sexual descriptions in *Quiet Days in Clichy*, shows little obscenity and even little sexuality. Where most of the sex in *Cancer*, at least for the sophisticated reader, appears grotesque or comic—but hardly titillating—that of *Capricorn* and *Sexus* shows more teasing aspects. In these books

Miller places emphasis on a dubious super-virility, female frenzy and degradation, generally exaggerated physiological responses, group sexual situations, and a lack of limiting, "realistic," qualification and contradiction in sexual experience.

While I shall not pursue Miller's handling of sexual scenes in any detail here, several general comments might be appropriate. Millerian obscenity—in contrast to that of Lawrence, Joyce, and many others—presents almost purely masculine responses. Because of Miller's mixture of energy, candid detachment, and lack of sexual morality, he especially catches hilarious incongruities. That male ethos which he so well represents views sex in unholistic and amoral terms.[24] It insistently, perhaps with overstated iconoclasm, emphasizes the physical to the exclusion of most subtleties of psychology and sentiment. Like much common male humor, the comedy often depends on hostility towards women as well as on the mechanically pervasive autonomy of sexual longing. The "boys" all suspect, or hope, that everybody, all the time, wants and loves it.[25] Miller's use of sexual variations, as nearly as I can tell from the usual literature on the subject, belongs to the limited "normal" range—sometimes "normal" fantasy.[26] Homosexuality seems absent. (Some refined, suspicious readers might want to include under homosexual rubrics the lower-class male ethos of sharing prostitutes and sexual privacy with buddies, as well as some of the hostility towards women.) Most dominant, of course, are that pervasive alienation and egotism which result in an acrobatic, wilful, grotesque, voracious, and verbally exuberant treatment of sex.

Whether or not the sexuality of *Capricorn* and *Sexus* and *Quiet Days in Clichy* (and a few episodes in other works) should be judged as "pornographic" must, of course, be a matter of debatable definitions. My argument would be that pornography should be defined as the exploitation, warping, and repression of sexuality, in whatever forms, for commercial, political, and moral purposes. (I find such pornography in advertising and the "mass media" generally, in the rituals of socio-political authoritarianisms, and in many of the covert processes used for identification with our dominant bureaucracies and other ideological institutions.) From this point of view, Miller's use of the obscene is not pornographic, though there are elements of exaggeration, titillation, and fantasy in some of his sexual scenes. Arguments about the use of the so-called "four-letter words" are, however disguised, simply questions of social decorum (we patently do not live in a society with a genuine taboo structure). Generally, the vocabulary of "good manners" is in our time in inverse proportion to the vocabulary of good literature. Miller's use of the disputed terms, whether as physiological description, epithets, or curses, usually seems to be appropriate to character, scene, or tone—indeed, they are sometimes used with apt poetic effect. Some of Miller's sexual scenes, as I have already suggested, deserve artistic censure because they represent confusions about his themes and materials. Some of the sexual descriptions might also be criticized for not being obscene enough—for not exploring more fully the contradictions between sexual desire-and-fantasy and emotional and social realities.

That ethos of the American streets which underlies Miller's sexuality and language also controls much else in his work. For example, there is a representative comic episode in *Plexus* which illustrates the characteristic weakness of his art. He tells the story of working as an assistant to Lundgren, "a human adding machine" (365) compulsively dedicated to self-defeating projects. This traditional American eccentric—a basement inventor, backyard mystic, and suburban fanatic—is the proper butt of Miller's street-corner skepticism; the narrator's gusto of contempt applies well to his technological mentor with his "cold-blooded nonsense" who cannot enjoy the tangible verities of food, drink, dreams, and laughter. But much of Miller's comedy becomes a forced joke, as when the earnest Lundgren and the Schweikish Miller go to shingle a roof and Miller spills hammer, nails, etc., in a predictable slapstick crescendo. Then, too, Miller uses Lundgren not only to set off his own response humanity but also as a dull foil to develop his own explication of Nostradamus—a representative figure of wisdom to crank intellectuals like Lundgren and Miller. The humor in this egotistical silliness seems unintentional. Lundgren's mother provides an excuse for Miller to play with words and to effuse an arty two pages of rhetorical free-associating praise—rather imitation Rabelais—while forgetting to show us the actual woman (376-77). Finally, Miller gets back into focus, in the Lundgrens' filthy town apartment which has everything, including worn-out shoes, properly indexed and filed. But there the story stops and Miller flees, covering his drawn-out but disintegrated anecdote with hyperbole, a grossly satiric note which ends, "To be filled under C, for catarrh . . . cantharides . . . constipation, cirlicues . . . cow-flop . . . cunneform . . . Czoglas . . ." (379-80).

The whole episode might also be filed under "corn-doctor comedy." For the comic possibilities of Lundgren and his mother are lost in free association, easy slapstick, petty sadism, occult mumbo-jumbo, and Miller's lack of discipline and his indifference towards anything but Miller. The episode is all too paradigmatic for hundreds of pages of Miller's ostensible autobiography. The occasional satiric shrewdness and the endless self-indulgence characterize a garrulous joker gone on too long in telling the anecdotes of his one passion: his desire to transcend a narrow American ethos. But he has fallen back into being just one of those boys from Brooklyn.

III *The Imaginary Jew*

In his longings to transcend the Brooklyn boy ethos and himself, Miller sought a new identity—in an exotic Europe, in the roles of artist and sage, in memory and fantasy—which would separate him from a tediously bland America, provide a communal heritage, and create a richer and more responsive self. The American ghetto Jew, alien yet with a community, bottom dog yet intellectual, suffering and ecstatic yet living in Brooklyn, provided an antitype of what Miller could become. Miller puts in the mouth of one of his oldest friends, in his autobiographical romance, the announcement: "You're no *goy*. You're a black Jew" (*Sexus*, 87-88); and Miller claims to have often passed for a Jew (*Nexus*, 226). In attempting to create a myth of himself, the fascinated gentile also makes his Dark Lady of passion Jewish, proclaiming to her, "I love you just because you *are* a Jew" (*Plexus*, 39).[27] And, almost in the same breath with which he rejects his Brooklyn-boy alter ego, MacGregor, he gives a Jew, one of his last remaining American friends, the power of dubbing him: "Miller . . . you're what I'd call a good Jew" (*Nexus*, 358).

Now Miller is also aware that his inversion of his anti-Semitic heritage into Jewish identification poses some curious ambiguities. He aptly develops several of them near the end of

Sexus when Eisenstein, a superior "cloakie" (from Odessa, of course), mistakes Miller for a Jew, and lovingly expounds to him the magical power and resiliency of the mélange which constitutes Jewishness. When Miller informs him that he is not a Jew but intends to become one, Eisenstein gets upset, insists that Jewishness is only a religion, and properly notes that Miller may only be searching for exotic repentance—"violently in love with what he once hated" (532). Then follows a set-piece of apocalyptic prose, to give the Jewish-gentile relation cosmic proportions (534-39). The former Jewish ghetto of New York, which Miller describes in his hyperbolic fashion, becomes the best part of the city.[28] The rest of New York he views as an inhuman "abstraction" gone "*insane*." The description emphasizes the rich physicality of the Jewish community—the food, the sexuality, the talk, the crowding, the suffering, the pervasive intensity—and ends with a chiliastic apostrophe to the gentiles: "Build your cities proud and high. . . . Underneath, below the deepest foundations, lives another race of men . . . dark, somber, passionate . . . the scavengers, the devourers, the avengers. They emerge when everything topples into dust" (539). Thus Miller's rather effective lyrical praise of an historical actuality, the ghetto, turns into mythical invective. The humanity of the Jewish saving remnant somewhat obscurely becomes the demonic vengeance of the underground pariah against the soulless megalopolis.

While we need not argue the obvious point that Miller's fascination with Jewishness contains, like the Jewish heritage, odd mixtures of love and hatred, the imaginary Jew role also expresses Miller's love of the grotesque and apocalyptic for their own sake. Miller identifies with the Jew—"Whenever I bump into a real Jew I feel I'm back home" (*Nexus*, 227)—not just because of the warmth, humor, and intensity of the community, nor just because of the lost gentile's desire to join the alien, but also because the Jew often plays the major role of bittersweet clown. Many of these grotesques appear in Miller's work, such as "Crazy Sheldon" who always loans money to Miller. A grimacing, kindly refugee from Cracow pogroms, he carries secret money and jewels, and a hidden revolver and terrors, which come forth in paranoid gestures (*Sexus*, 251-54; *Plexus*, 171-74, 178-86). Miller's favored mad innocents naturally include relatives (Tante Melia) and gospeling Christians

(Crazy George); but all of them, and especially the Jews whom he treats with passionate interest partly born of repulsion, express the nearly irreparable cruelty of the world. Miller reverentially praises the intuitive wisdom of the forlorn, outcast, and defeated.

Of the many other Jews touched on in *The Rosy Crucifixion,* perhaps the most self-sufficient dramatization is that of Elfenbein near the end of the first volume of *Nexus* (276-86).[29] Having renounced his gentile world, Miller spends most of his time with Jews. During a Jewish family party, Elfenbein drops in. Miller, sensing a kindred clown, asks, "From Minsk or Pinsk?" "From the land of the Moabites," replies Elfenbein, and the elvish Jewish monologist, the burlesque "Yiddish King Lear," takes off on his flying sequences of "Old World Talk, his crazy grimaces, his stale jokes" (281). Dialectician of the mad city streets, "leaping from subject to subject like a chamois," he discusses Elizabethan drama, Yiddish actresses (of half a century ago), and Old Testament patriarchs, as if they were all contemporary. An apocalyptic moralist, he also discusses "the sickness of the Gentiles, which he likened unto *eine Arschkrankheit,*" and the modern lost world, in one long song of mangled English. With wry passion, he presents Miller's real moral doctrine—of a kind of comic Sabbatai heresy: "Drown yourself in the pleasures of the flesh, but hang on [to the vision of God] by a hair" (282). Elfenbein is also the mouthpiece for Millerian theology: "man has been chosen to continue the work of creation"; but of the collaboration with God, the "Jew has forgotten . . . and the Gentile is a spiritual cripple" (281).

A Brooklynized Old Testament denouncer and rabbinical clown, the fervent monologist and joking, raging, sentimental old Jewish actor provides one of Miller's more charming portraits. In his pastiche of genre sketch and self-conscious folk parable, Miller presents the gesturing Jew both as *"meshuggah"* and as the portentous figure from Deuteronomy 13 (the unheeded prophet) who longs to dance at the funeral of the sick *goyim.* And so does Henry Miller. For Americans as such lack, among other things, a collective origin and rich folk history; and wherever Henry Miller goes—Paris, Greece, Louisiana, Big Sur, or the Brooklyn of memory and fantasy—he hungers for a community and communion which appears not as the "traditionalism" of the genteel authoritarian in the academy but as a sensuous, comic, intense, tangible world. Miller's ghetto, of course, arises from a synthetic nostalgia—the return to a Jewish world to which he never belonged and which, at the time of his writing, had become submerged in nationalistic and suburban pseudo-communities. But for Miller to have passion in Brooklyn meant to create an identity as an imaginary Jew, so long as the Jew was vital and marginal American.

Part of the Jewish identity, Miller explains in a long speech on the subject, arises from the Jew's relating himself to those who are "in distress, hungry, abused, despised" because of his knowledge of "poverty, misfortune, disgrace, humiliation." In short, Miller and his authentic Jews belong to the communion of "pariahs" (357). But pariahs face two ways in this gentile world: into warmth, zest, responsiveness—as Miller illustrates with such Jews as Eisenstein, Yood, Essen, and Elfenbein—and into the underground, "the deep subcellar of the human heart" (*Sexus*, 539)—as Miller illustrates with Max, Boris, Sheldon, and especially Kronski. For with many of his Jewish characters, we return to Miller's savage grotesqueries and to the tortured psychic shape of both the Jew and the gentile's dream of him.

Dr. Kronski, for example, first appears in *Tropic of Capricorn* as an intern working for the Cosmodemonic Telegraph Company and as one of Miller's buddies in the pursuit of food and underground experience. In an only partly developed episode, Kronski, whose wife has just died, walks in the park with Miller, alternately lamenting her death and mockingly discussing with Miller a girl they have both been pursuing. He also informs Miller that he has the making of "a Jew bastard . . . only you don't know it" (88). Miller, fascinated with Kronski's destructive friendship, listens to Kronski announce that Henry Miller will be a great man if he only learns to "*really* suffer"—a lesson which Miller seems never quite to understand. Miller's fascination with Kronski, as with Max, turns about the question of suffering; the "hopeless Jew" is a strikingly miserable summation of the calamity so alien to Miller, the "dumb and lucky goy" (95). In a long and outrageous monologue Miller thinks about suffering, about the Jews' special mission to gentiles who lack both suffering and joy, and about the dead wife of Kronski and the longing for death—and "the more I thought about it, the happier I grew" (93). Miller approaches the existential boundaries, only to flit fantastically away.

We see Kronski more fully in *Sexus* where he appears as repulsive, a "leering, bantering pale-faced toad" (91), always talking compulsively, always helping Miller, even moving him into a lugubrious room in his own place, "Cockroach Hall."[30] Miller sees Kronski as the secular Jewish fanatic who wishes to understand and reform the world rather than to accept and enjoy it. To the Brooklyn boy's street-skepticism, Kronski seems the neurotic intellectual "full of crap" and a bore with "a screw loose" (96). Yet Miller, himself a *lumpen* intellectual, remains peculiarly fascinated with the neurotic Jewish intellectual while he mocks him as a "walking cemetery of facts and figures," a sick reformer "dying of statistical indignation" (98). But the most grotesque misery of the Jewish intellectual—one not noted by Miller—is that an exuberant, sly, predatory *goy* is both his disciple and his tormentor.

Miller also sees Kronski's malaise as a destructive *Weltsch-merz*, an endless hunger for love which turns into "anthropoph-agous tenderness" (205). Such a "perverted Galahad" would "pull the house down about a friend's ears in order to rescue him from the ruins" (203). And Kronski helps Miller, for the reward of endless insults. It is Kronski, not the actual men that Mara/Mona has, whom Miller fears as a sexual competitor in a long, detailed fantasy he has about the slobbering Kronski and the nymphomaniacal Mara (103ff.). Kronski also insists, despite the Dark Lady's denials, that she is Jewish; he thus incites Miller's passion both by the sense of rebellion from a cold, niggardly lower-middle-class Protestant (and anti-Semitic) German-American background and by the exotic-demonic sense of the Dark Lady myth.

Kronski appears, as a gross, knowledgeable, Jewish voice, several times in *Plexus* as well as in *Nexus*. But his penultimate appearance, and the systematic revenge that Miller reserves for his friends, comes as an interpolation in the latter part of *Sexus*. Apparently drawing on materials from a decade later (Miller's return to New York in 1936), the narrator presents a Dr. Kronski grown fat and pathetic in a neurotic withdrawal from life. Although a practicing psychiatrist, Kronski lets Miller talk him into being psychoanalyzed—by Miller. As analyst, Miller shows great confidence; his willingness to play analyst is height-ened by the desire for comic revenge on Kronski, by the need for money, and by the bland conviction that Henry Miller rightfully belongs with Sigmund Freud and Mary Baker Eddy as a "healer." He insists on charging Kronski ten dollars an hour, following the usual hilariously specious logic of the profession that the height of the price will raise up the patient. The compulsively talking Kronski suddenly falls silent, and Miller further deflates the patient with a mild parody of the usual analytic double-talk (414ff.).

As so often, Miller short-circuits the comedy by drowning the episode in one of his apocalyptic essays, an excursus on psychiatry and religion. Kronski's illness, Miller ruminates, comes from knowing too much—far more than he can feel or truly live with (418). His layers of obese fat, Miller suggests, are layers of pride, and the doctor further protects himself by the false superiority of being conscious of every weakness and misery around him. Kronski also becomes a monster "because he always saw himself as strange and monstrous" (421), and he remains miserable because he picks his friends (such as Miller?) to play Judas to him. Miller poses an acute analytic question for the patient: *"What kind of drama do you want to stage?"* (421). In sum, Kronski "wanted a failure so brilliant it would outshine success," and only to use his intelligence destructively. He succeeded in failing. It is too bad that Miller does not dramatically develop his intriguing analysis of this paradigmatic case of the Western intellectual.

Miller's main concern turns to the religious role gained from his own shaman-power over Kronski: "I realized at once that by the mere act of assuming the role of healer one becomes a healer in fact" (415). It is Miller's fundamental belief that any gesture produces a role, and any role produces the reality. The earnest exposition frequently becomes hilarious, as when Miller, of all people, announces that *"everybody becomes a healer the moment he forgets about himself"* (425). Miller, in the fragment we are given of the mock-analysis, never forgets the role Miller is playing, though he forgets Kronski easily enough. This, of course, does not deny his perceptions, as when he notes that some people, such as Kronski, exist primarily as cripples, and must go on being cripples. For, following D. H. Lawrence and related artists of malaise, Miller finds the main psychic disease to be rooted in self-consciousness; thus modern intellectuals cannot confront the reality that "is here and now, everywhere. . . ." Thus, too, the greatest analysts are not psychiatrists and artists but "awakeners," like the Buddha, who "electrify you by their behavior" (426). And the real cure means both self-confidence and "an abiding faith in the processes of life" (427). Once again, Miller draws the moral of amoral acceptance—one of the main gestures of his work from *Tropic of Cancer* to *Nexus*. Those who are truly well will have "confidence in the fitness and rightness of the universe. When a man is thus anchored he ceases to worry about the fitness of things, about the behavior of his fellow men, about right and wrong. . . ." Miller does rebelliously add that this religious acceptance does *not* mean "Adapt yourself!" to this "rotten state of affairs" but *"Become an adept!"* (427).

Miller's verve in restating this wisdom pays the literary price of junking all art of narrative and character, and perhaps of intimate human concern. Poor Kronski! He seems to have drowned in the tidal deeps of Miller's prose, to have become one of those "Piscean malingerers" with "fluid, solvent egos . . . in the uterine marshes of their stagnant self"—a fish of "surrealist metempsychology" (422). Such types may even be beyond the "plastic job" done by the usual psychiatric therapist, for they themselves are therapists: "Their most successful disguise is compassion. How tender they can become! How considerate! How touchingly sympathetic!" Such is the guise of the "egomaniacs" who act as "professional mourners" glorying in "misery and suffering" so that they finally reduce "the whole kaleidoscopic pattern of life to a glaucous glue. . ." (423).

As so often with Miller, he stirs some genuine profundity in with such silliness as Mary Baker Eddy and literary religiosity in an uncertain mixture of parody and perception. On the serious side, he expounds the modern religious rebel's theme of the illness of reformist moral benevolence. Giving a rotten system a humanitarian gloss destroys essential vitality, freedom, and joy. Blake, Thoreau, Nietzsche, and Lawrence, among others, attacked just such moral sentimentalism. But Miller, simultaneously the mawkish and unitive salvationist, should bleed a bit from his own sharp awareness.

The Kronski fragments—unfortunately badly scattered through four books, unlike the story of Max—show a powerful suggestiveness, and nothing more. Miller longed to be an imaginary Jew, to transcend *goyische* America. Well equipped, at least by fervent individualism, fundamental alienation, and uninhibited vigor, not to fall into the American Jew's defeating labyrinthine self-consciousness and assimilative softness, Miller yet again does not follow through in creating literature or re-creating himself. He dallies, sentimentally and satirically—and occasionally effectively—with the imaginary Jew as a parabolic outsider and intense prophet of a richer life. But Miller, apparently unable to take on the heritage of suffering and day-by-day commitment, always ends by escaping into easy roles of ersatz healer and joker. He makes some gestures at being an imaginary Jew, throws out candid fragments of his sensitive American's love and repulsion for the saving remnant, even tries to fuse it with his myth of a passionate destiny, via the Dark Lady as Jewish witch and muse; but he always dissipates his powerful theme. Miller settles for being only that quaint and amorphous self-hero, Henry Miller.[31]

The autobiographical romances bunch some bits of poignant documentation of the Brooklyn ethos and the longing for a fuller identity with occasional brilliant or playful flashes, but it all adds up to a tedious testament of Miller's lostness.[32] Ostensibly writing the history of how he gained the experience, the suffering, and the imaginative knowledge to break out of his narrow time and place to become a saintly artist, Miller reveals that he never did get out, never did learn, never did fully become an "artist." Much of *Sexus, Plexus,* and *Nexus* fails because Miller does not seek to comprehend the Dark Lady, the Brooklyn boys, or the Jewish pariah archetypes but only his artist role: "What a wonderful life, the literary life!" (*Nexus,* 297).[33]

Miller thinks of art as an escape from the ordinary life of "a paid employee" into a will-less world of personal whimsy where one can "revel in one's thoughts and emotions" (*Sexus,* 43). He aims, despite occasional ponderous claims, not at truth, not at meaning, not at art, but at his role (*Nexus,* 158; *Plexus,* 410; *Sexus,* 313, etc.). Literally dozens of passages illustrate that Miller has experiences for art's sake, and the major meaning of what did, or could, happen to him was that he would someday write it. He literally had a "frenzy to live the life of a writer" (*Sexus,* 55), and that, almost only that, is what all the fuss was about. Miller sometimes had a hard life, "struggling to visualize on the faces of all my coming readers this expression of unreserved love and admiration" (*Sexus*, 37).[34]

While he may have succeeded in playing the role of artist he did not so generally succeed in producing art. Miller believes that art must be inspiration, frenzy, free-association, comic flow, and the supercession of intellect, effort, criticism (*Sexus*, 307-13; *Plexus*, 612; *Nexus*, 235, 297, 389ff.). But for these volumes the inspiration was long gone and far removed. The two decades and more devoted to it were a willed, arbitrary violation of Miller's own esthetic. In the forced style of much of *The Rosy Crucifixion*, Miller's colloquialism becomes dominated by triteness (note the dozen stock clichés on the *first* page of *Plexus*, and throughout). The thought, lacking confrontations and defiance, becomes equally trite. The earlier Miller drew outrageous but sometimes suggestive analogies about America; now he often falls into cantankerous stock moralizing, as when he says that earlier generations of American "men were made of sterner stuff . . . more industrious, more persevering, more resourceful, more disciplined" (*Plexus*, 80). The prophet in the purlieus has moved downtown to preach in the clubrooms, in painful self-parody of the very things he supposedly despises.

Part of the verve of *Tropic of Cancer* and some of his burlesque sketches and apocalyptic essays depend on sheer revolt. But, in the self-satisfaction of resurrecting his past and trumpeting his garrulous role-playing as Artist in his six-volume "book of life," he loses his saving humor and defiance. Egomania without the struggle and immediacy of a crisis or the shattering confrontation with the actual, tends only to bloated posing; and the only surprise is that in spots Miller forgets his self-congratulatory romance of memory and fancy to achieve the amusing and the suggestive. On the whole, these volumes provide neither adequate art nor significant document. They are just a mildly weird ruin, a willful monument of egotistical verbiage, from which can be extracted some stray bits of grotesque wisdom and some archeological curiosities about a dubious Brooklyn passion for playing, at any price, the artist.[35]

CHAPTER 4

The Outsider at Home

I "Reunion in Brooklyn" and Tropic of Capricorn

MILLER'S PASSION to escape the Brooklyn ethos by the identity of an artist-outsider—with such aliases as the cancerous rogue, the lover of the Dark Lady, and the imaginary Jew—swells into polemics and burlesques about America as Nemesis. In Miller's prolix writings of three decades, no matter what the ostensible subject, we repeatedly find his gestures of rage against his birthright. While the rediscovery of America furnishes one of the obsessive themes of our literature in the twentieth century, Miller makes his eternal return as an artistic Columbus in chains, shouting that he will be imprisoned on a vast desert island blocking the way to the China of the imagination.

The world of the good old Brooklyn days changes, leaving the rebel-voyager adrift; but America, he always hollers, remains the one certain place of shipwreck. Put another way, Miller's role-playing as Artist becomes a compulsion in which America *must* play the villain. But much of this polemical game is bad and clichéd since Miller takes it with stock literalness rather than with rich seriousness. Fortunately, a few of the American pieces show confessional and burlesque verve. *Tropic of Capricorn,* his most ambitious journey into his native wasteland, is usually taken as the key document of Miller's America; however, I find that "Reunion in Brooklyn"[1] provides a better and more nuclear confession where we poignantly see him at home. This autobiographical sketch and ruminative essay, written largely in his plain colloquial style, draws upon the author's return to his family from Greece in 1940. Because he had mixed feelings in confronting the reality of his Brooklyn, he achieves a significant sense of anguish. When he looks at his family's puritanically ordered, lower-middle-class home, it is both "the same modest, humble place it had always been" and the "polished mausoleum in which their misery and suffering had been kept brightly burning" (68). More generally, Brooklyn is both the place where he found everyone "dying of malnutrition of the soul" (76) and the locus of his own vision of paradise where he fuses memories of childhood and adult dreams around an obscurely sacramental street scene (100-2). In these curious mixtures of the maudlin and the sardonic we may detect the outraged sentimentality which infuses Miller's relation to everything American.

Some of Miller's best art comes forth in the bittersweet portrayal of his all-too-ordinary American family life. With painful candor, he sketches the fastidious, nagging, penurious mother whose one moment of "tenderness" comes when she picks a thread off his coat (86); the pious, resentful half-witted spinster sister; and the weak, kindly, dull, father slowly dying of cancer of the urinary tract. The family life centers around radio programs, household appliances, and ritualized little anxieties, sentiments, and hatreds. It all provides a devastating portrait— quite without the doctrinaire qualities of the prevalent "naturalistic" treatment of such a milieu—with highlights on the trivial "stupidity, criminality and hypocrisy" which form the sad epitomization of a death-in-life domesticity. Yet, for Miller, this is home, and a heartracking part of himself, as well as the frustration of every fuller self: "By the time I was ready to leave my throat was sore from repressing my emotions" (86).

In the animus of such devotion, Miller attempts touching gestures of expiation. Burdened with guilt (93), he brings gifts, longs to do more to "prove" himself, and rages against the machines and mass culture which both enmesh and reflect his representative family. He hopefully contrasts a supposedly richer European way of life, and alternately weeps over and flees into fantasies from his identification with that narrow Brooklyn world. He cannot, of course, prove himself to his family; his flight into the role of artist merely confirms his failure in their eyes. Reliving the humiliation of his attempts to write at home, when his mother insisted he hide from a visitor in a closet because it was shameful for a full-grown man not to be more usefully employed, he still feels "like a criminal" (67) and sobs like a guilty child.[2] What can he do but wildly rage at

the befuddled mixture of abundance and emptiness which
provides the American way of family life?

The complementary alternative is flight into the subject of
his writing, the romance of memory which attempts to remold
the past into some now lost significance. The one bond middle-
aged Miller can establish with his dying father is to listen, enchanted, to the old man's reminiscences of the 1880's. Life
then, before son Henry ever existed, must have been richer
and fuller. Or, harking back to a horrendous episode in his
past when his second wife threatened suicide, Miller escapes
the actual by involuntary memory. His anxiety triggers a vision
of "the whole of my life" (89), which obliterates all actuality.
As with the involuntary memory which some people have when
drowning, the fearful connection with the present snaps and life
becomes an uncontrollable surge of the past. Only then, he tells
us, does he find himself "alive again"; the whole significance of
life becomes the surrender to the non-present, and it is "marvelous to have lived, to remember so much" (90). Should the
memories be too painful, the mind will make its own distortions:
Brooklyn, he says, becomes for him a "dream" which "was far
more vivid than the actual scene" (100). And if not the dream
of the past, then there is the dream of the future. In his
fiftieth year Miller displays the spontaneous egotism of the
very young. He sees himself moving toward a future which
will reveal him to be a "great man" (98). So down with the
mere Brooklyn actuality! He ends the piece by trumpeting his
separation from family and America and by insisting grandil-
oquently on his "allegiance to mankind," to "God," and to his
"private destiny" (106)—all apparently the same thing. This
vision separates him from the painful reality of time and place.
Hence there can be no reunion in Brooklyn.

Despite his bombast and muddle, and because he remains
the sobbing child who flees into spastic memory and fantasy,
Miller testifies with considerable effect to some of the most
pervasive and crucial American experiences. His bedrock personal America—our most fundamental social pattern of lower-
middle-class triviality, acquisitiveness, sentimentality, vacuous-
ness, repression, and petty virtue—remains unacceptable to anyone's intelligence and sensitivity. Such family life can never
achieve, can never be given, authentic passion, heroism, or
style. To accept such a way of life is death-in-life. But to break

with it is to be sundered, forever outside oneself, essentially outside of America which can apparently only be defied, not transcended. With this implicit insight, Miller's art of artless confession sometimes achieves a poignant documentation superior to much art. To see this, we must not take Miller literally as the great artist-prophet from Brooklyn; when self-consciously the artist-prophet, he becomes painfully bombastic in style. But we can recognize his artist-prophet gestures as a pathetic part of a dramatic confession, as a part of the buffoonery of anguish of one who testifies—perhaps with an art he did not intend—to the lack of "inside" in America, the "home" of the outsiders.

The earlier *Tropic of Capricorn* (1939)[3] may fairly be seen as a more ornate description-confession of the outsider at home in America. While *Capricorn* provides the first of Miller's half-dozen volumes of autobiographical romance—some motifs of which we have already discussed—it is also a work of more elaborate and peculiar artifice. In *Capricorn,* the outraged artist-prophet most fully escapes into involuntary memory and auto-fantasy, thus providing a pathetic-grotesque document of a self-alienation which aims to describe hyperbolically the spiritual climate of America. Or, to put it in terms of one of Miller's own metaphors, he creates in *Capricorn* a fantastic, monstrous verbal construct which parodies the communal American imagination: "Perhaps I regret not having been able to become an American. *Perhaps.* In my zeal now, which is again *American,* I am about to give birth to a monstrous edifice, a skyscraper, which will undoubtedly last long after the other skyscrapers have vanished, but which will vanish too when that which produced it disappears" (56).

Some of the fantasia, apparently, misleads readers as to the nature of the book. The title, for example, may suggest parallels with *Tropic of Cancer* which do not really exist. Where *Cancer* was a series of roguish episodes, *Capricorn* carries anti-art a step further in its free flow of fantastic associations and disassociations, to express the transcendental power of the subjectivity of Henry Miller. Reality, in most senses, is rather less in *Capricorn* than in *Cancer,* while an ornate poetic-prose—of the type Miller calls "dictation" or "cadenza"—takes greater prominence.[4] The purgative process in *Capricorn,* covering a more variegated time, space, and attitude, often lacks the incisive ges-

tures of *Cancer;* and it certainly lacks much of the humor of the
first book. The Parisian of *Capricorn,* turning back to memories of
more than a decade earlier in distant America, dallies with
his materials and his perplexities. The mixed feelings about
his Dark Lady and about his own identity in the pre-artistic
days, including the uncertain jumbling of repulsion, nostalgia,
gusto, injury, rage, and confusion, allow less exuberant, sly defiance of a hopelessly cancerous world. In the home of memory
Miller does not just confront chaos, he *is* the American chaos.

In the more or less prefatory essay opening of *Capricorn,*
Miller insists upon his hatred of America as the most degrading
and humiliating of all places. "I wanted to see America destroyed. . . ." The motive, he says, is "vengeance" to force
"atonement for the crimes that were committed against me
and against several others like me who have never been able
to lift their voices and express their hatred, their rebellion . . ."
(12-13). We see in this statement one of Miller's most basic
pervasive motivations; it is, as Nietzsche might note, the religiosity of resentment. Most simply, of course, he resents his
heritage: "My people were entirely *Nordic,* which is to say
idiots" (11). They had, that is, most of the miserable virtues
of the dominant American culture. They were of northern
European, Protestant, *petit bourgeois* stock. They had the
appropriate ideology of cleanliness, righteousness, prudence,
literalness, and hard-work—Americans of Americans—and were
unable, therefore, to live richly, openly, fully in the present.
Miller accuses them, and himself as well, of being cowards,
self-aggrandizing hypocrites, and spiritless somnambulists unable to embrace life.

Yet, in most of the remaining three-hundred-odd pages, Miller
avoids talking much about any such mere reality as his family,
except for one fine scene about his father; and when he does
it is to insist on his disconnection—he "was born in the wrong
household" (326). What he does discuss intermittently in the
first section of manic flowing, ruminative narrative is his
work as messenger-employment manager for the "Cosmodemonic
Telegraph Co." Though essentially intriguing material, Miller's
years with "Cosmodemonic" are not well told. Besides the
usual defective characterization—such a crucial figure as the
Negro woman Valeska lacks detail and is even killed off without
our knowing why and how—Miller's account suffers more gen-

erally from disproportions between rhetoric and reality.[5] The job as messenger-employment manager turned out to be a "hideous farce" of the stupid bureaucratic hiring and firing of a marginal population of pathetic and grotesque people. Miller treats the experience as unique, when much of the point should have been that hundreds of thousands of other American jobs were, and apparently still are, equally absurd. Any sensitive and intelligent person who has held a variety of urban jobs could report similar details of frenzy, inhumanity, grossness, and farce. With the exception of some hyperbole, such as the sexual scenes, Miller reports the ordinary; but he so loads his scattered details by comparing American enterprise to a sewer, an endless war, and a contagious ward, that the fragmentary narrative will hardly carry the burden. His responses become arbitrary shouts of manic compassion and depressed resentment. He makes too much of the fact that the horrors happened to *him;* he does not probe the more profound truths of just *how* and *why* they do happen.

Crudely sketching in a few of the more extreme cases of violent messengers, Miller provides no sense of motive, no rounded figures, no rich immediacy. These inverted Horatio Alger caricatures—"the dream of a sick America"—culminate in the self-portrait of one who succeeded in bullying his way into a job because one official was maliciously out to get another, then proved himself as a company spy, and ended by becoming a properly frenzied, griping, submissive, and self-punishing underling with sick dreams of glory: "If I had had real power . . . I could have used the Cosmodemonic Telegraph Company . . . as a base to bring all America to God . . ." (27). In some of his other burlesque gestures Miller perceives that his madness is part of the system: a communication "service" speeding up things not worth communicating; "personnel policies" which are simply wild fluctuations of depersonalization and bigotry. In short, he portrays an archetypal American enterprise as not only stupid, fraudulent, and cruel but horrifyingly meaningless as well.

Miller also discovered in the Cosmodemonic mechanism that D. H. Lawrence was right in seeing the "lawless, violent, explosive, demonical" (41) under the bland efficiency and optimism of America. Miller's best case in point is Henry Miller, whose euphoric frenzy—"violent and phlegmatic at the same time" (76)—becomes the key response. Miller serves as a weather vane for the American climate in which the "whole continent is sound asleep and in that sleep a grand nightmare is taking place" (42). But perhaps Miller's most apt responses, and style, may be found in his laconic common-sense asides, such as "nobody knows what it is to sit on his ass and be content." In either case, Miller's reactions, usually flip-flopping from violent rages to fantastic sentimentality, do not present the real nature of the Cosmodemonic mechanism. There is a large, ostensible pattern: "Everything I endured was in the nature of a preparation for that moment when . . . I walked out of the office . . . to liberate [myself] from a living death" (64). This Brooklyn Sherwood Anderson theme doesn't quite fit the facts as given in his autobiographical romances; for Miller only slowly withdrew from his job, from his embittered domestic arrangements, and from the desperation of ordinary life. The transformation from employment manager to expatriate bard depended more upon the years of underground bohemian life than upon mad American enterprise.

In Miller's touchingly confused account of his quest for a private salvation from the purgatory of ordinary America, there always arises a didactic and Thoreauvian moral fervency: "I want to prevent as many men as possible from pretending that they have to do this or that because they must earn a living. *It is not true.* One can starve to death—it is much better" (37). The nihilistic twist at the end, of course, is what separates the nineteenth-century, self-sufficient provincial individualist from the twentieth-century, anxious megalopolitan rebel.

Miller's amoralism and rhetoric of roguery occasionally serve him well. His bemusement and gusto at moments amidst the dreariness of the Cosmodemonic mechanism, or his comic over-adjustment when he is willing to buy everything on the install-ment plan, or his kaleidoscopic wanderings through dance halls, burlesque theaters, vaginas and many other odd corners, provide his best gestures of defiance. Sadly, these scenes remain sparse. Much of what he supposedly presents is *not* present, such as his summary of Myrtle Avenue, Brooklyn, which only emerges as a long series of negatives—"this street no saint ever walked . . . nor any poet" (311). Miller too often simply asserts the American drought; he fails to let us see the land-scape. Broadway, however, does call forth the dadaist poet:

From Times Square to Fiftieth Street all that St. Thomas Aquinas forgot to include in his magnum opus is here included, which is to say . . . hamburger sandwiches, collar buttons, poodle dogs, slot machines . . . orange sticks, free toilets, sanitary napkins, mint jujubes, billiard balls, chopped onions . . . patchouli, warm pitchblende, iced electricity, sugared sweat and powdered urine drives one on to a fever of delicious expectancy. Christ will never more come down to earth nor will there be any law-giver . . . and yet one expects something, something terrifyingly marvelous and absurd . . . (98-99).

There are half a dozen pages of this, and much of it is good—not just because of the shrewdly rich surreal Whitmanianism, but because he also catches the mixture of feverishness and negation that constitutes the crucial city experience. The "frenzied nothingness" makes Miller sing; but the melancholia that follows the mechanized orgasm of the city-vision also provides him with the awareness that nothing—nothing short of apocalyptic violence—can make a Christian, or any other, order out of the modern megalopolis.

Miller's strength as an urban poet, though weakened by his near epic pretensions, is not simply primitivism. Near the end of the book he recalls, with the pathos that overwhelms much of *Capricorn,* his being frightened and alone in the North Carolina countryside during one of his few flights from the loved and hated city. In this episode Miller realizes "what a terribly civilized person I am—the need I have for people, conversation, books, theatre, music, cafés, drinks, and so forth" (308). Such ruminations, which run through all of his works, and his concern for elaborate meals, varieties of wines, books, painting, as well as his endless geniality and garrulousness, reinforce the self-aggrandizing myth of being an artist. Caught between "complicated needs" and "this infernal automatic process" which demands too much, he must find a devious path in which outraged rebellion itself can become a profession within the comforts of society—thus making him a man of letters.

In contrast, his simplest rebellion and his direct flowing colloquial laments often give his best stance:

I'm here to live, not to calculate. And that's just what the bastards don't want you to do—to live! They want you to spend your whole life adding up figures. That makes sense to them. That's reasonable. That's intelligent. If I were running the boat things wouldn't be so orderly perhaps, but it would be gayer, by Jesus! You wouldn't have to shit in your pants over trifles. Maybe there wouldn't be macadamized roads and loud-speakers and gadgets of a million-billion varieties. . . . there certainly wouldn't be any cabinet ministers or legislatures be-cause there wouldn't be any god-damned laws to obey or disobey, and maybe it would take months and years to trek from place to place, but you wouldn't need a visa or a pass-port or a *carte d'identité* because you wouldn't be registered anywhere and you wouldn't bear a number and . . . you wouldn't own anything except what you could carry around with you and why would you want to own anything when everything would be free? (281-82).

Natural skepticism about the social fraud arises, through native American exuberance, to natural anarchism. But both the modern rebel and his modern world inevitably achieve a more complicated alienation. For both are disorganized, and so a more fundamental violation becomes necessary. Thus Miller connects the "lucid" and the "daffy" and becomes, he claims, "the unique Dadaist in America" (286). The ultimate negation of society and of any possible larger order becomes an ultimate affirmation of himself, and Miller can then say "yes, yes, yes" by acts of annihilation. The rebel who goes all the way into the modern chaos comes all the way up into a new sense of life: "New beings, yes!"

Confronted with the urban chaos and meaningless frenzy of life, Miller, by a kind of "implosion" of the psyche, finds him-self back in the land of childhood. For a major example, he recalls that he and his cousin, in a boy's fight in a park near Hell Gate, accidentally killed an eight-or nine-year-old opponent with a rock. They then returned to Miller's Aunt Caroline, whose sour rye bread provides "tacit but complete absolution" (128). Like Proust's cake—unquestionably Miller's source here —the dark bread, used as the memory key, opens corridors of enchantment into "a primitive world ruled by magic" (129) with the numinous power of incomprehension and non-respon-sibility.

Miller pours out a long run of fragmented anecdotes about his Brooklyn childhood. One whole series centers on magical companions—a Jewish boy, a French lad, an exotic Cuban—who carried some penumbra of enrichment not yet throttled by the Brooklyn daily world. These figures represent the escape from that ordinariness which provides Miller's great curse but also his identity; they also stand for the whole childish ethos, the "enlarged world" of "anarchic man" (145). Childhood was "crazy and chaotic but not [as] crazy and chaotic as the world" of adults. The last of the series of youthful heroes, arriving and departing when Miller was twenty-one, is Roy Hamilton, a self-educated young man out of the West in search of his father. For him, Miller claims the heroism which he attributes in general to childhood heroes—and later to literary saints and madmen—of achieving "a minimum of discord between the truths which were revealed to him and the exemplification of those truths in action" (147). This didactic point actually underscores Miller's own overwhelming split between his "truths" and his "actions."

Miller's trip to the West, which follows, is weakly described, and apparently was ineffective in restoring the sundered world of maturity to magical wholeness.[6] Many of the other episodes are further elaborations on the same theme. Miller's amusing description of his father, who swore off drinking too fast and fell into, and then out of, the inebriation of bland Protestant religiosity, and then finally into gross somnambulism—his snoring gets a burlesque two-page description—illustrates one of the losses of authority in the child's world: *"Father, sleep, I beg you, for we who are awake are boiling in horror . . ."* (167). Since all maturity becomes alienation for Miller, the very sequence of memories, leading inevitably into adulthood, destroys the magic of the child-vision of life. Other mantic flights become imperative; other methods for producing a manic "euphoria" must be found if the chaos of America is to be overcome.

Music, sex, and a dada-like derangement of sensibility provide a jumble of ecstatic epiphanies. *Capricorn,* outside of one early chapter division and a number of irregular breaks in the free-associating run of prose, has only two formal divisions. Drawn on musical analogies, these are an "Interlude" of fantasy composition and the concluding apocalyptic essay about the Dark Lady entitled "Coda." Music—Miller's piano playing as a youth—also provides a burlesque subject matter. His first sexual conquest of his piano teacher at fifteen, ostensibly leads, also via music, to the next seven (or more?) gross and amoral seductions which are presented with the traditional American male exaggeration.

Sexual epiphany more explicitly provides an organizing trope in the irregular development—perhaps on some vaguely musical analogy—of the motto for *Capricorn*: "On the Ovarian Trolley." On one level, this simply refers to the compulsive train of sexuality, the pursuit of several dozen pudenda, that runs through most of the book. But the trope intends much more than this; the ovarian trolley, beginning with Miller's bemused comments about his reluctance to leave his mother's womb, in the opening pages, to his final violent assertion of nailing on the wall the black womb of his Dark Lady, would seem to be Miller's wildly splayed version of Otto Rank's *The Birth Trauma*.[7] While Miller intermittently exploits some of the metaphoric possibilities—being misborn, regressive states, a changeling child, burrowing back into the womb of memory and fantasy, the metaphysical womb-journey into rebirth, and so on—Miller's mind and art depend upon fortuitous, even gratuitous, exfoliation of metaphors rather than on elaborate Dantean or Joycean metaphoric architectonics.

The "ovarian trolley" image has several forced developments in terms of auto-fantasy, ending in an apocalyptic vision. The starting point comes from that kind of gross literal fact Miller delights in; his Cosmodemonic clerk, Hymie, is married to a woman with diseased ovaries. While on a trolley ride, Hymie asks Miller to explain ovaries to him. In Miller's state of associative mania and intentional derangement, this request starts him off: "from the idea of diseased ovaries there germinated in one lightning-like flash a sort of tropical growth made up of the most heterogeneous sorts of odds and ends . . ." (49-50). A few pages later he revealingly explains that "I had never done what I wanted and out of not doing what I wanted to do there grew up inside me this creation which was nothing but an obsessional plant, a sort of coral growth, which was appropriating everything . . ." (53). *Tropic of Capricorn* and, indeed, the whole autobiographical fantasia are the verbal equivalents of that obsessional growth.

Miller writes to purge his failures as a human being—not to understand or to transform into a meaningful structure but explosively to unload in bursts of heightened language. At times he grows pretentious in the process: *Capricorn* is "the equivalent of that Purgatory which Dante has described" (208) (he also compares *Cancer* to Dante's *Inferno* and his Big Sur writings to a description of Paradise). Actually, a kind of schizophrenic verbal gesturing remains central. I have previously noted the defining self-alienation which Miller cultivates with his discreet actions (theft, sex), discreet things (vaginas, words), discreet feelings (sentimentality, malice) which are given heightened isolation from a full human context. In *Capricorn,* discussing his fascination with the image of ovaries, he writes: "Only the object haunted me, the separate, detached, insignificant *thing*" (54). His cannibalism of the sensibility he neatly perceives as "a perverse love of the thing-in-itself." And it rests, of course, on romantic inversion; where William Blake found truth only in "minute particulars," such as the symbolic grain of sand, Miller finds his in "minute particles" which always take form as a "blemish" or a "grain of ugliness which to me constituted the sole beauty of the object." From such fragments he compiles his obsessive growths which give shape, such as it is, to his world of dismembered imagination, mixing times and fantasies, books and Brooklyn, rages and longings. This self-alienation can be given continuity and identity only by the insistent rhetoric which tries to create a distinctive voice for that naturally surreal being, Henry Miller.

Thus, though Miller will attempt, rather unsatisfactorily, to claim the American way of life—Cosmodemonic labors, Brooklyn philistinism, the loss of innocence—as the purgatory which explains him, just as he claimed the down-and-out inferno in Paris as the explanation of *Tropic of Cancer's* gestures, the ostensible causes explain very little. Miller would remain self-alienated in paradise—and his testaments there would be equally fractured and fragmented. His lively nihilism, his "ferocious gaiety" that he occasionally achieves by "balancing at the edge of the abyss" (62), may sometimes provide appropriate comic comment on the more general alienation, frenzy, and loss of center of the twentieth-century world, but it inheres most fully in the subjectivity of the author. The longing in the *Tropics* for cataclysm, for destruction and annihilation, is also the longing for the metamorphosis into new being and purpose—the desperate lunge out of partial chaos, as in modern wars and social manias, into the ultimate chaos.

The "ovarian trolley" trope is replayed in the "Interlude"

section which Miller also calls "The Land of F——." In meditating on the impersonal compulsion of life represented by sex, "my soul would leave its body and roam from place to place on a little trolley such as is used in department stores for making change. I made ideological changes and excursions; I was a vagabond in the country of the brain" (202). And what he finds, *Cancer* style, is that every exit is marked "ANNIHILATION." He again exploits the destructive process, a "Gentile Dybbuk." In this section impersonal and dehumanized sex with an idiotic baby sitter turns into a monstrous growth of fantasy to reach toward some sort of meaning. In yet another variation on the "ovarian trolley" trope, he makes the actual pudendum into a super-pudendum "not of this land at all" but of the "bright country" of the imagination (196). More specifically, he imagines the womb at hand to be an ornately furnished Pullman car. By such fantasy processes the fragmented and nearly meaningless experiences can be turned into something portentous—"eschatological, ecumenical"—and the gross, pathetic, and compulsive become excitingly rich. The man of resentment creates his own universe of memory and fantasy.

However, the Miller of *Capricorn* is not quite the Miller of *Cancer*. During his years in Paris, he became increasingly influenced by the visionary in a more impersonal sense—astrology, Zen Buddhism, and several occultist doctrines (Swedenborgianism, Jewish mysticism, etc.).[8] As we noted of the *Colossus of Maroussi*, Miller's return baggage from his European sojourn included several more or less traditional unitive visions. Some of this crops up throughout *Capricorn*. In the fantasy ramble of "Interlude" the ovarian trolley seems to carry a fundamental occultist principle: "everything is sentient" (204). Miller's wry way of developing the animistic view shows characteristic downward animation: "Once this fact [of universal sentiency] is grasped there can be no more despair. At the very bottom of the ladder, chez the spermatozoa, there is the same condition of bliss as at the top, chez God. God is the summation of all the spermatozoa come to full consciousness." Perhaps, then, an increase in sexual intercourse will provide an increase in divine consciousness—a charming idea. But rather than pursue further implications of Miller's methods of fantasy, now incremented by the usual occultist acrobatics around "the self and the not-self" (207), the emptiness which is unity, the change of heart in which degradation becomes angelic, etc., or Miller's insightful asides ("all department stores are symbols of sickness"), let us return to the lesser tropics of America. For it is quite likely that the occult myths so popular with twentieth-century literary visionaries are but fragments shoring the ruins of more human and social passions.

Miller's demand on America for "a life more abundant" (300), by which he means a life more individually comprehensible and humanly joyous, is transformed into a monstrous purgative edifice. Its backyard baroque shape derives partly from the over-assertion of one who discovered himself a nullity— "just a Brooklyn boy . . . which is to say one of the last and least of men" (48)—and his change of heart becomes partly that of the underground man, resentful and perverse, and partly that of the homegrown sage, didactic and prolix. The mechanical glitter and the alienated thingness of America reflect his self-alienation, and of course deny the mystery of grace as well as of creation. Miller, with his shapelessness, often inadequate presentation, and his confused stridency raises rather than commands his interesting material. His simple story, occasionally obscured by his rhetorical gestures, is merely sad: his lost first adolescent love; the pathetic affair with a maternal older woman; the disappearance of childhood heroes; the rapid breakdown of the ineffective father; the fading of the innocent vision of the primal neighborhood; disillusionment with the boy's dream of American opportunity; and the descent into the compulsions of work, sex, domesticity, and Broadway excitement.[9] By going, in his mind anyway, to the extremity of resentment and rejection, of anger at maturity, he dismisses America and the all-too-ordinary, inverts reality to memory and fantasy, and becomes *"an angel"* free to create his own country and cosmos.

Though Miller is all too willing to dramatize himself as criminal and saint, both gratuitous acts and grace, despite hyperbolic prose, tend to buffoonery. One source arises from apparently unintentional literary parody: "I was really a brother to Dostoyevsky, . . . perhaps I was the only man in all America who knew what he meant in writing those books" (211). His peccadillos, however, are rather more those of the timid opportunist and the polymorphously perverse child—in *Capricorn,* the quick sex in the back room, the swiped pennies, the fanciful lies, the sly obscenity at a funeral, the mixed affection toward and exploitation of buddies, the puckish cheating on job, wife, friend, and principle—rather than any Dostoyevskian anguish. Always the literary man, he must make large claims for his small stature in the effort to make himself monumental.

"I should have been a clown," he properly notes early in his laments of how the world misunderstands him; and so, as both mock-underground man and synthetic angel, he is. While Miller would have achieved more art if he had stuck to direct clowning in his writing, his wrath against the American he was does sometimes provide a curious testimony of a fragmentation and a longing which belong to much of America as well as to Miller. The incomplete rebel, he suffers from the very compulsions, stridency, righteousness, ambitions, and inchoate yearnings he denounces. He does sometimes effectively present, almost in spite of himself, the mixture of glittering surfaces and soft centers which make the American experience almost incomprehensible. His cry of the heart is for the means to put the cosmic and demonic pieces of America and Miller back together. Certainly, despite some wonderful responsive flourishes, that curious documentary mélange, *Tropic of Capricorn,* does not succeed in doing it. This Brooklyn Columbus must remain perpetually at sea in the tropic of his self-pitying rages about the America of his dreams.

II The Air-Conditioned Nightmare

Miller's frequently brilliant gestures—his metaphors, titles, and roles—go in search of a context. As he travels, in memory and in fact, back and forth between Europe and America, he does not so much describe his experiences as turn out rhetorical markers indicating partly submerged fears, longings, and fancies. Of one of his trips back to the United States in the 1930's he wrote a hortatory dirge, "Glittering Pie," in which he labeled America a "nightmare" of uniformity-conformity.[10] The endless American re-doing of the cityscape, the proliferation of bland "skyscraper souls," of automated aloneness and gregariousness, of glittering and vicarious lives, end in nothingness. Only the artist, apparently, can escape, for he joyously *"plays the role of undertaker"* (345). Typically, this apocalyptic essay neither describes anything as such, nor argues any problem or point of view, but simply strings out labels, vestigial anecdotes, names, and tropes; it ends with an all-encompassing condemnation of America, except for the artist-condemner. There are many similar pieces. They point to an interesting vision of America but never actually present it, and even the sloganizing becomes prolix and irrelevant.

The apt title of *The Air-Conditioned Nightmare*[11] covers two volumes of miscellaneous pieces (*Remember to Remember* is "Vol. 2 of The Air-Conditioned Nightmare").[12] The major subject is art and artist, and most of these sketches are marked by the point of view of the professional literary prodigal. Miller's encomiums of his artistic friends and his editorials on the state of American art show him at his weakest as a writer, thinker, and person. Among the other pieces are several of Miller's best burlesques. But first, the frame. *The Air-Conditioned Nightmare* is ostensibly organized around Miller's year-long tourist travels in America, via automobile, a year after his return from Europe in 1940. Actually, except for the summary remarks in the "Preface" and a few sketches loosely connected by the sequence of the highway, the linkage is vague and arbitrary. Another, and unintentionally amusing, frame may be seen in the epigraph and appendix to *Nightmare*. Miller starts with a long passage from Swami Vivekananda about the Sattvika (unknown and silent hero). Not only with his usual aggrandizement and noise but also in the appendix and in a number of sarcasms along the way (115, 247), Miller shows what an anti-Sattvika he himself is by displaying his anger at not being given a Guggenheim fellowship in 1941 for his trip around America, though he had a sizable advance from a commercial publisher.[13] He appends a list of representative Guggenheim projects, of the usual pedantic sort, "for the reader's delectation." The persistence of the author's righteous sarcasm may puzzle readers: shouldn't Miller, a long-time mocker of genteel institutional frauds, have expected the refusal, and taken it as a compliment? The ideal audience for whom he writes, however, consists neither of Sattvikas nor of sophisticates; like Miller, they apparently delight in bumptious naïveté and in playing the sly child among the earnestly fraudulent adults.

Righteous stridency runs thickly through the preface of *Nightmare*. Miller's reactions to America on his return from Greece, he tells us, were full of dread, disgust, and anger; but a passing comment of typical candor, about his "wretched, sordid memories" (11), gives us the awareness that his miseries were really more internal than public. The inhospitality of America to the artist, its materialism and gewgaws, and other stock charges are sprinkled through the miscellaneous personal details of arranging the trip. Then follows a list of the best experiences of the trip, in which the primary one, for this eternal literary man, is reading a book. That year's Miller awards for best man, best woman, best soul, etc., show the usual overstated quaintness—a Hindu swami, the wife of a Negro poet, a Jewish philosopher, and a theosophist. He names some other friends, gives tourist-style praise to gas-station jockies, lists the best bookshops, and notes the obvious experiences of the touring littérateur—boring academic wives, terrifying landscapes, and the "monotonous fabric" of American life. The concluding half-dozen pages consist of an editorial against American mediocrity and for heroic revitalization. He finds, of course, no place in America for the "poets and seers" who people his dream vision of a literary man's America.

"Good News! God is Love!" is an angry sermon in which Miller impatiently dismisses the largest part of his American nightmare, and the largest part of America: all that represented by Pittsburgh, Cleveland, Detroit, Chicago, and points between; all that personified by "futilitarian salesmen," Walt Disney's coy monsters, and fatuous, clean, anxious American faces; all that found in the cruel slums, the sterile hotel rooms, and the frightening industrial landscapes. With too much thrown in— and thus not adequately realized—the occasionally apt rhetoric generally turns blatant in dealing with the discrepancies between the rich and the poor (corporations create these with their "tentacles"), the frenzied productivity and the feeble culture, the moneypower and the individual blandness, and the more evident forms of dullness, ugliness, stupidity, and soullessness. While Miller is not altogether wrong, neither is he quite right; and a good many of his slap-dash caricatures miss the actual America, as in linking the United States "status quo" with "Czarist Russia" (24), or in using the Southern poor as the praiseworthy antithesis of the machined souls of Detroit—as if they weren't literal brothers!—or in holding up the synthetic religiosity of the suburban Bahai Temple as the answer to what is wrong with the South Side in Chicago (51). For the "Good

News! God is Love!" which Miller saw chalked in horrible irony on a Chicago slum building is, for him, stock doctrine as well as bitter mockery.

Occasional bits, though never an extended piece, of invective are well turned, such as that directed against the business-busy American: "the fat, puffy, wattle-faced man of forty-five who has turned asexual is the greatest monument to futility. . . (41). Or the condemnation of mass culture, which doesn't even have the virtue of narcotics: "Real dope gives you the freedom to dream your own dreams; the American kind forces you to swallow the perverted dreams" of those with only the cheapest of longings (31). Agreed, too, "Souls don't grow in factories," or in the slick, bright ruthless ambience of technological idolatry (37); but they may also not grow in the Indian reservations and European slums which Miller sentimentally counters with. The sense of American actuality will run out rapidly with such large spouts as Pittsburgh, "symbol of brutal power and wealth," vs. Ramakrishna, "incarnation of love and wisdom" (24). Miller, of course, pours less of his feelings through Oriental love-and-wisdom than through the literary hysterias of Celine, Patchen, and other *prophètes maudits* that he imitates.

When Miller sees America, his memory sees France, as in the third sketch, "Vive La France!" This wandering bit of rumination finds everything equally hideous in Jacksonville, Cleveland, Milwaukee, St. Louis, and Ruston (Louisiana), though not much is presented; but in the nostalgic memories of France everything is beautiful. The contrast is spurious since Miller compares his rage against Americans as "clean clots of phlegm" with his magical associations around *Le Grand Meaulness*.[14] The literary dream-life, not the ordinary world, American or Parisian, is the real base of the Francophiliac frenzy with which he concludes this tiresome essay.

"The Soul of Anaesthesia" consists largely of didactic ruminations triggered by his visit to a prison in the South (Atlanta?) which he connects with an ex-convict. Neither place nor man gets presented in any significant detail, though Miller reacts violently to the prison and sentimentally to the ex-convict. Several suggestive motifs peep through—the sexual cruelty of prisons, the innocence that the social victim acquires, the crime in every man's heart, the sedate torture characterizing modern institutions—but none of them are significantly developed, perhaps because frightened Miller has two all-encompassing answers: First, "There is only one word to remember, as you pass in and out of life, and that word, as every great soul has said, is LOVE" (81); and second, some pages of ornate apocalyptic prose whose verbal delirium anesthetizes Miller's fright at nightmarishly inexplicable suffering.

At this point we might comment on Miller's long sketch, "The Alcoholic Veteran With the Washboard Cranium." Though published in *The Wisdom of the Heart* anthology, this seems to belong somewhere in the middle of the first volume of his American trip.[15] The "veteran" is a grotesque character whom Miller and his painter companion reputedly met one night in New Orleans. By his own report, a badly scarred and disillusioned hero of World War I, this loquacious drunk also claims to have been a successful lawyer, doctor, legislator, commerical writer, convict, poet, builder, adventurer, song writer, desperado, and so on. As Miller presents himself, he took an absurdly long time to figure out that the down-and-outer was a fraud. He then draws some lengthy morals to the case.

The handling of the anecdote is weird in more than its' naïveté. As given, much of the veteran's fluid, fragmented, and quaint monologues on war, politics, modern society, and American food belong to Henry Miller. Yet the skidrow philosopher is treated with hostile detachment by his alter ego, and the moralizing is even more contradictory than usual in its mixture of condemnation and sympathy. The narrating author admits being cruel in the way in which he dismisses the veteran; when questioned about this by his companion, Miller gives the shoddiest rationalization, insisting (in reference to the Cosmodemonic days of several decades earlier) that he had "heard so many terrible tales, met so many guys like this . . . that I've hardly got an ounce of sympathy left in me" (128).

Yet Miller launches into lengthy philosophizing about the necessity for a true revolution of the heart, as against other forms of ameliorative change; and he attempts to demonstrate the point in a confessional double-ending. With some slyness, the author seems to admit that he belongs to those who "always know how to muster a thousand reasons for withholding their aid" to the unfortunate, as he did with the "alcoholic veteran." Yet he decides to write of the veteran, he tells us, for the didactic purpose of making "people more kindly and tolerant" (137-

38). (Just how his presentation of the alcoholic veteran as a fraud will encourage charity must indeed remain a puzzle.) Then comes the memory of when Miller walked the streets of New York, himself a garrulous moocher, and a man in a cape and opera hat threw some change for him in the mud of the gutter. Miller's anger, before he picks up and washes off the thirty-six cents, is therapeutic. He later announces to his wife that he is joyous: "I've just been humiliated, beaten, dragged in the mud and washed in the blood of the lamb." He buys her an Easter morning hamburger in a "greasy spoon on Myrtle Avenue," and makes "a vow to remain wide awake and if possible to wake up the whole world, saying in conclusion Amen! and wiping my mouth with a paper napkin" (139).

Curious, what! as Miller loves to say. He might also *say* that the Easter morning revelation proved that human sympathy comes from suffering. However, the ostensible moral is mostly a paper napkin to finish the literary meal. The tale, as we have it, belongs to the true confessional tradition in that it undercuts its own moral. Miller's hostile pretense at patient listening to his own mirror image (the veteran spouting Millerian doctrines); his cruel dismissal of the man and what he stood for, and his absurdly transparent justification for witholding human sympathy; his candidly admitted exploitation of the man for literary-didactic purposes, and his contradictory moralizings—these show a rather different understanding of his own heart. The personal anecdote of humiliation which Miller suddenly inverts into joy we can also recognize—it takes the same form in *Cancer* and *Capricorn,* and in the volumes of *The Rosy Crucifixion*—as showing his usual perverse strategy for turning misery into ecstasy. Unlike the earlier and parallel story "Max," the "Alcoholic Veteran" is about Miller, his inability to suffer, his inability to sympathize with the sufferings of others, and his casuistry by which, representative sentimentalist that he is, he has inadequate tangible sentiments. Avowedly concerned with the wisdom of the loving heart, his superb candor reveals the joy and the "wisdom" of the loveless heart. Quite a confession!

There may be some analogical connection between this motif of the sentimentalist who cauterizes most personal sentiments and the motif of the anti-artist who spends much of his time shouting about artists. When we return to where we left off in the first volume of *The Air-Conditioned Nightmare,* we find a series of five pieces about art and artists (the two just before the end, numbers 17 and 18, are also on the same subject). The longest centers on the character of Weeks Hall, who is described as a compulsive talker, full of gusto, responsiveness, and eccentricity—the same type as the Greek poets of *Colossus of Maroussi*—and who is also the proprietor of an old mansion, "The Shadows," in New Iberia, Louisiana. Miller's stay leads to a fairly straightforward, if touristic, adulatory account of the place and its proprietor, both seen as part of a mythic Old South of rich and bizarre culture.

Miller broadly generalizes the same theme in the concluding brief section of the book, "The Southland." "This world of the South corresponds more nearly to the dream life which the poet imagines than do other sections of the country" (248). What he has in mind are *not* the Gothic nightmares, which in point of fact American poets have found appropriate to the South, but the fancy mansions of tourism which evoke "magical names, epoch-making events" of a supposedly plantation economy which produced a "great symphonic pageant" (252). He has, of course, granted that it was based on a vicious slave culture, but so were "India, Egypt, Rome and Greece" (250). What Miller blandly fails to emphasize is that the South never produced a good minor culture, much less a great one; however, dream can substitute for deed, for "who knows what splendours might have blossomed forth . . ." (251). But in the long piece on "The Shadows" he noted, with rather more perception, that the idiosyncratic custodian-artist of the Southern heritage "was a self-convicted prisoner inhabiting the aura of his own creation" (101). Even with pious and pernicious Southern mythology set aside, Miller does not recognize the genuine, if narrow and vestigial, enchantment and real mythos of the South—its tragically violent and earthy folk culture. The refugee from Brooklyn ordinariness comes looking mostly for the bizarre fantasy; and, in his eagerness to grasp the exotic fruit of art, he ends with nubbins of quaintness.

Miller's perceptions, as well as his genial mixed bag of artists and culture-fantasies, seem fortuitous. "Dr. Souchon: Surgeon-Painter," links a few details of New Orleans with some ranting about American philistinism and the seventyish medico-businessman who became a primitive Sunday painter. Since, for Miller, an American artist is a social eccentric "who has faith in himself" (104) and in self-expression, his qualities of mind, feeling, and art become secondary. Besides, this Sunday painter links in Miller's mind with New Orleans, "the most congenial city in America," whose tourist section seems to sentimentalist Miller the one place "on this bleak continent [where] the sensual pleasures assume the importance which they deserve" (111).

The "artists" in "Arkansas and the Great Pyramid" are two cranks, Albert Pike, nineteenth-century Masonic Potentate and occultist, and William Hope Harvey, who wanted to build a multi-million-dollar pyramid. Miller's artless praise of them consists largely of miscellaneous information and quotations. At the other end of the American artist spectrum is a surreal apologia for *avant-garde* auditory experimentation, "With Edgar Varese in the Gobi desert," which mostly sloganizes: "THE WORLD AWAKE!" (146); "Be more and more like God" (147); "Nothing is deader than the status quo . . ." (147); "if one *believes*, miracles occur" (148); "*We are all filled with murder*" (154)—and so can only be redeemed by violently magical artists. The euphoric praise of Steiglitz as a culture-broker and of John Marin (whom Miller imitates in some of his own paintings), or the brief blurb praising an old Paris friend. "[Hilaire] Hiler and Murals," (161) produce only sentimental indulgence.[16]

So, for the most part, does the "Letter to Lafayette," a fragmented personal polemic in which Miller praises the "genius" of several of his devotees. The center of this work seems to be righteous hyperbole, perhaps including some fractured self-pity, directed against America. If an American has any talent, shouts Miller, "he's doomed to have it crushed" (136); if the sensitive citizen of these States is "dedicated to beauty," he will spend the rest of his life "in a straight-jacket" (137). His advice to the artistic American: "Shoot yourself, young man, there is no hope for you!" Alternate advice is: "Do anything, be anything that comes into your head because it's all cuckoo . . ." (139).

The mélange of provincial swindlers and corn-doctors, twentieth-century eccentrics and off-beat artists, in Miller's sentimental and noisy rebellion against American dullness, is a kind of home-grown dadaistic salesmanship. The art of the blurb, with the usual overstated asides about nightmarishly wicked

America, also dominates the tediously written pieces on artists in the second volume, *Remember to Remember* (pieces 2, 3, 5, 6, and 11): painters Varda, Beauford Delaney, and Abraham Ratner (probably, in its digressions, the best of the sketches); sculptor Benjamin Bufano; and theater director Jasper Deeter. His personal friendship with them does not encourage any complex, critical, or subtle response—thus demonstrating the very provincialism he rants against. The clownish defiance of disinterested awareness—the complete lack of humility in taking his own experiences, his friends and his responses as definitive and absolute—is not confined to art and artists. In the thirty-page preface to *Remember* he also does passing "homage" to a series of friends, though the lack of development means that they can have little interest to a reader. Miller's avowed affection for "the salt of the earth"—bootblacks, AWOL soldiers, and other outcasts—seems to be only sentimental since he does not bother to portray them in any detail.

The same limitations apply to the following pages of invective against America. Though he rages against nationalism and statism, Miller tumbles into an amorphous mixture of the occult, Jules Verne, and millenarian populism. Thus he predicts a "new realm of consciousness" bursting forth in the worst of all possible worlds: Japan soon taking over Europe, the world-wide revolution of the "little man" ushering in a utopian "new age," and fantastic inventions which will straighten out all practical and psychic perplexities. Miller can get pretty silly when he practices the American vice of positive thinking and subsumes every difficulty under an indignantly vague and literalist fantasy.

The matching escape into memory provides the long title sketch of *Remember to Remember*. The main subject is remembered France, not the France of *Cancer* and "Max" but of a righteously romanticized nostalgia. The main motif comes from the didactic novel, *The Renegade*, by his Paris companion, Alfred Perlès, in which the libertine hero is saved by the occultist's message, "The mission of man on earth is to remember" (295). Following Perlès in believing that the escape from the present into memory provides both "identity" and "eternity" (292, 300), Miller uses a few instructional aids, such as maps of Paris and France, to get himself into the proper humor for his anecdotes and exhortations about the natural religiosity and

culturosity of France in contrast to America. Miller's overstatement of the merits of French wine, whores, scenery, spirituality, food, and books results in loose Francophile prose which
lacks real discrimination.[17] Sometimes Miller sounds like a
DeGaulle of bohemia.

Another way of being outside America while in it—the ap-
parent therapeutic function of much of Miller's writing—is
to see only the dream of America. In "My Dream of Mobile"
the bookish child's version of Marco Polo starts off a series of
ruminations which include a fantasy of Farragut's Mobile. A
few curious details about the actual South join the exotic
substitution, though Miller prefers the dream to actuality,
especially when he can finally collapse both into the self-
mystagoguery of Henry Miller someday disappearing into
Tibet.

A less wilful version of Miller's child-centered cosmos appears in "Day in the Park" where he tells several anecdotes
about children. The first briefly focuses on a tough, eight-year-
old Negro in Charleston, but Miller's natural preference is for a
softer image and so he develops a contrasting anecdote about
a younger pair he takes to the zoo in Albuquerque. The dia-
logues and details show the wryness and coyness we might
expect from a lonely, genial middle-aged tourist. He develops
a tearful longing for children. Also impressed with the child's
indifference to moral values— "the gift of detachment" (177)—
Miller finds yet another way out of anxiety and guilt besides
memory-fantasy. The sketch concludes with the children out
of sight, the rain coming down, the magic of the day dissipated,
and the sense of empty depression of the solitary and homeless
American in an auto court.[18]

The next three sketches in the *Nightmare* also belong to the
Americana of highway culture, and they culminate appropriately
in the burlesque world of Hollywood. On the way we have a
pleasant comic set-piece, "Automotive Passacaglia," in which
unmechanical-minded Miller burlesques his own naïveté with
the motor troubles of his old Buick and ends by satirically
asking for good old American kindness to animals and auto-
mobiles. But the Buick seems to get him to the Grand Canyon
which provides the scene for several anecdotes, the major one
about the entitling figure, "A Desert Rat." The first few anecdotes shrewdly mock the crassness and vapidity of some

standard American tourist types. Quite antithetical is Olson, the talkative, "philosophical" old-timer from the desert who tells Miller of his outsmarting the professors, of his fantastic theories about diet, of the magic power of the Indians, and of how to straighten out World War II. A typical weakness appears in the sketch: only rarely does Miller succeed in separating his *persona* from himself to give him independent and adequate voice. With apocalyptic hatred Miller-Olson delights in the view that Indians are better than the white Americans who are a "swiftly decaying people . . . degenerate and degraded in every way" (198). This gesture of inverting the usual tourist sentiment is elaborated in a good bit of cantankerous mythology.

Better done is the loosely woven but intensely felt next stage west, "From Grand Canyon to Burbank." The tension that gives immediacy to the descriptions here depends on the sharply changing scene as one progresses into California by anxiously pushing on overheated car across the desert. Miller's fluid prose and sharp eye for incongruity, which accords so well with the southern California materials, aptly projects the discomfort and the time and place.

So, too, with the next and best piece in the first volume of *The Air-Conditioned Nightmare,* the surreal satire "Soirée in Hollywood." Miller's fragmentation and free-swinging provide proper tools for the comic vision of Los Angeles. The Millerian catalogue of oddities, leveling religion and Coca-Cola, fusing the Marquis de Sade and right-wing Americanism, linking the "faérique" and the neon, provide the reality of Sunset Boulevard, which he describes as being "like a strip-teaser doing the St. Vitus dance" (225). With wry colloquialism, surreal metaphors of incongruity, and a speeded-up comic violence indebted to slapstick cinema, Miller presents a wealthy Hollywood dinner party where everyone is "soused," righteously phony, and childishly outrageous. The iconoclasm, the spoofing, and the earthy shrewdness of the boy from Brooklyn with an *avant-garde* verbal dexterity here find their natural milieu. And the ever so appropriate irreverent and irrelevant give one a Los Angeles which gives "a feeling of the future," a "bad future" (224), and the corny penultimate of the open society and the pluralistic culture.

"Astrological Fricassée," the longer parallel party sketch in

Remember to Remember, is one of Miller's best burlesques. Given the natural grotesques of an absurd Hollywood, and a host, Gerald(-ine), who is a snobbish, malicious, exploitative, homosexual astrologer—a dead ringer for "The Red Queen"— Miller is not distracted by ambiguities, his doctrinaire view of a stock America, or the need to defend himself from ordinary reality. We get detached observation and dialogue, plus comically artful metaphor, for each of the caricatures at the party: a rich, sickly, and officious upper-class American lady, who "might have been the twin sister of Carrie Nation done by Grant Wood in a moment of Satanic illumination" (222), with a heart "ticking away like a rusty Ingersoll" and blood "running through her veins like mucilage soaking through blotting paper"; Lady Astenbrooke, mad, trivial, rigid, British authoress, with three cherries on her hat and deflated leathery breasts, who bows like a "broken hinge" and stands like a "tipsy Gainesborough to which Marc Chagall had put the finishing touches" (224). Other guests include a "portly, interior decorator type of homosexual" (230) with a "yoo-hoo" voice; a strikingly beautiful and self-aggrandizing dancer, Lolita, "blank and flawless as stainless steel" (237) and with a similar hard and shiny vanity; Humberto, pawing and bewildered drunk, whom Miller introduces to a name-dropper as "the assistant gynecologist at the Schizophrenic Sanitarium in New Caledonia" (262); an ornate and sweating Cuban lady, whose posterior hung over "the seat of the chair like a piece of limp liver" (234), and who had a suspiciously dapper husband with "butter-colored gloves" and the threatening asperity of a "Neapolitan barber" (235); a pack of yapping "trained poodle" females, "terribly psychic," who talk of their reincarnations towards Karma (229) while nibbling tea cookies and thrilling to Miller's occult "aura" ("Violet . . . with a touch of magenta"); and varied other "psychopomps" of the nether world.

Miller's bemused detachment and mocking contempt, and, perhaps most important, his general lack of pretension to being an American prophet, a unique personality, or a Great Artist—the bloated ambitions which mar so much of his writing— give him a brilliant comic command of his material. The fantasticality and incongruity of surrealist epithets, verbal displacement, and violently playful yoking produce stylistic power when turned to such concrete farce. Perhaps, too, the purlieus of Hollywood provide a most suitable locus for the more disciplined pyrotechnics of surrealist style, as we see in these two party pieces of Miller's and in the more bitter-pathetic *Day of the Locust* of Nathanael West. For the disjunctions of surrealism aptly convey the appropriate violence, sexual warping, ruthless longings, and empty dreams. While Miller sometimes falters, such as in the coy burlesque of himself as a writer with Hollywood possibilities (something he quite lacks), he usually stays within the shrewdly limited comic point of view. Even with the counterpointing little vignette midway in "Astrological Fricassée," when Miller brings in a charming young innocent, a true pathetic visionary in contrast to the occult fakers, he manages, for once, to stay short of sentimentality in contrasting dream with dream.

The final long episode of "Astrological Fricassée" centers satirically on Mrs. Rubiol, pretentious wife of a rich American petroleum engineer-inventor. Miller uses most of the "stand-up" comedian's amusing repertoire in mocking her: parodied name dropping, learned *non sequiturs,* highfalutin jabberwocky, dead-pan fantasia, and more of his translation of surreal, visual incongruities into comic rhetoric. The sequence ends with farce deflation, the petulant homosexuals making love, drunk Humberto imitating a whale under the couch, Mrs. Rubiol in an alcoholic daze ("her eyes twittered like two desynchronized song birds" [268]), and, as a Marx brothers' fillip, a complacent undertaker arrives searching for a corpse. At the genial conclusion the characters are all looking for something to eat— Miller's common-sense focus—and are prepared to turn the place upside down.

The wild word is all. The burlesque rhetoric of "The Staff of Life" broadly satirizes American bad taste in monuments as well as in bread, inadequate spice in conversation as well as in salad, sugary weak sensuality in sex as well as in beverages, and lack of tang in life-style as well as in cheese. The comic techniques include mock-logical sequences: "poor bread, bad teeth, indigestion, constipation, halitosis, sexual starvation, disease and accidents, the operating table, artificial limbs, spectacles and baldness, kidney and bladder trouble, neurosis, psychosis, schizophrenia, war and famine" (36). Then onward and downward through "the decay and dissolution of our once glorious republic"—all because of standard American bread.

The outsider's gusto for food provides the vantage point for hilarity against the American fear of "the zest for life" (51).

From the burlesque vantage point Miller can mockingly play with clichés, instead of falling into them: "it's the pie that takes the cake" (46), that standarized American machine pie with its piece of fruit "surrounded by a clot of phlegm" (47). Using the traditional device of comic displacement, it is the birds of North America, fed on our crusts, who decline—"beaks have become dull, their wing-span shortened; they are pining and drooping, moulting in season and out. Above all, they no longer sing as they used to; they make sour notes, they bleet instead of tweeting, and . . . have even been heard to cackle and wheeze" (53). The actions that take on their own mechanism— what Bergson labeled the "snowball" device; the scenery-collapsing finale of vaudeville—becomes a favored device of Miller's in such comedy. Towards the end, he has a long parody recipe, in outrageous mockery of both our bread and our earnest desire to jazz things up, where he uninhibitedly throws in ketchup and kerosene, anchovies and urine, to improve "the staff of our unsavory and monotonous life" (52). There are appropriate asides on American fruit salad and salesmen (our crassest dishes), on the uniformity of our stock restaurants (try to get a herring or a grape, nuts, good cheese, or Jewish bread), on how America melts down the rich foreign-born diets into the automated pot of bland stew, and on the closely related tastes for Hollywood funerals, Christian marriage, war production, and conspicuous garbage. In describing much of our grossness, Miller again displays his Thoreauvian touch, even some parallel verbal conceits. "Earning a living," the major excuse for our hurried, prefabricated diet, "has nothing to do with living. It's the beltline to the grave, without transfer or stopover" (40).

In the hyper-logic of burlesque, Miller's sweeping condemnations of everything American become meaningful in a way that his petulant rages cannot possibly become when he poses them in more earnest forms. In comedy he can properly ignore the multiple shadings and nuances of awareness which his naïveté, egotism, and alienation deny him in efforts at more serious writing. "What do I find wrong with America? Everything." Only from the perspective of the saint or the fool can the total rejection of a given order of society take on authentic shape and meaning. The rebellious wisdom of the wise buffoon is in the detached simple-mindedness and absolute logicality with which he can annihilate all. Unfortunately, Miller frequently does not recognize his essentially comic perspective and limitations. But when he does, he comically follows out the American logic (though not the mixed American realities) which hates human communion even more than communism, suspects rich responsiveness even more than regal simplicity, and, in creating the world center of conspicuous garbage and hygienic nihilism, makes us super-esthetes who let our machines and organizations live for us.

Miller often relates his gestures of buffoonery to dadaism and surrealism—no doubt they did provide liberating elements for natural American hyperbole and fragmentation—and rather questionably links himself to Petronius and Rabelais. But some more native roots nourished his vulgate zest and wise-fool iconoclasm. Much can be found in Miller's beloved burlesque theaters and vaudeville; in the great American silent film comedians; in traditional American male obscenity, exaggeration, and deflating jokes; and in similar urban folk styles.[19] Part of this richly mimetic and mocking heritage goes back through several thousand years of the popular arts of fools, jesters, clowns, and buffoons. Miller's literary revolt was less a negation of Puritanism and Philistinism and Americanism than of the restrained style, genteel sensibility, and understatement so essential to the main Anglo-Saxon literary traditions. Miller adapts more folkish traditions of direct and outrageous humor, full of obscene and blasphemous energy, into literature. And this humor is drastically antithetical in tone and appeal to the prevailing castrated amusement of the mass media or to the impotent urbanity of cultivated wryness (à la New Yorker).

Until recently, much of the hyperbolic and iconoclastic, mock-heroic and verbally fantastic comedy—except as rural folkloristic humor in writers like Faulkner—has, like sex and profundity, been covert in our literature. The rough comic heritage which Miller helped rediscover for literature, along with an increasing number of recent continental dramatists and American novelists, provides valuable laughing defiance at a world constructed on anti-human logic. The gravest limitation of Miller as comedian is that he doesn't stick with it but instead pursues romantic, metaphysical, and other literary ambitions which provide a

ponderous and masked buffoonery—as when he casts an obtuse
clown named Henry Miller as the tragically passionate lover in
The Rosy Crucifixion. Except for some asides, only the few
pieces just discussed, from the two lengthy volumes of his
American trip, have intentional humor. This lack is unfortunate
for if Miller had been able to confront more American reality
and to give it comic shape, instead of fleeing into indulgent
dreams, fantasies, prophecies, rages, and vanity, he might have
produced several good books instead of two weak anthologies
that are only partly redeemed by a handful of good epithets and
three or four burlesque sketches. For comedian-Miller is right:
America *is* absurd. Artist-prophet Miller demonstrates well
the pathology of American culture in which a little is made
into too much, thus ending in even less.

The concluding fillip to the two-volume anthology is a
joke gone ponderous, a two-page prose-poem epilogue, "The
Most Lovely Inanimate Object in Existence." The provocative
gesture of the title has only a synthetic context, a catalogue of
allegorical (and capitalized) mythic American journeys ending
in a "cold, dead mystery, like Mesa Verde" (427). The revelation is that "we are on top of the Mountain that was God, and
it is extinct. . . ." What is really wrong, then, with America,
the natural home of the "inanimate object," is that its God is
dead. And so Miller, the comic outsider who, in *Tropic of Cancer* wanted to give "a kick in the pants to God" (11), is left
rather spiritless on the Enchanted Mesa of America.

III *Horatio Alger at Big Sur*

After some American touring and an extended spell in Los
Angeles, Miller found his own enchanted mountaintop on the
central California coast and settled down for the better part
of two decades. The boy from the city streets who had, in his
forties, discovered himself as a writer, had, in his fifties, discovered the simple life in nature in the American West. He also
started rearing a family and identifying with a community, as
well as industriously working in various roles as a professional
avant-garde littérateur. Despite Miller's repeated confessions of
cowardice and confusion, there is some admirable quotidian
bravery in this determined pursuit of an identity and a place.[20]
That, at the end of this saga, his first book (*Tropic of Cancer*)

should become a million-copy best-seller, providing him with the proverbial pile of money and other appurtenances of celebrity-dom, properly rounds off this American success story. Henry Miller, indignant mocker (in *Tropic of Capricorn*) at the Horatio Alger "sick dream of America" where the indomitable youth rises from rags to riches, becomes a kind of paragon of the self-made American literary man. It is, of course, a success story full of aslant comedy: our smiling young hero is a some-what odd seventy-year-old man whose public success depends on notoriety as an ostensible pornographer—Horatio Alger *en marge*.[21]

In literary fact, Miller's later writings have not only little obscenity but often little of the earlier verve, though some ele-ments of idiosyncratic charm always remain. The later writings can conveniently be divided into the endless "autobiographical romance" (already discussed), into the equally endless literary ruminations (discussed in the following chapter), and into the writings focused more or less on the Big Sur present. The main miscellany here is the one entitled *Big Sur and the Oranges of Hieronymous Bosch* (1957).[22] This volume, divided into twenty-two pieces (jottings, sketches, prose-poems, autobiographical fragments, and sermons) cannot readily be given systematic discussion. The one sustained piece, of over a hundred pages, is "Paradise Lost," a perverse memorial to Conrad Moricand (1887-1954), French astrologer-occultist and derelict-dandy, friend and intellectual mentor of the author. Miller knew Mori-cand in Paris in the 1930's and had him as his guest at Big Sur for three months in 1948. That visit, for which Miller brought the nearly destitute Moricand from Europe, is less a study in the tribulations of friendship than a portrait of decadence and another documentation of Miller's bumptious naïveté.

With a frequently effective turn of detail, Miller sketches Moricand as an elegant conversationalist, fastidious parasite, meticulous pornographer, sickly old snob, and utterly impossible person. Images of his running psychosomatic sores, of his sexual and moral perversions, of his collaborationist wanderings through wartime Europe with two suitcases of occultist manuscripts, and of his absurdly threatening and whining demands, enlarge into a pervasive sense of the sickness unto death. Miller's motives in bringing this small-time urban decadent to his rural American retreat seem compounded of nostalgic sentimentality for his

Parisian days, uninsightful sympathy, and, apparently, some obscure guilts about his own relation to suffering. Wryness—to invite Moricand was "like inviting Melancholia to come and perch on your shoulder" (296)— mixes with fascination.

In his usual chaotic way, Miller drops in scattered autobiographical musings, descriptions of memories, fragmented sensations, food, books, and sketches of several fantastical friends (a grossly energetic and lavish Hollywood cameraman, a neurotically earnest Christian Science healer, an enigmatic—undeveloped—learned recluse),[23] and several sermons on living simply and wisely. As with Miller's earlier portraits, running from "Max" through the "Alcoholic Veteran," there appears in "Paradise Lost" the usual odd mixture of Miller's sympathy and righteousness, including again the compulsive anecdotes from his own days of beggary. Yet the genteel, neuresthenic, rigid, depressive Conrad Moricand—friendless but unable to be alone, paranoiacally suspicious but totally dependent—remains trapped in a misery quite alien to the healthy, garrulous, sentimental, shrewd, self-delighting, and self-appeasing Henry Miller. While the mean and miserable have no monopoly on suffering, Moricand, as Miller makes fulsomely clear, starts miserable and has only one direction to go. An implicit theme here, and through most of the self-congratulatory later writings, is that "whosoever hath, to him shall be given."

Rather than discuss again the weird synapses of sensibility characterizing Miller's sketches, we might consider some larger dimensions of Miller's portraits of grotesque outcasts. Sometimes mistakenly viewed as naturalistic documents, they are essentially studies of bad-luck figures, black fools, sacrificial blemish scapegoats. The author's rhetorical distance, underlying both the too-general moralizings and the nasty, precise detail, may, in literary terms, be related back to a pre-Christian, classical stance, as in Apulieus' Socrates episode in the *Golden Ass.* Charity in such stories is poisonous; sympathy simply increases the parasite's demands and produces outrageous results because it violates the magical order of the universe and of the magician-author which such tales presume.

Miller's portraits of Moricand also belong to a type whose finest twentieth-century example is D. H. Lawrence's portrait of Maurice Magnus.[24] The similarity between Magnus and Moricand is striking: quasi-aristocratic background, incongruous Foreign Legion service, left-handed intellectuality, compulsive fastidiousness, genteel mooching, "unnatural" vice, resentful authoritarianism, pretentious literary ambitions, dandyism, verbal charisma, total disloyalty, miserable lonely death, and so on. Lawrence and Miller even use some of the same comparisons—the lost figure of melancholy against the beautiful landscape, the desperation of the trapped rat. But whether Miller, a devoted student of Lawrence, derives some of his treatment from the Magnus portrait is of less import than the awareness that Moricand-Magnus belongs to a fundamental type. The grotesque dandy of literary cultivation and spiritual degradation becomes a major exemplar of decadence, repulsively fascinating to Miller and Lawrence who seem to sense a kind of diabolical parody of their exacerbated and outcast sensibilities.

Miller, especially, having less character—which means less style —must defend himself at length against the diabolist who would destroy his paradisaical vision.[25] In a long lecture in which he accepts the "poetry" and basic principle of astrological occultism ("as above, so below"), he rejects some of its arid abstractness and dehumanization. In the process, he emphasizes his being "very much of an American. That is to say, naive, optimistic, gullible . . . a product of this land of plenty, a believer in superabundance, a believer in miracles" (319); he is equally a believer in "experience," in a self-righteous *quid pro quo* ("I made all the mistakes . . . and I paid the penalty"), and in the divinity of the ego and the actual world. While Miller's rather boozy exhortation in itself need not concern us, it does provide a vulgate and anti-tragic American rejection of unrebellious European pessimism, sickness and despair, as appropriately represented by Moricand. The Devil is a decadent European, and Paradise is still the traditional American dream.

Most of the other pieces of the *Big Sur* volume lack art at any level—Miller, now secure in his identity as an artist, no longer produces either art or anti-art but simply casual jottings—and his praise of Big Sur becomes jumbled ruminations on artists, misfits, children, faith-healers, and the author's friends and followers. While some of this could be interesting material, Miller usually just names it rather than presents it. Though the book is filled with shadowy figures of aspiring autobiographical writers, or their letters in which Miller can smell "genius a mile off" (169), almost all these people seem exceptionally pathetic, confused, self-centered, and pointless. While part of this emphasis may be the covert side of Miller's egotism, it may also characterize the rather passive bohemian modes of the 1950's.

In ostensibly defending Bohemia-by-the-Pacific as, rather weakly, a millennial interpretation of the pious medieval painter Bosch,[26] Miller aims to defend individuality, a contemporary Thoreauvianism of wise and simple living. He does a poor job in carrying out this admirable purpose. Several examples from the final sermonic piece of what he rightly calls his "potpourri" may characterize the whole. Aware of the non-ideological stance of most of his fellow outsiders—bohemian privateerism—he wryly observes that if they were running things "there would be no need for revolution, they would run the country into the ground in no time" (256)—and the country would be better off for it. But most of his gestures lack humor and finesse, as with his gross praise of two other groups who do not conform: gangsters and "call girls" (270). This casual, and irrelevant, attempt to up-date his earlier sentimentality about rogues and whores overlooks the fact that gangsters and call girls are, for the most part, notable examples of over-conformance to the very things Miller rages against.[27]

After a burlesque catalogue of things patently wrong with America (250-51), Miller gives a curious counter-list of how to truly live—curious because he cannot decide whether to be serious or comic in recommending flight from money, mass-culture, etc. Among his stock adages about doing everything in moderation are such dictums as "don't irritate your boss . . . don't use bad language" (252). Miller's admonitions to be neighborly and loving occupy the same rhetorical margin between blandness and buffoonery. Though Miller always tripped into triteness in his writing, he now wades in clichés. Even when aware that he is trite, he is only tritely aware: "The greatest problem is . . . how to get along with one's self. Trite, you say. But true, nevertheless" (145). Similarly, his invective against America—against reading *Life* and the *Reader's Digest*, against installment buying, and against joining organizations (262)—appears as easy and empty gesturing when it is undeveloped.[28] The pervasive deadness of writing, thinking, and awareness is rather sad; for by it Miller does a disservice to the individualism he supposedly defends—to the "lone-American" heroically will-ing "to live *en marge*" (255).[29] A literary rebel gone flatulent may well be the least rebellious of all.

Miller is, with a few small exceptions, not much better than mildly quaint in his later small collection of literary and moral pronouncements, *Stand Still Like the Hummingbird* (1962).[30] Once more the message of the artist versus America, the indi-vidual versus conformity, and God versus Americanism, lacks body and development. Why he is against the artist being "still regarded as a menace to society" (ix)—if the society is anywhere near as bad as Miller says—remains perplexing. That foundations aid mediocre and bad artists (viii), that conformists are "petted and pampered" (ix), and that America is often in the vanguard in creating a mad world may all be true enough, though Miller does nothing with those commonplace assertions. Besides miscellaneous discussions of literature, *Hummingbird* contains some sermonic essays. "Children of the Earth," starting with rather obtuse praise of France as against America, ends homiletically on the "inner peace" and "atoneness" Miller found in America but should not have according to his evaluation of America.[31] "When I Reach for My Revolver" also finds Europe a "honey comb" and America a "desert," and ends by apocalyptically quoting Isaiah. There are many other rhetorical gestures that belong to an age several generations back in defying a stock reality of a provincial America and a Brooklyn crassness. The world so seen is vestigial and so, perhaps, is the seer.

There, indeed, seems to be the crux about Miller in the con-temporary United States: he really is the outsider, far more so than he knows; he is so far out he rarely gets near, in per-ception, art, or understanding, to any sort of tangible America. It is not just the clichés about conformity and materialism and gewgaws and machines (and literally hundreds of other things), nor even that most of his later writing about America comes out as assertion rather than presentation, but the deepest of disrelations. Miller, as I have repeatedly pointed out in analyzing his writings—and could elaborate at endless length—has a fun-damental horror of and separation from ordinary reality. Miller's obsessive and fractured sensibility is no pose. Miller was always in childish flight—abroad from America, abroad into memory and fantasy and the occult, abroad into "Art," magical gestures, and rhetorical distance. Even when ostensibly describing America in the *Air-Conditioned Nightmare* volumes, he elaborately describes his fantasies, France, and the atypically bizarre (Hollywood parties), or he fell into second-hand bombast. In *Big Sur* he only gets significantly concrete with the visiting European, Moricand. The only tangible unclichéd material in the pieces collected in *Hummingbird* is some digressive description of France in an essay on Ionesco. His major effort during the more than twenty years back in the United States was the willful digging into the America of three and four decades past—the volumes of *The Rosy Crucifixion* ("Reunion in Brooklyn" is simply an appendix to this). Then, too, Miller's rage against America—the compulsively repetitious denunciations which, with some updating of clichés, actually reflects the artistic and social situation of the 1920's rather than that of the 1940's, 1950's, and 1960's—clearly seems an extension of his traumatic alienation in the Brooklyn days. Whether or not Miller should be in contemporary America is not the point—he does pretend he is writing about America, though the writing gives the assertion the lie—but there is something totally disconnected about Miller's ostensible later relation to America.

In attacking the inadequacy of Miller's attacks on America, the critic is not defending America against Miller. For example, Miller's repeated stock charge of "materialism" not only does not inform but misses the point; as, in various ways, Santayana, Lawrence, Huxley, and many others have noted in making the same charge, American "materialism" is outrageously idealistic in ways incomprehensible to a French shopkeeper and that often may lead, I would add, to its hypocritical viciousness. The American best-seller system which Miller rages against (at least half a dozen times in the books discussed in this chapter) is obviously a gross mechanism, though one—I think unfortunately—so valueless that it will indifferently boost all sorts of books into irrelevant sales, including *Tropic of Cancer*. Miller's attacks on the surface conformities of Americans, such as identifying themselves with organizations and their jobs, concern the deplorable; but Miller, who does the same thing in his identifying with Big Sur and with the role of "Artist," fails to note that the conformity is really pathetic because it indicates a terrible isolation, a vagueness of identity, and a lack of basic community.

When Miller is not foolishly asserting his role as American

sage, he may show us something significant. We might conclude with several points he does show: His success in playing the role of the angry American adds an interesting variation to the Horatio Alger story of how the American boy makes good, for Miller's not very adequate denunciations have never brought him much other than a distinctive role and fame, followers, and profit. If we were cynically to suppose that Miller altogether chose to play that role, we would have to admit that the choice would have been personally shrewd and artistically bad. But Miller seems generally simpler than such chicanery would require, and the official role as angry American outsider fits well not only his obsessive flight from the ordinary but also from the perplexities within a comfortable nightmare. From Brooklyn to Big Sur, what *is* this America to which Miller is always announcing he doesn't belong? Miller, least of all, seems able to tell us what America is, but Miller's writings perhaps uniquely show us the American. And what is the American? Apparently the result of an outrageous trauma when he discovers the antithesis between American dream and actuality; thus he is someone in complete flight from both himself and America. The further outside America and self he gets, the more American he becomes.

CHAPTER 5

The Rebel-Buffoon

I *Heroes From Books*

MILLER'S MAJOR ROLE is the buffoonish one of substituting writing for life. While his literary endeavors focus almost completely on the exploded ego which constitutes his life, his major experiences and longings are obsessively tied to the literary process. As he confesses in *Tropic of Capricorn*: "I realized that I had never had the least interest in living, but only in this which I am now doing" (13)—that is, writing. For Miller, the yearning to "express" himself becomes a total end in which *what* he has to express is the yearning to express himself. In rebelling against any limits to that role, he searches for rhetorical identities which culminate in the buffoonish literary hero Henry Miller.

Since Miller views self-expression as his heroic achievement, it also becomes the implicit (and sometimes explicit) prescription for others—a kind of religious therapy for the sensitive, the injured, and the rebellious. In this respect, apparently, Miller has had some effect as a hero of the literary life. Miller also seems to have believed that his way of self-discovery of self-expression provides enlightenment for materialistic, hypocritical, meretricious America. In this literary religiosity, reading provides the forms of devotion, art and artist the ark and priest, and writing (or painting) the sacramental acts. While literary bohemia should provide the community of true believers, and sometimes does (as in his Big Sur ruminations and his comments on artist-friends), Miller rightly suspects most modern sub-societies—they do lack genuine autonomy and difference—and so vicariously finds true community only in communion with the saintly artists of past and present.

Miller's commitment to self-expression is sometimes mistakenly seen as making his work the verbal residue of an unusual

life. However, his autobiography is of more rhetorical than fac-
tual interest, even to Miller. His life, with the partial exception of
the flight to Paris, has been the fairly ordinary one of a not especially adventuresome or profound literary bohemian, American
style. Miller has, of course, been unusually persistent, and fantastically lucky. Actually, his ordinariness provides Miller's
appeal to many; in his role as literary cynosure he uninhibitedly
combines common American pathos and muddle with the grand-
est yearnings to play artist and saint.

Miller's literary-religious role is an unusually direct adaptation
of his own early longings. It is also an amazingly simple adop-
tion of earlier romantic-subjectivist notions of the literary life.
An apparently avid and responsive reader in childhood, Miller
sought for experiences in literature to transcend ordinary life
and to provide heroic feelings of aliveness for one terrified by
the meaninglessness of life and self. Because, as he often acknowledges, he is not very heroic in action on any level, the
personal process of reading and responding to reading becomes
for him the self-fulfilling way. All literature for Miller is literal
personal propaganda. From adventure stories and romanticized
history and biography, he moved on to chaotically diverse reading in which the two major directions seem to have been exoticism and artist-hero worship. The exoticism included (and still
does) the more fanciful sort of history (Crete, China, Atlantis),
popular romance (Haggard, Sienkiewicz, Bellamy), and inspirational philosophy. The artist-heroes were generally the
extreme, alienated "moderns," such as Nietzsche, Lawrence,
Strindberg, Van Gogh, Dostoyevsky, and Rimbaud. While Miller's
major interest in literature lies where literary biography and
rebellious religious quests meet in the artist as hero, he often
strikes one as a reflection of the perverse geniuses as seen in
the distorting mirrors of an American carnival funhouse.[1]

The process of Miller's literary responses, and a considerable
volume of writing, may be represented for convenience by three
writers, taken in the chronological order of Miller's enthusiasm:
Lawrence, Balzac, and Rimbaud. Apocalyptic Miller went to
school in the writings of D. H. Lawrence. In *Tropic of Capricorn*
he says that Lawrence was one of his obsessive concerns in
his early days of artistic groping. After completing *Tropic of
Cancer* he worked on a book announced as "The World of
Lawrence," which he never finished. He did publish.over the

years a half-dozen essays on Lawrence drawn from his abandoned book, plus a great many scattered remarks. It is characteristic of his interest that Miller never refers to Lawrence's novellas, stories, and travel writings (his best work), nor to his poetry, nor to most of his novels. Miller's Lawrence may be found almost entirely in the violently metapsychological polemics, from "The Crown" to *Apocalypse*, plus the early memoirs about the man. Miller is only interested in the artist-prophet.

In "Creative Death"[2] Miller insists on the religious uniqueness of the artist in dealing with modern spiritual malaise. By his "criterion of passionate experience," Lawrence became a major diagnostician of the fundamental failures of our time. Miller, rightly I think, recognizes that "creative death" (positive nihilism) is the nuclear Lawrencean meaning.[3] Miller, in another essay, praises Lawrence's "sacred" view of sex;[4] and he sometimes sounds off on sex in a similar manner, though his own hyperbolic naturalistic view of sex makes his Lawrencean stance rather buffoonish. But Miller's most insistent point, as in the weak article "Apocalyptic Lawrence,"[5] is that Lawrence had a violent awareness of twentieth-century alienation which he profoundly recognized but perversely refused to transcend. In Miller's most absurd piece on Lawrence, "Into the Future,"[6] he earnestly poses a saintly trial consisting of Jesus Christ, Saint Francis, and D. H. Lawrence; but he also indicates that Lawrence failed in spirituality because of his destructive separateness.

In "Shadowy Monomania,"[7] Miller's best discussion of Lawrence and one of his most coherent essays, he analyzes some of the dualities of his apocalyptic hero. Lawrence, he argues, failed badly as a man but, aware of his own sickness, his obsession with "always smelling corruption" (271), he recognized the need for drastic individual regeneration. Miller also aptly notes Lawrence's eager search for "symbols of destruction" (234); his self-portrait in his polemic against Poe; his Oedipal and spiritual crippling which led to his compensatory phallicism; his highly feminine yet insistently intellectual sensibility; and his often ridiculous but intensely alive nature. In sum, Lawrence is appropriately viewed as an extreme sensibility and as the intellectual artist and faltering religious man warring with the modern world.

In "The Universe of Death,"[8] a suggestive general literary essay from his abortive Lawrence opus, Miller argues that Lawrence struggled far more intensely against death-in-life than the other major moderns. Proust and Joyce substituted art for life to produce a literature of "onanism" and a "head-culture" with a "mortuary odor." The later Joyce turns out to be a sensitive "sick scholar" seeking to escape into a womb of words. Proust was disintegratively "ultra-civilized." In comparison, Lawrence is the real life-affirmer, though in "Shadowy Monomania" Miller wisely qualified this by emphasizing that Lawrence's obsessive concern with death and destruction is his creative perversity.

As his best remarks in these early essays indicate, Miller showed a lack of interest in literature as such but an interesting dialectical sense about the perplexed quests of his literary heroes. Lawrence provided Miller with a good many of the felt ideas about his own alienation and iconoclastic rages about the inhumanity of modern life; he also exemplified for Miller the role of the artist as God's angry man. Emphatic echoes of Lawrence occur all through Miller's work. Yet it was Proust, with his process of involuntary memory and his obsession with re-creating a lost world, and Joyce, with his shrewdly sordid details of urban life and his grotesquely elaborate verbal play, who more affected Miller's methods of writing. Put another way, Miller follows Lawrence's major lines of assault—against intellectual idealism, against middle-class culture, morality, and personality, and against the whole Western emphasis upon the rightness and power of "Will" and its culmination in mass-technological society—but Miller develops these by imitating or adapting the embalming rhetoric of the major twentieth-century decadents.

Miller's Lawrence significantly searched for a unity which he could never achieve. So, for Miller, does Balzac, as we see in a later phase of Miller's quest for a literary-religious hero. Again we find what would by most standards be considered an eccentric emphasis upon the minor works. Miller dismisses most of Balzac's "realism" and the novels of the *Human Comedy* to focus on the two occult tales, *Seraphita* and *Louis Lambert*. These are hardly the major works of Balzac. Miller has an altogether extravagant and permanent admiration for *Seraphita*.[9] Miller's real concern with Balzac's works, besides their personal effect on him, is as autobiographical documents of a tragically unsuccessful occultist.

In "Balzac and His Double"[10] Miller thoughtfully views the French novelist as a victim of a cold mother and harsh schools, of conventional literary ambitions and success, of a maladapted genius close to schizophrenia, of spiritual art in an unsympathetic world, and, especially, of the disease of Will.

> The study of society and the psychology of the individual, which form the material of the novel in European literature, served to create the illusory world of facts and things which dominate the neurotic life that began with the 19th century and is now reaching its end in the drama of schizophrenia. At the back of it is the Will, reducing through the powers of analysis all life to ashes. Balzac was himself aware of the disease which is killing us. It is the mind which is poisoning us, he says . . . . Dostoyevski gave expression to the conflict even more forcibly. Indeed, it is with him that the novel comes to an end, for after him there are no longer any individuals to write about, nor is there any society which may be said to possess a body. Proust and Joyce epitomize the dissolution of our world in their great epics. With Lawrence the novel becomes a vehicle for the Apocalyptic visions which will occupy us for the next few hundred years, as our world fades in blood and tears (216).

The portrayal of Louis Lambert, a hypersensitive and self-destructive occult genius, Miller sees as Balzac's cry of the heart against his own illusory intellectual and social will. Seraphita, an hermaphroditic Swedenborgian "Angel" who ascends to heaven in pure spiritual love, Miller sees as Balzac's answer and cure, but one which Balzac was incapable of accepting.

Miller's essay "Seraphita"[11] consists of summary, quotation, and paraphrase; like most of Miller's ruminations, it suffers little from the ashy "powers of analysis" he condemns. "Balzac and His Double," more than forty pages about the problems of Balzac-Lambert, is more informative, analytic, and interesting. In neither essay does Miller give any attention to the literary characteristics of these novels. Miller, of course, is opposed to "literary" standards. But even as occult documents it would seem that Balzac's novels must suffer from their artistic defects—gross melodrama with stock characters—as well as from a mechanical and unimaginative presentation of Swedenborgian doctrine. In the dialectical battles waged against dubious ideologies by "modern" literature, Swedenborgianism,

in its very eccentricity of engineered Protestant super-ration-
alism, provided perverse weapons, as we see in its peculiar
adaptions by such writers as Blake and Baudelaire. But Miller
certainly, and Balzac probably, confused the occult means with
the writer's ends of enlarging awareness and passion in ways
quite antithetical to occultism. The major literary occultists
of the past century and more seem, after all, to have been anti-
occultists in their twisting the doctrines into esthetic means
("symbolism"), into polemics (the critique of middle-class society), and into this-worldly subjective exaltation (their responsiveness to the actual). Occultist writings rarely achieve any
literary merit, and our literary men, even when trying, hardly
ever achieve occult ends—fortunately. The major appeal of such
"marginal" religious experience is in its heterodoxy, not its
piety, in a world of inadequate or of viciously manipulated
rationalisms.[12]

In Miller's writings on Balzac there appear a number of
implicit parallels with Miller's image of himself; in his writings
on Rimbaud, some years later, a major concern is with expound-
ing the parallels between Rimbaud and Miller. That also becomes characteristic of many of Miller's writings on literature.
He makes much, for example, of the repressive mother in the
lives of Lawrence, of Balzac, of Rimbaud, and of Miller. According to him, all were poorly adapted to society and its institutions,
obsessed with questions of religious power, and ridden with
egomaniacal dreams of literary-religious glory. The parallels
seem too vague to help define the writer-heroes, except perhaps
the intriguing implicit suggestion that repressive mothers produce
sons who long for the cosmic womb of occultism.

Miller's book on Rimbaud, *The Time of the Assassins*,[13] insists on many parallels between genial old Henry Miller, who
did most of his writing in middle age, and the violent adolescent
Arthur Rimbaud, who quit writing before he even grew up.
Miller's identification is almost comic for, unlike Rimbaud,
he has nothing of the violent thug about him: a homosexual
Miller involved in assault, or running guns in the misery of
East Africa, or grimly accumulating money, or contemptuously
renouncing literature, and so on, seems inconceivable. Miller's
garrulous and rambling confession-burlesques provide as much
of a contrast with Rimbaud's hard and often obscure lyrics
as do the biographies of the two men, or their physical appear-

ances, or their sense of themselves. Some may find the comedy irritating when Miller goes so far as to insist that his sufferings "far outweighed" Rimbaud's—they patently have not—or when he implies that Miller is a better man and writer. But really, Miller's identification with Rimbaud is but another grotesque gesture of self-aggrandizing innocence and an outrageous parody of the vicarious cultism of literary hero-worship which so many have centered on adolescent Rimbaud.

Some of the cruxes of the Rimbaud "problem" come from the fact that that *voyant* turned anti-poet with a devastating clarity. Taking poetry as both a weapon of total revolt and total salvation, Rimbaud explored its limits only to discover its inadequacies for either, and, I believe, accordingly renounced it. When Miller writes, "I call that man poet who is capable of profoundly altering the world" (39)—it is a basic doctrine of his—he uncomprehendingly explains the metaphysical side of Rimbaud's renunciation of literature: Rimbaud had pretty well finished with adolescent literary egotism by the time he was nineteen. This renunciation may be the motive power of Miller's ruminations on Rimbaud—he can't believe it, though he sometimes makes his own gestures of renouncing literature as a substitute for life. Therefore, Rimbaud's "failure" must have been his mother's fault—"she who denied him, betrayed him, persecuted him" (139). Or Rimbaud's flight from poetry must have been modern society's fault, for it denies the "vision" of the artist, thus silencing him (131). Or Rimbaud's later life must have been a reverse spirituality, an "angel's" overdone demonic reversal into "*total* conformity" (147). Or, finally, the misery of Rimbaud is history's fault—the whole ideological assassination of the artist-saint in the modern age. Why else would a great poet-hero-visionary go under like a small bourgeois adventurer?

The major revelation in Miller's rather prolix ruminations on the Rimbaud legend might be found in what he never considers. Rimbaud, after all, was rather lucid in giving up the pretentious ambitions of the literary visionary to become, in the age of imperial capitalism, the most logical of "poetic" entrepreneurs, trading in guns and slaves in Africa and finally ending with a gangrenous body and a pious soul. The man was reasonably human, all too human, in his renunciation of large literary ambitions, in his simple longings, in his ordinary corruptions, and in his pathetic death. Directness and truth may be far more destructive than amorphousness and pretension.

For Miller, Lawrence seems to have failed in that his hard sensibility overrode his piety; as Miller rather neatly puts it, Lawrence proclaimed the "Life abundant" with "hymns of hate."[14] Miller's Balzac failed in that he could never renounce his literary and personal obsessions with society and all its powers to become an occult angel. Rimbaud failed in that he, unlike Henry Miller, renounced literature and came to a miserable end. Both the continuity and, I would say, the decline in Miller's literary perspective are evident from this pattern, which runs from the early 1930's to the mid-1940's. Miller generally misses the point that it is the perplexity, not the piety, of his literary figures which gives them their value. To all he applies the standards of the artist-prophet, the literary saint—an interest that may seriously be called cultish in that he judges each of the writers primarily for his qualities as a charismatic religious hero. When Miller treats art as a cultus, he baldly does what many do more covertly. The religiosity of culture is widespread in our time; once again Miller's muddled candor provides intriguing testimony to the malaise.

In his most extended discussions Miller also raises the poignant problems of why our cultural heroes are not more heroic human beings. But most of his writing on artists—"artist" must be taken very broadly to include novelists, painters, quasimystics, belle-lettrists, autobiographers—lacks significant religious dimension because it is merely literary hagiography. Most often he simply writes blurbs on his personal enthusiasms—frequently his personal friends—as in the dozen or so encomiums in *The Air-Conditioned Nightmare* and in *Remember to Remember*. Books on astrology, Dostoyevsky's *The Possessed*, children's potboilers, scholarly studies of oriental religion, Van Gogh's *Letters*, Nostradamus' prophecies, *The Divine Comedy*, Nijinsky's *Diary* during his madness, popularized histories, the *Tao Teh Ch'ing*, and a minor Jewish mystic[15] elicit similar praise for the magical enlightenment and personal inspiration they provide. While Miller once in a while turns a phrase, perception, or whimsical response in a curious way, most of this vast writing is mere verbiage—paraphrase, not particularly apt quotation, cranky fashion, personal blurb, disorganized autobiography, or just drifting rumination in which Miller demonstrates his contempt for dis-

crimination, standards, analysis, complexities, and even awareness of reality. Enthusiastic personal response is all.

While Miller's treatment of literature varies fortuitously from
casual remarks to fragmented pedantry to ornate appreciation,
there is rarely any developed argument, principled effort, or
full and deep range of response and commitment. Sometimes
Miller belligerently defends or insistently recommends, but
more often he simply and repetitiously says that he liked this,
was influenced by that, or bemusedly remembers this and that.
Miller's literary essays comprise some hundreds of thousands of
words of the overflow of a heavily literary life, a purely arbitrary
personal history of miscellaneous reading, undifferentiated enthusiasms, and endless recall of the many bookish years of a
garrulous littérateur. He takes literary culture as literal personal
experience, yet not seriously.

Certainly some of the pieces have charm, usually of a genial,
reminiscent sort—"Ionesco," "Anderson the Storyteller,"[16] some
passages in the earlier pieces in *The Books in My Life*. However,
many of the reminiscent essays are very badly written—witness
the long, bodiless, and nearly meaningless catalogues of theaters,
plays, and actors in "The Theatre."[17] Many of Miller's discussions—such as the repeated ones of Cabeza de Vaca, Spanish
explorer in the American Southwest who earnestly played witch-
doctor to save his life—lack elementary awareness; for Miller
takes an exaggerated interpretation of the man as a faith-healer
while ignoring the other sides of this ambitious courtier-soldier-
adventurer.[18] What Miller wants, especially in his later years,
is the easy enthusiasm for the simple messages of redeeming
spiritual powers.

Miller's rebellious and buffoonish asides, not his ponderously
inadequate and quaintly irrelevant discussions of his literary
heroes such as Whitman,[19] provide the merits of his literary
rambles. For example, *Books in My Life* makes some thoughtful
points about literary education. For literature to become meaningful individual experience, he points out, the young should
start not with classics (as Miller did) but "with his own times"
(32). Literature is not the crux of what the young should be
taught (43) since it is the one thing that must be self-taught;
besides, too much of a literary education will reverse itself since
"every genuine boy is a rebel and an anarch" (82). Literature,
contrary to most of the professors and other bland culture-sales-

men, is a matter of "possession" and "obsession" (70), which can only be falsified by the genteel authoritarianism of most of official education (178ff.). The "spiritual poverty" of America, by which Miller seems to mean both its Philistinism and its lack of social and spiritual density, is the real obstacle to genuine literary education.

As for the buffoonery, the later Miller is poorest at it when most elaborate. In "Reading in the Toilet"[20] he reverses his usual sense of incongruity to give a burlesque of middle-class American compulsive reading which is rather snidely cute. The hidden joke is that the late Miller is contemptuous of reading in the toilet, even righteously against it, while the more gusty Miller of *Black Spring* highly recommended it (57). A less intentional but even more elaborate buffoonery may be seen in Miller's constant catalogues of authors and titles throughout *Books in My Life.* He concludes with an appendix of "The Hundred Books Which Influenced Me Most." Here obvious broad parody is uncertainly stirred in with fundamentalist earnestness in mixed lists of literary and religious classics, good-bad books from his childhood and later, the works of friends, and various nostalgic incantations. As "influences" the list should not be taken seriously; it does not include Dreiser, Lawrence, Sherwood Anderson, Anais Nin, Michael Fraenkel, and many others who patently influenced him, consciously as well as unconsciously, in ways much more important than those listed. The self-importance assumed in this straightfaced comedy of Germanic pedantry and the do-it-yourself short catalogue was to find fuller expression in another volume in which Miller was to list *all* the thousands of books he could remember having read. Miller, of course, does not have a true subject; thus a quaint notion snowballs into a monstrous joke; this particular one, fortunately, he seems to have dropped.

In all of this writing Miller regularly makes pious affirmations of life over literature while he is actually and even pedantically exalting literature over life. The crux of this literary solipsism may most simply be explained as a series of deeply imbedded puns, a magical naming which is part of the widespread literary theology of our times. It is the method by which Miller can resolve his surface contradictions of literature and life. In brief, it goes something like this: "Art" means knowledge and writing; therefore, writing is knowledge. "To imagine" means to realize and to pretend; therefore, to pretend is to realize. "Creator" means god and artist; therefore, the artist is god. And so on. Once we recognize the hidden puns in the rhetoric, this contradiction of Miller's alternately exaggerated claims for art, artists, and imagination, and his violent disavowals of literature for "direct experience of life" (11) disappear. He wishes to suppress the more mundane, bookish, intellectual side of the rhetoric to exalt its religiosity.

Thus, too, Miller has little to say about art and writings as such. His pronounced esthetic usually takes the shape of an almost purely personal religious therapy, despite his later efforts to read the cosmos in the same terms. In "Reflections on Writing"[21]—a representative piece of dozens of such ruminations—he says that the "telling itself" (20)—the process of being the artist, not the art—is the important thing. And by the "telling" Miller does not mean the craft, the order, the knowledge, the awareness; he means the unconscious, fortuitous, and purely personal associations and effects on himself while doing the writing. He catalogues the things he could say about the conditions in which he wrote, nothing about the things he wrote or their relation to any fuller reality or truth (26). For Miller carries out the logic of art as a subjective process rather than as a product to its near extreme.

However, unlike some lucid French practitioners of anti-art, Miller is no more serious or consistent here than in most other things. He goes on writing, quite concerned with publishing and with being identified with the by-product. As to why he really writes, he may have much more accurately described it when he said that the artist was "between the hero and the saint," longing for "power—vicarious power."[22] Thus he can make of his "shattered and dispersed ego" (28) a new egotism and a process of revelation. What is finally revealed is not art, truth, or actuality, but a state of powerful personal being, of religious seizure or megalomania, in which the artist becomes "a god in fact and in deed" (24).[23] Such exaltation and such subjective transformations of the ordinary—whether in reading art, admiring art, making art, or contemplating oneself as artist—are the essential meaning of life for Miller. At his best Miller enthusiastically affirms the role of the writer as rebel and of literature as powerful personal experience. But as artist Miller is rarely at his best because he renounces literary heroism to move up the blessed hierarchy, though what in this world a god does is less clear than ever.

II *The Literary Saint*

In his first significant publication, "Mademoiselle Claude," the author was already busy, amidst his pimping, with a comic renunciation of the desire to be a "saint."[24] But when not putting aside his sainthood for lesser or higher being, Miller has had a goodly number of pronouncements to make on the religious life. Some few of his early sermonic pieces have a bit of the verve that belongs to his cancerous rhetoric; not so the later ones. Self-made Brooklyn boy, American innocent, and earnest refugee from lower-middle-class respectable piety, Miller longed for exotic cosmic notions to transform mere reality. At the times when he sweated hard over the disparities between ideas and living, and over his art, he gave verbal form to a significant attitude. But when he takes an idea as reality, or sees reality only through the brine of his exotic borrowings, he falters badly. Ideas of the saint and seer provide some of his most coy, and buffoonish, self-dramatization.

Miller's best religious speculations insist on the "antinomian quality of life." In the "Enormous Womb"[25] he sees life as a horrendous conflict between illusion and fear (96) with the actual world as the total reality which one must intensely and religiously accept. Thus he demands absolute engagement and response to "the idea which has obsessed all the religious maniacs, the very sensible one that only in living a thing out to the full can there be an end. It is a wholly unmoral idea, a thoroughly artistic one. The greatest artists have been the immoralists, that is, the ones who have been fully in favor of living it out" (98). It is a Nietzschean affirmation: *"The best world is that which is now this very moment"* (99). The comic-rebel side of this nihilistic yea-saying comes out in a short related piece, "Uterine Hunger."[26] Defiance gets put in aslant gestures; born wrong, he says, he naturally became "a rebel, an outlaw, a desperado. I blame my parents. I blame society. I blame God. I accuse. I go through life with finger lifted accusingly. I have the prophetic itch. I curse and blaspheme. I tell the truth" (188). And in yet another apocalyptic essay from the

1930's, he takes his title from Father Divine (a spectacularly self-indulgent leader of a fanciful American-Negro religious cult): "Peace! It's Wonderful!"[27] Here Miller insists, drawing yet again on womb-imagery, that in his Paris experiences he "touched bottom" (2) and was reborn into the acceptance of his outcast role. No longer suffering the illusions of "hope" (a "sort of spiritual clap"), he has reached cosmic self-sufficiency and self-acceptance: "Since I have become God I go the whole hog always" (3).

This overreaching, in which the Brooklyn underground man becomes the cosmopolitan and cosmic *öbermensch*, adds a footnote to Nietzsche's discovery that "God is dead." It reads: Hence I am God. By such blasphemy, Miller aims to go beyond, including beyond art ("kill off the 'artist'" in himself), and "simply *be*." Unfortunately, I think, Miller did not stay with his role of total rebel. "The rebel," he later wrote in unconscious epitaph, "is nearer God than the saint."[28] But Miller went in for literary sainthood and spent far more time being the moralist than the renegade, not going beyond art but spreading the gospel of it.

One of his many pronouncements as holy littérateur, "Artist and Public,"[29] will serve as an example. In it he urges not better art but more artists, and every artist in America should be given $2,500 a year for life (ca. 1946—it should be approximately doubled to get its useful equivalent in the early 1960's). Since he has a strong libertarian suspicion of governments, the money is somehow to be provided only by "the people" to the artists. Since he also suspects all critical standards (his own work, of course, was outside the usual accepted criteria), the money is to be given "to every artist, good or bad, deserving or undeserving" (409). Miller naïvely assumes that there are not very many would-be artists in America. But given the many millions of Americans with yearnings to play the glamorous role of artist— just like Miller—and his and their pervasive discontent with most forms of work and routines of living in contemporary America, the cost of supporting all self-proclaimed artists would be such as to make nuclear weapons appear cheap. Even if, contrary to Miller's suggestion, the stipends for self-declared artists were kept at a minimal subsistence level, invidiously far below prevailing economic rewards, so as to limit the number by requiring a price for assuming the role, would it not still be unfair to would-be philosophers, would-be religious men, would-be good men, and all the other honorific roles?

Miller makes some weird assumptions: one can establish vast social institutions without forms, standards, qualifications, judgments, or limits; asserted roles, and not actions and products, determine identity; and money is a prime encouragement for significant art and authentic individuals. No doubt many besides Miller do make these assumptions, though usually theirs are a bit more obscured. However, this is to take a representative argument of Miller's literally. He might be better understood as somewhat confusedly advocating an atomized brotherhood of religious adepts, called artists, who are publicly supported, somehow. The issue of a non-utilitarian and non-authoritarian religious caste, which only exists in disguised and attenuated forms in America, might merit further exploration. But Miller, so lacking in a sense of social realities and in intellectual rigor, is not the man to do it.

In the same essay Miller also vaguely propounds the rather antithetical traditional libertarian demand for an organic society of pre-industrial craftsmen and general self-sufficiency which will "foster the artist in every human being, see to it that everything one handles, sees or hears is imbued with art" (513). This serves less as an argument than as one of Miller's gestures of protest against the prevailing system in which esthetic values are outcast or over-assimilated into the bureaucratic and mass-industrial markets. One can fully sympathize with Miller's anger against systems which reward and encourage the mediocre and mendacious, such as ours (there appear to be worse ones), without taking his confused and righteous ruminations very seriously. Indeed, he does his own best role of "ordained defiance" a disservice when he pompously plays the "art-ridden" cultural game which he earlier denounced.[30]

It would be mere pedantry to discuss more than a representative few of Miller's ideas since his discussions are so badly written: prolix, fragmented, grossly inconsistent in tone, perspective, language, and argument. The rare interesting notions and metaphors simply set off the general bombastic weakness. In one of his long, confused rambles in the 1930's, "An Open Letter to Surrealists Everywhere,"[31] he starts with his Brooklyn verve: "Below the belt all men are brothers" (151). He then intermittently attacks living by, for, and as intellectual abstractions. His main purpose in the following ruminations seems to be the defense of an extreme religious individualism and the consequent refusal of moral and social commitments in this age of "spiritual famine." His ethic is to "live out the maximum of our potentialities" (154). Carried to the rebellious but decisive test, this means we should commit individual crimes—personal violence instead of mass war, individual hatred rather than such collective ideal hatreds as fascism and communism and Americanism. Though the prose does not make it very clear, I should guess that Miller was profoundly aware that the lies, frauds, miseries, cruelties, and murders of recent history are far less a product of immoral individual desires than of righteous collective ideologies. Thus the true artist, individual, and saint—Miller makes them synonymous—owes allegiance only to what "is active, immediate and personal" (160).

This is the position of the rebel, not the revolutionary; of the dadaist, not the surrealist; of the antinomian individualist, not the religious prophet-leader. Unfortunately, Miller buries these points in the usual irrelevant verbiage, a pastiche of long quotes and miscellaneous shouts about art, his favorite prejudices (Anglophobia and astrology), and various side-swipes at his contemporaries and his times. Such tiresome idiosyncrasy may be the too-literal application of the individualism he defends, and the best argument against it.

Despite the fancy literary locus, most of Miller's moralizings quite clearly come out of native American radicalism. In the late 1930's Miller wrote: "I was always an out and out pacifist, and still am." His cogent explanation is straight individualism: "I believe it justifiable to kill a man in anger, but not in cold blood or on principle, as the laws and governments of the world advocate."[32] But Miller seems incapable of developing this admirable and lucid view. A few years later he elaborates, for nearly a hundred pages, his position on war: "Murder the Murderer."[33] Miller's view of the ostensible war against fascism-Nazism remains the same refusal to commit himself to "any group or nation or cause or ideology" (129). He rings in a considerable amount of the native radical—"populist"—bombast of an earlier day: war is a product of the "vested interests" and the "munitions makers"—which may show lack of insight into the peculiarities of ideological and totalitarian wars. Part of his pacifism is put in traditional American individualist terms:

the right and "authority" of the "individual conscience" (179) is the only rule. However, he also increasingly glorifies his position of "detachment" as being the wisdom practiced by the great religious saints. With more piety than in his earlier writings, he does not put his emphasis upon individualizing evil and engagement but on self-purification. The title points up this motif: one should "murder one's own murderous self" (178) rather than anybody else. (The same argument is repeated and elaborated in a shortly following monograph, ostensibly about Wasserman's novel, *Maurizius Forever*.)[34]

Most of "Murder the Murderer" is prolix autobiography. There is also some of the usual burlesque overstatement; he is weakly comic about super "Flit" (insecticide) weapons and earnestly silly about America ("the worst democracy that has ever been tried out"[169]). Amidst other stridencies, clichés, and wanderings, there are casual provocative points. For example, Miller attacks the hypocrisy with which modern societies go to war. They never act consistently or genuinely; they never go "the whole hog" in carrying out their ideological claims to destroying dictatorship, defeating the enemy, establishing a different world, or whatever. It may be objected by political "realists"—not to mention obviously cynical rejoinders—that Miller fails to understand the complex relations between ideology and institutions; this is true but misses the point. Within his muddle, Miller simply recognizes a more basic truth: the labyrinthine discrepancies between ideologies and actions produce an increasing *sense* of futility, and, probably, in fact increases futility. Some truths, best recognized by saints and fools, are simple.

It is the wisdom of his naïveté—the occasional insight in the bombast, rambling, and clowning—which gives what substance there is to Miller's role as a saint. No increased proportion of wisdom, or good writing, seems evident in Miller's latest collection of mostly sermonic pieces, *Stand Still Like the Hummingbird*. "The Hour of Man," for instance, quotes and paraphrases several arguments that man needs to meditate on the religious nature of the world; and, if men do, the world will be paradisaically transformed. His negative arguments, as when he rants against conformity in "Lime Twigs and Treachery," are equally stock. The latest sermon, "Stand Still Like the Hummingbird," takes a few usual loose swings at America as seen from a jet plane (what is Thoreau-Miller doing in one?), then advocates replacing current mechanical technology with psychic technology (telepathy and celestial transmigration), though it ends with invective against a somewhat more likely future in which we become "one vast interlocking machine of a machine" (194).

Probably the best written, though somewhat pompous and hardly probing, is the antihomiletic homily, "The Immorality of Morality." The argument is that Jesus, the Oriental saints, and a roguish friend of Miller's who takes life easy and is without principle, all make the point that one should follow spiritual impulses and not moral laws. While the later Miller is drastically inconsistent as to whether life should be aimed at the intense present (his early view) or at the unitive spiritual future (occult stock in trade), he does make clear that the saints he admires subordinated morality to the affirmation of a way of life, self-accepting and self-delighting. Thus Miller still does battle with his, and America's, Protestant-guilt heritage. His insistence that such religious affirmation denies both suffering and rebellion seems dubious, but it is an essential part of his late and undialectical emphasis upon occult technology and unity.

Much of Miller's literary religious role is characterized by his dabbling with various styles of occultism. Dabbling, I say, because he rarely seems whole-hearted, even moderately consistent, or at all thorough or devoted in his use of the occult.[35] From the popular romantic mystifications and exoticisms taken from literature, Miller apparently moved into Theosophy in his early twenties, then into doctrines derived from writers he admired such as Hamsun (*Mysteries*) and Lawrence (*Apocalypse*). But in his post-*Cancer* days he went in for literary religions on a big scale, acquiring a fantastic, and perhaps incompatible, series of occult interests: Swedenborgianism (via Balzac), Zen Buddhism (via Alan Watts), magic and madness (via the surrealists), alchemy (via Blake?), mysticisms (Jewish, Christian, Hindu, Egyptian, Tibetan, etc., via all sorts of books). Indeed, he nibbles at so many cosmic doctrines that it might be easier to list the few for which there seems to be no evidence. One such would seem to be Jungianism (he was a devotee of Rank); another would seem to be any form of Protestantism (except for Christian Science). Others he passed over are ritualistic Catholicism (his violent Protestant antagonism to it usually crops up), the "orgone" mysticism of Wilhelm Reich (he mentions it several times, but to Miller there is really nothing mystical about sex), and those highly specialized occultisms (numerology, cabalism, cryptograms) which have elaborately rationalized methods (though he several times praises the *Tibetan Book of the Dead,* which is much the same thing). But perhaps his most persistent doctrine for restyling actuality and gaining a literary sense of holiness and a cosmic rhetoric is astrology.

Astrology has a considerable place in Miller's writings, though probably not a crucial one. Titles (*Cancer* and *Capricorn*), satiric sketches ("Astrological Fricassée"), grotesque character studies (Moricand in "Paradise Lost"), and many burlesque passages (the "observatory" scene in *Colossus of Maroussi*) draw heavily on astrological lore. Miller also apparently thinks of himself, and of his inordinate good luck, in terms of heavenly conjunctions. However, to the sceptical observer, Miller's astrological exploitation has the following functions: a fancifully ornate language; therapeutic incantations for his personal fate; arcane specialization to costume his role-playing as miraculous prophet; an occasional parody device; and a pious hope that the universe is not the nihilistic comedy presented in *Tropic of Cancer* and similar writings.[36]

I do not mean to deny that Miller puts some faith in astrology as a psuedoscience of prediction, though his statements about that tend to be ambiguous. But there is considerable pose and even *jeu d'esprit* in his use of the astrological. He is refreshingly unaffected by social status in his religious tastes. In America, the vulgarity of astrology (it lacks the sanctions of honorific history and class) would seem to control most educated responses to it, as with superior literati who have a fashionable smattering of Zen, or Jung, or Reich, or the Upanishads. It is, of course, as difficult to separate astrology from its social context—fortune-telling for the poorly educated, usually of the narrowest lower-middle-class circumstances and taste—as it is to separate Christianity from suburban churchgoers.

While in a number of remarks Miller mocks astrology, and in his reported discussions with astrologer Moricand at Big Sur he accepted astrological principles but denied their fateful applications, his main discussion of astrology draws on other sophistications.[37] He places his interest in astrology with general occultism as having the poetic utility of expanding one's "vision." The later Miller also blandly asserts that "every man who is honest and sincere with himself will admit that all is not chaos, not chance, not accident" (119). Astrology, he says, provides one of the microcosm-macrocosm patterns of order with particular emphasis on periodicity and repetition. While he grants that the cosmic "mystery" is not fully open to human interpretation, astrology, poetically used, provides "inexhaustible symbols" —"wheels within wheels"—for the contemplation of individual destiny. Astrology also provides him comfort in showing the mixture of "the divine in everything" (127) and in promising "miraculous" power which could be used to "transform the world overnight" (123). One's horoscope, rightly read, will allow one to "so live each day that with fullness of being and total awareness we may enjoy the privilege of giving expression to the glorious uniqueness" (124) of each self. Astrology, then, is mainly inspirational rhetoric.

Why one should follow astrology rather than some other inspirational rhetoric is not a matter that Miller considers. His implied answer would seem to be that there are not such divisive intellectual distinctions and that all occultisms would be equally valid since "common sense would decree that any role, if entered into wholeheartedly, is the right one" (126). Miller makes the usual bland fallacy of inspirational writers and of occultists especially: the denial of tragically human limitations. Though astrology, displacing this awareness to a cosmic design, tends to be deterministic, Miller's optimistic American disposition inverts it into total power and freedom. While we need not mock Miller's argument with the multitude of sadly common, and inevitable, inappropriate choices (not to speak of the ambiguity implicit in "wholeheartedly"), we should not overlook the main point: the dialectical sense of life as a conflict between who one is, who one wants to be, and a malignant or indifferent universe, is totally alien to the later Miller's awareness. He has, as his later work testifies, very little sense of dramatic conflict, either within one's own feelings or in relation to others and the cosmos. After all, Henry Miller, an aging Brooklyn "nonentity," chose to be a writer and literary saint—wholeheartedly, no doubt—and was not only right in his choice but publicly successful. And it is only here that his doctrine really applies, to the nether world of art-role and literary gesture.

All we have to do is understand that artist really means saint: the "artist is alway surrogate for all men everywhere . . ." (127).[38] Since the artist has no other obligations than self-discovery and self-expression, it is hard for Saint Henry, who alternately recommends quietism and rebellion, artistic production and pure spirituality beyond art, encompassing love and total detachment, to decide what to do as surrogate for all mankind. In the meantime he has faith. And when it comes to faith, as against lesser utilities, one might, of course, just as well believe in astrological science as in salvation by statistical knowledge from the social sciences or in the automatic beneficence of the physical sciences. As religion, the psuedo-sciences may be much less dangerous—as well as more pleasantly fanciful—than the modern technological sciences. Historically, astrology has been mistakenly viewed, I think, as being transitional between science and magic. Actually, as Miller seems to demonstrate, magic can be found at all historical points, which is also confirmed by the naïveté of the believers in scientism. Astrology, after all, is so ineffective as to be mostly compensatory dream, and thus it is less efficiently authoritarian and cruel than, say, Pavlovian conditioning or "scientific" weaponry. Horoscopes tend to be cheaper than rockets and astrologers may do better than astronauts in giving human significance to the stars. While some of us might dramatically prefer cults that produce festivals and artistic monuments rather than the occultist nostrums of astrology and the technological nostrums of astrophysics, the very inhumanity of lunar pathologies seems to be an essential part of their appeal.

Miller's treatment of astrology—and that may fairly represent all his religious concerns—is fanciful and inspirational, a thin jumble and an egotistical self-glorification.[39] Perhaps more important, his religiosity upgrades the artist at the expense of his art. His occult portentousness damages his comic verve. Case in point: Miller wrote, as one of his very few excursions into traditional literary form, a clown fable, *The Smile At the Foot of the Ladder*.[40] In it a circus clown discusses, rhetorically, some tribulations of self-discovery and ends, after a few vague adventures, destroyed in "seraphic" bliss by a cruelly uncomprehending world.

Ignoring the aggrandizing self-pity of the fable's autobiographical dimensions, the religious portentousness makes the art bad. The language is absurdly heavy for a fey tale ("ineffable," "simulation," "ascension," "infinitesimal," "inexplicable," "reminiscence," "pursuance," "formulate"); the phrasing is ponderous euphemism ("bring his plan to fruition," "become more manifest," "revolved his dilemma backward and forward"); the imagery is tritely melodramatic (dusk is violet, blood bubbles, truth is a fire, reality is a veil); and the allegory is multi-prestigious (the clown is Christ, the tragic artist, the archetypal scapegoat, the simple saint, the illuminated mystic). In an essay-epilogue Miller indicates that the story has literary-religious sources and purposes, as is too evident; and he insists that clowns are really angels and artists are really saints. (His moral dictums—"We have only to open our eyes and hearts, to become one with that which is" [111]—do not fit the tale in which the totally anxious and unhumorous clown receives his illuminations only through punishments.) Miller sadly confesses, "Perhaps I have not limned his [the angelic clown's] portrait too clearly" (114). Indeed not. The trouble may be put thus: Miller and his clown have not stuck to his own clown's revelation—"If he were really a clown, then he should be one through and through . . ." (99). Much of Miller's work suffers from not playing it straight but attempting to make a natural American clown into a literary saint.

III *The Legacy of Henry Miller*

Miller started, as it were, with an apocalyptic "kick in the pants" at the dubious and dying heroic verities. To fill the void left by the collapsed idealisms, he turned out a vast and miscellaneous stream of boozy egotistical verbiage which included a small stream of good iconoclastic and comic rhetoric. Where his pyrotechnical style and buffoonish gesturing come together, he produced, I believe, work of intrinsic merit. But when he played the self-aggrandizing fundamentalist of the imagination, he produced only the *blagueur* man of letters and the cornball literary saint. The wordy by-product of that effort, as a poet candidly put it, turns out to be "inspirational chats for semiliterate bohemians and rebels with 'C+' minds."[41] But our primary concern is with the writings of Miller, and not with his apparently ambiguous sociological and religious effects and with the personal therapy of Saint Henry. In Miller's case, we may take his word for it that the artist is the clown.

One way of sketching out a perspective of evaluation is to suggest an anthology of the better writings. Though it has obvious unevenness and prolixity, *Tropic of Cancer,* but no other book-length work of this essentially fragmented writer, might stand complete, or almost so. From the sketches in the 1930's an anthologist should certainly include "Mademoiselle Claude," "Max," and perhaps "Via Dieppe-Newhaven." "The Tailor Shop" and some excerpts from the earlier sketches and the conclusion would be a sufficient selection from *Black Spring.* Miller is not an important or good literary essayist, but "Shadowy Monomania" and "Balzac and His Double" ("The Universe of Death" would be a lesser choice) could be included to represent that aspect of his work. Little would be lost in completely ignoring *The Books in My Life, The Time of the Assassins, Maurizius Forever, Stand Still Like the Hummingbird,* and the many dozens of other literary polemics and ruminations. From the volumes on America, the comic pieces—"Astrological Fricassée," "Soirée in Hollywood," "The Staff of Life"—plus "Reunion in Brooklyn," are the good pieces, and the rest could well be ignored.

If one were producing a fat anthology, he might reasonably add some purple, scarlet, and black passages from Miller's other works. From *Tropic of Capricorn* might come a representative bit of the "ovarian" fantasia, some burlesque descriptive passages, such as those of his father and Broadway, and perhaps some summary remarks about selling, working, dreaming of art, and other American vices. From the other volumes of "autobiographical romance," *The Rosy Crucifixion,* the selection would be small, and it might require some editorial work: most appropriate would be an obscene fantasy episode (this is one of Miller's significant contributions to American letters) such as Mona's rape narrative in *Sexus,* or a similar piece about the narrator's first wife. One might include the Elfenbein portrait in *Nexus* (perhaps filled out by a bit of the other Jewish material), a description or two of some of his Brooklyn friends, and some brief bravura bits such as the good-by to America. (Except as curiosities, all those forced and tedious volumes cannot be taken as wholes, and most of the set-pieces are poor or bad.) Several burlesque and ruminative passages from *The Colossus of Maroussi* could be included with his better writings.

Of the later work in America, only the portrait of two grotesques, "Paradise Lost," might merit inclusion, despite its prolixity, but certainly nothing else from *Big Sur and the Oranges of Hieronymous Bosch.* The arty pieces, such as "Scenario" and *The Smile at the Foot of the Ladder,* are best forgotten. For other descriptive passages, one might consider that of Lourdes from the last of the *Hamlet* letters and perhaps a bawdy episode from *Quiet Days in Clichy.* Certainly Miller's long essays, *The World of Sex,* "Murder the Murderer," "An Open Letter to Surrealists Everywhere," and others, don't bear rereading. None of the shorter essays are outstanding, though if one wished to document Miller's home-brew philosophy, he could include one early essay such as "Peace! It's Wonderful!" and one late essay such as "The Immorality of Morality." The ambitious anthologist might well include a number of titles, asides, wild comparisons, and odd dictums scattered through the letter, sketches, and ruminations to make an intriguing section of *pensées.* As for documenting Miller's life, it does not merit it, despite his thousands of pages of sometimes amusing and poignant but more often misleading, confused, and tedious rhetorical discussions of himself. One could, of course, document other quaint concerns of Miller's, or quite reasonably use him as evidence for one or another representative peculiarity of American sensibility and pathology. But, after all, there is an endless supply of such curious Americana.

The point here is not to urge such an anthology—the profits of publishers, the prejudices of authors, and the pedestrian mentalities of most anthologists stand against it—but responsively to suggest an appropriate view of Miller's work. Another evaluation can be posed by considering the role of Millerian literature (not the role of Miller) amidst other American writing.[42] *Tropic of Cancer* and its appendages, I have already suggested, significantly belong with the idiosyncratic and rebellious poetic-prose testaments of Thoreau, Cummings, Agee, and others—a native extension of European traditions of Varronian satire and picaresque potpourri. On the other hand, Miller's major purpose of self-discovery—*"l'homme que je étais, je ne suis puis"* (*Black Spring,* 39)—and all the autobiographical rumination and burlesque that belong with this American-as-romantic-artist are part of the pathetic immaturity of American literature.

The tradition of self-sentimental and wordy naïve exaltation —best known in Sherwood Anderson, then self-parodying itself in Thomas Wolfe, William Saroyan, Jack Kerouac, and a host of lesser writers—may be the major tradition of American prose, quantitatively speaking, and the murky edge of the European *Bildungsroman* and the quasi-literature of confession and case history. In Miller, the confessional strain crosses, though not for the first time, with the vast sub-literature of homemade metaphysics and millennial exhortation which we find in the native radicalism of nineteenth-century American utopians, and in its predecessors, the antinomian tracts of seventeenth-century English Protestantism. But Miller, lacking demonic rigor and too patently the indulgent personal and artistic sybarite, is no major heretic. The garrulous American littérateur takes on an emphatically buffoonish cast when playing the rebel as well as when supposedly baring an anguished soul.[43]

When we relate Miller to the contemporary American literary scene, some effect on the literary rebels of the 1950's, the "Beats," seems evident. Lawrence Ferlinghetti appropriately borrowed a Miller title to label his collection of comic-pastiche verses, *A Coney Island of the Mind*.[44] Miller is a possible source as well as an admirer of the swelling and embracing "bop" prose of the confessional literary "saint," Jack Kerouac.[45] Possibly from Miller, but more likely translated from similar surrealist sources, come the epithets of incongruity and the fractured invective which provide the major stylistic distinction of such "Beat" poets as Allen Ginsberg and Gregory Corso. Miller's rhetorical gestures may be his main "influence," though certainly the personal fragmentation and the stylization of the obscene in his confessions have provided a standard for ornate "daring" and for strident confusion in the more literary mode of self-exposure, as in William Borrough's *Naked Lunch*. But at their best the Beats also follow Miller in grotesque comedy of defiance.[46]

More generally, and perhaps more significantly, Miller importantly contributed to the increasingly dominant and major poetic-naturalistic American styles—surreal, obscene, fantastic, iconoclastic, learned, colloquial, lavish, and desperate—which, in their mixing of low and high elements, provide an increased richness of language and awareness. Put another way, Miller's work—especially his early writings—have provided *ground* for such poetic-fantastic comedies of alienation as Algren's *A Walk on the Wild Side,* Ellison's *Invisible Man,* Bellow's *Henderson the Rain King,* and Heller's *Catch-22.* Miller's violent fantasies also appear to be having some direct effect on the early 1960's writing of Norman Mailer. And critics have rightly noted that a delightful bawdy comedy of American rebelliousness abroad, J. P. Donleavy's *The Ginger Man,* belongs to the *Tropic of Cancer* tradition of wild nihilistic humor.[47] Miller's best work partakes of this major direction of our literature—the sardonic, physical, rebellious, and expansive tradition of American comedy.[48]

For Miller's intrinsic merit as well as his significant contribution is in extreme comedy. Rational and moral comedy, the historians tell us, used society and its common sense as a norm to make the comic standard a golden mean. Irrational and amoral comedy, as with Millerian frenzy and bemused alienation, uses the sense of loss of authenticity and community as its fractured norm, and so instead of a golden mean we get a black extreme of humor. For much of twentieth-century experience, Miller may well belong to the more relevant comic mode.

The twentieth-century arts of defying despair take several directions; one is into comic rhetoric, as in the late Joyce and other self-propelled verbal machines, in psychoanalytic complete verbalization of recall, and in surrealism's absolute release of language and imagery from convention and logic. To this rhetorical comedy, Miller adds a colloquial looseness (and prolixity), a grandiose sentimentality (and paucity of rigor), and a naïve egotism (and self-alienation) which seem peculiarly American. Patently, the heroic epic and tragedy are not likely for these times. The large novel of the morals and manners of a viable and multi-dimensional society necessarily seems vestigial. The discordant lyric, the aslant picaresque, the personal revery, the satiric apocalypse, and, especially, grotesque poetic comedy seem the most likely and responsive forms for the present. Thus I suggest that, while Miller is a minor writer, he may—in his best work—have a major relevance.

One of Miller's silly bemusements is to preen himself before the mirror of an imagined future and see that great guy and artist Henry Miller being admired by posterity. However, Miller may have already reached his greatest popular and

critical reputations—given a boost by the censorship furor—
considering that his reputation must bear the burden of an im-
mense amount of bad writing. Even leaving that aside, Miller at
his best is limited in scope, experience, imaginative form, insight,
human types, range of feeling, intelligence, and gesture; in
short, he is a minor writer. This is not intended as simple
denigration but just as an indication that it would be specious
to discuss his work as if it were fulfilled and fulfilling, a major
style and attitude in itself, a primary force and form of sensibility. To the degree that Miller found himself, it was by
a commitment to the grotesque and marginal; both a strength
and a weakness, his oddity must remain his definition. Naturally,
to predict what the future will do with him, as a means of
evaluation, is dangerous; literary history is probably no more
honest and wise than the rest of history. We need not, then,
seriously locate his place in some American factory-style literary
pantheon, even though it is mostly filled with anomalous and
weird writers with whom Miller would be at home.

Miller's main creation, I suggest, is the rhetoric of grotesquerie.
In a sense there is little behind his rhetoric—not much dramatic
world of autonomous characters and patterns, not any major
moral or social engagement, and not a unique way of knowledge or of life-style. His distinctive quality may be the Amer-
icanization of the literature of the absolute rebellion in which
defiance is modified by bumptiousness, bombast by candor,
extremity by geniality, nastiness by earnestness, and so on. In
short, Miller's American ordinariness does qualify him from
the extreme explorers of sensibility; he is a buffoonish version
of the great tradition. The mindloose and fancy-wild American
talker, he transcends the fatally ordinary family, ethos, and self
—and our perplexing, threatening, and dubious world—by his
eloquent and grandiloquent gestures. Miller's rhetoric becomes
his one identity, hiding as well as holding his irregular insights.

His words exaggerate all, including his own foolishness; and
thus he achieves the basic principle of buffoonery. Such a role
has its own poignant assertion, but it most displays, as do every
one of his portraits and self-portraits, the loss of all authentic
heroism. His figures lack almost all tragic, moral, and organic
consciousness. Miller, of course, is a bit of a fraud about his
comic nihilism, declaiming all sorts of artistic, social, and religious values. His poses as artist and saint, while hardly vicious,

do not need to be taken very seriously. In a way more willy-nilly than a great artist or person, Miller testifies effectively to the loss of values, to a drastically incomplete humanity, to the anti-heroism so pervasive in our genuine literature. Such grotesqueness has its profound truths in a world in which individuality is increasingly marginal and heroic patterns increasingly gratuitous. Adventure into a closed world and rebellion against amorphous doom are obviously foolish. But the Millerian grotesque makes the rhetorical gestures of adventure, and he rebels by refusing heroic poses as well as victimization. Thus to insist on one's grotesqueness is to insist on one's being—a residual, inverted, yet finally crucial heroism.

The buffoon is often a desperate and sly rebel. The more serious his poses, the more absurd he seems—is this why, knowingly or not, Miller plays at the most gigantic roles of great artist and prophet and saint and unique human being and god? While such buffoonery must be of ancient lineage, it is hard to recall anyone else quite so exhaustively playing the role as self-important writer. It must be granted that one curious interest Miller has is that he puts into books hundreds of thousands of bombastic, ruminative, casual, pretentious, disorderly, foolish words which have not usually been put into books at all. While the result is occasionally striking, but more often tedious, such literary buffoonery has a salutary charm and poignance. Especially poignance, for when we turn from Miller to many pretentious confessions and prophecies and art, they justly appear weak. The wisdom of the buffoon is to swell himself up until we see him, and everything else, in truer proportion. Miller is also a symptomatic American, as ordinary man and literary rhetorician; he is so far "outside," as it were, that he stands revealed as a central image of our peculiarity.

Miller's best writing and most original gestures also result in grotesquely humorous catharsis. The rebel-buffoon's one heroism is in his own defiant absurdity, and his reflection of it in others, as he dances in his torn rhetoric. Miller's verbal comedy, his one achieved art, is ragged but responsively open. It provides a legacy of motley for other rebel-buffoons, and for more sardonic comedians. The topsy-turvy gesture is all; but it is sufficient to be a suggestive and amusing affirmation of the lively human.

Notes and References

Chapter One

1. *Tropic of Cancer* (New York: Grove Press Black Cat Edition, 1961). All references are to this edition. There is, of course, no collected or standard edition of Miller's work. Because of unavailability of many volumes, citations in this study are usually to the most conveniently available editions.

2. No single or very reliable source exists for the biographical material. I am interpreting from a wide range of published, and some unpublished, commentary on Miller's life. As with the chronology for this volume, I have drawn on Miller's many chronologies, the longest of which appears in *The Henry Miller Reader* (New York, 1959), pp. 383-91. The only moderately extensive biography is the casual one by Alfred Perlès, *My Friend, Henry Miller* (New York, 1956).

3. See, among other examples, Edmund Wilson, "Twilight of the Expatriates [1938]," *Shores of Light* (New York, 1952), pp. 705-10. A detailed pedestrian discussion of this theme is Annette Kar Baxter, *Henry Miller, Expatriate* (Pittsburgh, 1961). For a more argumentative treatment, see Alwyn Lee, "Henry Miller—the Pathology of Isolation," *New World Writing*, Second Mentor Selection (New York, 1952), pp. 340-47.

4. George Orwell naturally overemphasized the sociology of Parisian and lower-class life, ("Inside the Whale [1940]," *A Collection of Essays* [New York, 1954], pp. 215-56). I have not been able to obtain a reported later attack of Orwell's on Miller in *Tribune* (1943), but even amidst his earlier praise Orwell shrewdly suspected tendencies that would lead to "charlatanism."

5. Emerson and Whitman crop up several times in *Tropic of Cancer*. In later years Miller explicitly identifies himself with the period of Emerson, Whitman, and Thoreau. See, for example, his editorial piece, "Henry David Thoreau," *Stand Still Like the Hummingbird* (New York, 1962), pp. 111-18.

6. The penultimate image of flowing water, probably derived from D. H. Lawrence's work, where it also represents the mysterious and amoral flux of life, appears elsewhere in Miller, as in the self-conscious affirmative conclusion to *The World of Sex* (Paris, 1959), pp. 124-25.

7. Miller's switch from "naturalistic" to "surrealistic" styles generally comes as the subjective culmination to an extreme episode,

the interior fantasia of associated images which provide a raging or joyous escape from the limiting reality. After describing a repulsive scene, then going to a movie, he will connect the two in a fantasy developing out of an associated image, such as the one of the eye, p. 57 (perhaps drawing on the film the *Andalusian Dog* by Dali and Buñuel).

8. George P. Elliot, in a rather ponderous memoir-essay parody of Miller, puts most of the emphasis upon the delight in "muck." "A Brown Fountain Pen," *Kenyon Review*, XXIV (Winter, 1962), 62-79. For an incisive description of the maternal compulsions Miller rebels against, see his "Reunion in Brooklyn," *Sunday After the War* (New York, 1944), pp. 67-106.

9. The attack on northern European consciousness, like the exaltation of Mediterranean vitality which follows later, is asserted rather than dramatized. Up to his visit to Greece in 1939, the main impetus to this must have been defiance of his own northern European and Protestant heritage and his literary influences, particularly D. H. Lawrence, about whom he may have been writing as he finished *Cancer*.

10. The scene has remarkably similar ingredients—in terms of excrement, the sentimentalized underdog, etc.—to E. E. Cummings, *The Enormous Room* (1922). We might also suggest that with its unstable fusion of harsh realism, subjective lyricism, and rebellious rhetoric *Cancer* belongs not only with *Walden, Moby-Dick*, and *Leaves of Grass*, but with the twentieth-century extension of that tradition of "eccentric" form in *The Enormous Room*, Agee's *Let Us Now Praise Famous* Men, etc. See Kingsley Widmer, "Timeless Prose," *Twentieth Century Lit.*, IV (July, 1958).

11. Miller's inability to accept "hum-drum" life has usually been completely overlooked by his devotees and commentators. One of the few to note it was Professor Paul Weiss, "Art and Henry Miller," *The Happy Rock*, ed. Bern Porter (Berkeley, 1945), pp. 133-35. It was also noted recently in a quite thoughtful article by Don Kleine that Miller's plain style—so overrated by Orwell and others—stultifies his perceptions and forces him into an excessively florid counterstyle ("Innocence Forbidden: Henry Miller in the Tropics," *Prairie Schooner*, XXXIII [Summer, 1959], 125-30).

12. In discussing titles, Miller appropriately praises one he sees in a bookstore window—*A Man Cut in Slices*—and favorably contrasts it with that of his previous, and unpublished, book "Crazy Cock." Miller's titles and slogans, as will repeatedly be noted, are often his best art. Underlying the concepts and negative imagery here is Miller's version of *Decline of the West*, though many of his gestures are most indebted to his taking on Nietzsche's Dionysian stance.

13. Miller's explanation of the title many years later was that "Cancer" was used because it is the zodiacal sign of the crab, who moves in all directions. Hear *Henry Miller Recalls and Reflects*, L. P. record, ed. Ben Graur (New York: Riverside Records, 1956). In a passage in *Black Spring*, quoted in Chapter II, Miller does draw upon the astrological point, but it has only minor relevance to *Tropic of Cancer*. I am concerned with the title in terms of the book.

14. I have largely ignored Miller's "womb" motif. He uses it briefly in *Cancer*—he is pregnant with this book, and Paris is an obstetrical instrument for birth and rebirth—but its main development is in post-*Cancer* writings, discussed later. Miller once wrote of *Cancer*, "The strong odor of sex which it purveys is really the aroma of birth . . ." (*The World of Sex* [New York, 1940], p. 19). Nonsense. The sexuality of *Cancer* is overwhelmingly impersonal, vengeful, grotesque, alienated—therein lies its perception. When Miller makes opposite claims, as *World of Sex*, p. 44, he is, at best, confused.

15. This rhythm of response would seem to describe the fundamental attitude of *Cancer* more than the "passivity" so emphasized by Orwell, *op. cit.*, (who is thinking in political terms), by Frederick J. Hoffman, *Freudianism and the Literary Mind* (Baton Rouge, 1945), pp. 299-305, and by others. Another part of Miller's attitude is shrewdly stated in his later statement that "Rome has to burn in order for a guy like me to sing." (*Hamlet* [New York, 1943], I, 109.) He is not above shouting "fire" to have something to sing along with.

16. The source figure for Boris seems to have been Michael Fraenkel, an erudite and obsessed speculative writer on death who unquestionably had a tremendous influence on Miller's ideas and imagery. Fraenkel touches on some of this, and on the book's imagistic structure of confinement and break-through, in "The Genesis of the Tropic of Cancer," *The Happy Rock*, pp. 38-56. See also some related comment by another skittish friend of that period, Walter Lowenfels, "A Note on Henry Miller's Tropic of Cancer," *International Henry Miller Letter*, I (June, 1961), 5-6.

17. The Kreuger episode, with Miller as the gross parasite, has an ironic reversal in Miller's tribulations as host to Moricand many years later (*The Devil in Paradise* [New York, 1956]). The point has been noted by Claude Mauriac who, however, foolishly overestimates Miller's self-consciousness and thus attributes to him intentional parody (*L'Aliterature Contemporaine* [Paris, 1958], p. 58).

18. Marlowe appears to be based on the late Samuel Putnam, who returns the compliments in his comments on Miller as coward, plagiarist, and "expounder of the Philosophy of Universal Filth" in

his memoir, *Paris Was Our Mistress* (New York, 1947), pp. 113-15. I am only indicating a few representative examples of the *roman à clef* pattern; the more general point is clear that Miller was, to put it kindly, doing caricatures of actual people.

19. The "dark lady" problem, poorly handled in *Cancer*, is discussed in some detail in Chapter III below.

20. For some further general discussion of the "American Joe" see my "The American Road and the Contemporary Novel," *University of Kansas City Review*, XXVI (Summer, 1960). Kenneth Rexroth has also noted the importance of the lower-class Brooklyn male ethos in his "Reality of Henry Miller," *Bird in the Bush, Obvious Essays* (New York, 1959), pp. 154-67.

21. Miller, apparently in reference to the prototype of Van Norden some years later, considers such sexual pursuit a natural state of youth—"to get at the mystery"—which, prolonged, becomes a destructive obsession (*World of Sex*, p. 30).

22. Of the many comments on *Cancer* later tossed off by Miller, two especially should be noted: 1) "hatred and vengeance were the main spring"; 2) the book was dominated by "the idea of separation. I had to break with the past, my own past particularly" (*Hamlet*, I, 354). Since we see Miller being driven into the admissions by his knowing correspondent, Fraenkel, the remarks are not as is so often the case, whimsical impositions. Part of the hatred no doubt refers to his harsh treatment of his friends.

23. The hundreds of discussions of sex in *Tropic of Cancer*, in relation to the issue of censorship, tend to irrelevant simplification or titillation. See, for a bad example, Eberhard and Phyllis Kronhausen, *Pornography and the Law* (New York, 1959), pp. 125-30. Some of this is inevitable, as I know from participating in the public and legal defense of *Tropic of Cancer* in San Diego in 1961-62. As Dr. Eleanor Widmer, main defense witness responsible for the San Diego acquittal of *Cancer*, noted during the trial: "There are fundamental disparities between sexual and literary facts and public and legal processes."

24. Fillmore was based on the late Richard G. Osborn. See his "#2 Rue Auguste Barthodi," *The Happy Rock*, pp. 28-37. This gives a different version of several of the episodes drawn on in *Cancer*, and necessarily highlights Miller's egotism.

25. I am not objecting primarily to the silly brutality but to the weak narrative: Marcelle, a prostitute with whom Miller (and perhaps the reader) becomes involved, just disappears; of Collins, never adequately developed, we are told at the end that "he was never to see America again," and are just left hanging in this confusion of personal life and narrative coherence. This weakness is also especially strong in the first two chapters.

26. For Miller's later lavish and trite francophilism, evident in *Black Spring* but not violently strong until after his return to America, see the entitling essay of *Remember to Remember* (New York, 1947); see also, "Children of the Earth" and "When I Reach for My Revolver" in *Stand Still Like the Hummingbird.*

27. Harry T. Moore properly notes a European part of Miller's heritage: "Descendant of Dostoevsky's Underground Man, without his nastiness, and of Rilke's Malte Laurids Brigge, without his fastidiousness" ("Tropic of Cancer," New York *Times Book Review* [June 18, 1961], p. 5).

28. The problems of *Cancer* do not come from careless writing (as in his later American publications) or from his adaptation of surrealist automatic writing (as in parts of *Black Spring* and *Capricorn*). Miller says of *Cancer*: "Original ms. three times size of published book; rewritten three times" (*Henry Miller Reader*, p. 385). While the style shows the intensification, it also confirms Miller's ineptitude at sustained dramatic analysis and integration.

29. Theodore Solotaroff, though misunderstanding Miller because of a social-moralist approach, strongly makes a similar point: "Miller's celebrated powers of acceptance often seem to rest on his tactic of withdrawing under a smokescreen of apocalyptic projections . . . from the nastier realities that he dredges up about himself" ("All That Cellar-Deep Jazz: Henry Miller and Seymour Krim," *Commentary,* XXXII [October, 1961], 319).

30. For an example of his sardonic gusto switching to a fatuous play with exotic words, see the end of the concert episode (70-71). Elsewhere, Miller has rightly noted his proclivity for "verbal jags" (*Time of the Assassins* [New York, 1956], p. 18).

31. There are fantastically diverse evaluations of *Tropic of Cancer,* ranging from the most vituperative condemnation to near-scriptural admiration. However, despite his complaints, Miller has long had reasonably sensible treatment from the more intelligent critics. Not only was *Cancer* well received by such writers as Blaise Cendrars, Cyril Connally, and others, but in the following period—perhaps the most crucial one for literary reputations—such critics as George Orwell, Philip Rahv, Herbert Read, Edmund Wilson, Herbert J. Muller, and others, gave Miller's early work discerning criticism. Edwin Muir briefly but aptly discussed Miller and his major themes in an academic survey in the 1930's, *The Present Age From 1914* (London, 1939), pp. 149ff. Some of the other criticism is summarized in Baxter, *Henry Miller Expatriate*, pp. 157-58. There has also been considerable praise and earnest discussion of Miller in other languages. Several friends have shown remarkable devotion to uncritically furthering Miller's reputation. Of Miller, Lawrence Durrell wrote: "American literature today begins and ends with

the meaning of what he has done" (*The Happy Rock,* p. 4.) For one of the more balanced recent discussions, see David Littlejohn, "The Tropics of Miller," *The New Republic* (March 5, 1962). These are only a few examples. The "obscenity" issues, and Miller's later bad writing, have of course sometimes muddied the discussion of *Cancer.*

32. The relation to Thoreau has been pointed to earlier; Whitman is obvious throughout; that of Lawrence will be summarized in Chapter V, below; Joyce is primarily important for his use of verbal high life and city low life. As scattered indications through Miller's work would indicate, some other obvious "influences" would be late nineteenth-century "confessional" literature (Strindberg's *Confessions,* and Van Gogh's *Letters*), surrealism (especially André Breton's *Nadja* and manifestoes, and the general ambience and many of the mannerisms of the group), Sherwood Anderson's grotesques and sentimentalized writers, and, quite strongly, some of the French late-naturalists (Phillipe, *Bubu of Montparnasse;* Celine, *Journey to the End of Night,* which evoked considerable discussion while Miller was probably still writing *Cancer*). The reason for emphasizing these is that Miller is a highly "literary" writer; books are often his most crucial experiences—a point not always duly recognized.

Chapter Two

1. *Black Spring* (Paris, 1958). The American edition (Grove Press, 1963) was published after this study was completed. Most of the sketches have been republished in Miller's various American anthologies.

2. *The Henry Miller Reader,* ed. Lawrence Durrell (New York, 1959), p. 3. Miller also said of this book that it "came nearer to being myself, I believe, than any book I have written before or since" (*The Books in My Life* [New York, 1952], p. 98).

3. George Orwell, while praising the nostalgic descriptions of New York, noted the tendency of Miller to slide into "mere verbiage" ("Inside the Whale," *A Collection of Essays* [New York, 1953], p. 218). Outside of repeated casual praise of the New York scenes, there has been little comment on the book, and no critical analysis. The 1963 reviews have tended to mild back-slapping—for reasons that have little to do with the book itself.

4. "The Angel Is My Watermark" has been reproduced with Miller's watercolors several times. A preface to one such version is reprinted in *Stand Still Like the Hummingbird* (New York, 1962), pp. 38-41. See also, *Henry Miller: "Watercolors, Drawings, and His Essay, 'The Angel Is My Watermark'"* (New York, 1962).

5. Wallace Fowlie discusses the last of this painting description as an example both of surrealist art and of surrealist theory (*Age of Surrealism* [New York, 1950], pp. 184-87). This also provides a summary introduction to some of the motifs of surrealism, though it should be supplemented by some of the fuller studies of that subject. Miller's adaptation of surrealism deserves separate study—the influence of surrealism on American writing in general has been vastly underrated—partly because it is the surrealist-tinged elements of Miller's writings which have had the most influence on other writers, and will probably continue to do so. Miller draws heavily on some French surrealist characteristics: hypnotic and automatic writing (or the pretense at them), dream structures, "free association," and labyrinthine verbal play; also, doom prophecies, hyper-logical and irrational sequences, amoral and immoral acts, black humor, and the role of the artist as alien, madman, child, and magician. However, Miller lacks some basic characteristics of André Breton and his followers, including absolute submission to "unconscious" mechanisms, extreme dandyism, political revolution, and real extremity of personal experience (suicide, drugs, violence, actual frenzy, etc.). With Miller, as with Nathanael West, the Beat writers, Ionesco, and others influenced by surrealism, the effects are most significant when adapted as images, motifs, etc., to literary forms larger and more coherent than those encouraged by surrealism.

6. Miller seems to indicate in several places that he was a devoted reader of *transition*. See, also, *Books in My Life,* p. 204.

7. In the realm of fact, considerable skepticism should be applied to this material. The title, among other things, seems to be derived from Anais Nin, who had considerable influence on Miller during the early Paris years. The narrative detail, also, plays free with autobiographical fact; the substitution of a half-wit brother for his sister is an obvious example.

8. Many of the details and motifs reappear in somewhat varying form in other works. Cleo, for example, provides a motif in *Sexus* (Paris, 1960), pp. 588ff.

9. A theme which appears much more clearly in the conclusion than in most of the other sketches is the "individual as against the collectivity"—in the Nietzschean sense. This statement and other jottings on material and purposes appear in some of Miller's notes from this period, published as "Work Schedule," *Henry Miller Miscellanea,* ed. Bern Porter (Berkeley, California, 1945), pp. 19-26. These notes indicate, incidentally, how self-consciously organized, personally ambitious, and earnestly in search of broad self-improvement (even to the point of planning to steal books from libraries), Miller was.

10. There is an "Epilogue to Black Spring," never published with the book. This run of surrealist images—"celluloid sky," "green carpet made of the foam and snot of the epileptic," etc.—occurs in *Henry Miller Miscellanea*, pp. 31-33. A similar piece and more readily available, "The Brooklyn Bridge," appears to have been written shortly after *Black Spring*. It draws heavily on that book—Tante Melia again—and employs surrealist images, disconnected assertions, and yet another rebirth announcement: "The thug in me is dead, and the fanatic and lunatic also" (*The Cosmological Eye* [New York, 1939], pp. 346-56).

11. Many of these pieces appeared in Miller's third book, *Max and the White Phagocytes* (Paris, 1938), and were soon reprinted, with additional pieces, in Miller's first American anthology, *The Cosmological Eye*. Examples of Miller's early, and quite unpromising, trivia appear as items 1, 2, and 4 in the *Henry Miller Miscellanea*.

12. "Mademoiselle Claude," *The Wisdom of the Heart* (New York, 1941), pp. 140-50. In the later *Tropic of Cancer*, Claude is unfavorably contrasted with Germaine because Claude was a too *"delicate* whore," p. 43. Another portrait of a prostitute, going back to the early 1930's but not written until much later, appears in the "Mara Marigan" series of minor sexual anecdotes in *Quiet Day in Clichy* (Paris, 1958). A revised version appears under the title of "Berthe," *Miller Reader*, pp. 190-99. In a prefatory note Miller links it with the Claude piece as praise of Paris prostitutes, though it is an extremely sentimental piece about the narrator's feeding a whore who was not used to being treated like a human being.

13. "Max," *The Cosmological Eye*, pp. 8-46. On this, as on most of Miller's best short pieces, there seems to be an absence of significant comment. Perlès, *My Friend, Henry Miller* (New York, 1956), p. 77, says Miller characteristically exaggerated both the good and the bad qualities of Max.

14. In a later prefatory note on "Max," Miller says that it was from such suffering ones that he "learned about life, about God, and about the futility of 'doing good.'" He adds that he does not know what happened to the original Max, though he assumes that he must have been killed by the Germans (*Henry Miller Reader*, p. 134). The great importance to Miller of his identification with Jews will be discussed in Chapter III.

15. "Benno, The Wild Man From Borneo," *Wisdom of the Heart* (New York, 1941), pp. 13-18. Perhaps a bit better, because more actually concrete, is the paean to the primitivistic *naïf*, his painter-friend, Hans Reichel, in the entitling essay of *The Cosmological Eye*, pp. 357-64. In a published letter to another painter friend in 1934, Emil Schnellock (the Ulric of the romances), Miller gives a long, gentle monologue attributed to Reichel who was trying to

teach Miller about painting and artistic order (*Miller Miscellanea,* pp. 27-30). See also, *Miller Reader,* p. 307.

16. "Scenario," *The Cosmological Eye,* pp. 75-106. Nin's rather lush prose-poem attempted to project a serious sense of narcissistic and incestuous longings. Miller unintentionally burlesques it by mechanical loading with dream symbolism and fantasy imagery from, I would guess, "*B*" movies, H. Rider Haggard, astrology, etc. The theme might be that love is an ornate mess, or that Miller has redundant nightmares.

17. Miller has published three essays on cinema in his anthologies: "The Golden Age," properly high praise of Luis Buñuel and a defense of cinema as art, in *Cosmological Eye,* pp. 47-62; "Reflections on 'Extasy'," an explication of Machaty's film, in *Cosmological Eye,* pp. 63-74; and "Raimu," some suggestive comparisons between America and France, loosely connected with film actors, in *Wisdom of the Heart,* pp. 47-62. These essays are in fairly direct discursive style, occasionally bombastic, and show an avid literary interest in the movies. Miller was obviously quite a devotee, and generally defends the "highbrow" position on movies. In a recent interview, Miller said that he gave up seeing films some years ago (some allusions in his writings would seem to contradict this); he still believes that cinema, rightly used, could be the great mass art (London, September 12, 1961, with Professor George Wickes, who has kindly furnished me a transcript of the interview). See also Henry Miller, "The art of Fiction XXVIII," ed. George Wickes, *Paris Review,* no. 28(Summer-Fall, 1962), pp. 129-59. During the 1930's Miller also seems to have taken a strong interest in jazz, which he occasionally drew on in his writing, but there is no evidence of a later interest.

18. *Money and How it Gets That Way,* "Booster Broadside No. 1" (Paris, [1938]); reprinted in *Stand Still Like the Hummingbird.* In "Foreword," dated 1936, Miller attributes the writing to a question from Ezra Pound. Perlès says that a wager he made with Michael Fraenkel that he could sound scholarly without making sense provided the impetus (*My Friend, Henry Miller,* p. 92).

19. Miller did some similar minor parodies for *Booster,* a periodical he co-edited in Paris. "Fall and Winter Fashions," portentous sounding nonsense in the manner of men's fashion notes of an earlier day, has been reprinted in *Miller Miscellanea,* p. 37-41.

20. *What Are You Going to Do About Alf?* (Berkeley, [1944]). Perlès says that Miller must have appropriated any contributions that came in, which is just what Miller justifies (*My Friend, Henry Miller,* p. 173).

21. In a letter written in 1939 he gave, as a conservative estimate of the full-sized letters he had written, twenty-five thousand (*Henry*

Miller Literary Society Newsletter. No. 5 [November, 1960]). Miller apparently continued the heavy letter writing for some years at Big Sur.

22. *Hamlet*, Vol. I (New York, 1939) omitted a number of letters which were included in the second edition (New York, 1943). The only edition of Vol. II (New York, 1941) is complete. There are a number of interesting matters in the letters which, for reasons of space, I cannot discuss here. In later years Miller published other letters from the 1930's. *Aller Retour New York* (New York, 1945) is a ninety-page quasi-essay, rather bombastic, directed to Alfred Perlès. A somewhat shorter and more genial letter-recollection is the parallel *Reunion in Barcelona* (Northwood, England, 1959). *Semblance of a Devoted Past* (Berkeley, 1944) contains a selection of Miller's letters to Emil Schnellock, written in the 1930's. Walter Lowenfels published Miller letters of the early 1930's in *The Outsider*, I (Fall, 1961), 62-66—a continuing series. Professor George Wickes has edited a selection of the Miller-Durrell letters (New York, Dutton, 1963). Some of these letters are much better than the forced draft essays published earlier because of being more topical, immediate, and directed toward an individual.

23. While discussing himself as a "genius" (as he often does), Miller notes: "When I write something I like extra well I smack my lips and look over my shoulder. I am already with the man of 2500 A. D. . . . enjoying this great guy Henry Miller who lived in the 20th century" (*Hamlet*, I, 313). Miller, I should judge, is at least half serious.

24. "Via Dieppe-Newhaven," *Cosomological Eye*, pp. 197-288. I know of no significant comment on this story.

25. *Colossus of Maroussi* (New York, 1941). The publisher's fly-leaf statement in the paperback reprint (1958) that Miller made an eight months' trip through Greece is not correct.

26. A Greek writer on Greece devotes a short chapter to praising and taking issue with Miller's view of his country. He particularly objects to Miller's romanticizing of the miserable poverty of the Greeks, his almost complete ignoring of the nasty Metaxas dictatorship of that time, and his failure to understand more fully the conditions he praises. Miller, of course, was quite the ordinary American tourist in these respects. (Minica Cranaki, *Greece*, trans. N. C. Clegg [London, 1959], pp. 77-90.)

27. In the 1961 interview with Professor Wickes, *op. cit.*, Miller said that the book that "came out best" was *Colossus*. However, he has made similar comments about *Black Spring, Capricorn,* and *The Rosy Crucifixion* volumes. He never seems to give such praise to *Cancer* and his best shorter pieces!

28. *Colossus* seems the most generally praised of Miller's books,

though usually in unanalytic asides. Paul Rosenfeld emphasized its eloquence, though with some reservations about Miller's philosophy, in "Hellenism," *The Happy Rock,* pp. 64-72. Nicholas Moore notes that *Colossus* is a considerably lesser work than his "best" (*Cancer*) and does not tell us much about Greece (*Henry Miller* [Wigginton, England, 1943], p. 20). Phillip Rahv praises *Colossus,* though as a lesser work than Miller's earlier books; and he notes Miller's role as a "fugitive from progress" and a "wholesale" mystic; rather dubiously, he claims to find a poetry of "concrete objects" (*Image and Idea,* p. 160). In a review of *Capricorn,* Roger Shattuck denigrates *Cancer,* criticizes *Capricorn,* and, as with a sigh of relief, repeatedly insists that Colossus is his "best book" ("A Loner's Lark Through Brooklyn," New York *Times Book Review* [September 2, 1962], p. 6). I think this is fairly representative of a large body of response. *Colossus* is generally well thought of by those who have an uncertain understanding of, or response to, the rest of Miller's work. Its "positive" attitude might have something to do with this.

29. "Today, Yesterday and Tomorrow," *Sunday After the War* (New York, 1944), pp. 107-15. In the same volume there is another bit of sermonizing on Hellenism in a vague discussion of a Greek writer, Anghelos Sikelianos, "The Gigantic Sunrise," pp. 57-62.

30. As Miller suggestively put the point in one of his essays, "The American is a born anarchist; he has no genuine concern with the ideals of the European," (*Wisdom of the Heart,* p. 61).

Chapter Three

1. *The Henry Miller Reader,* ed. Lawence Durrell (New York, 1959), p. 384. In *Nexus* (Paris, 1960), Miller wrote that he was working at an easy clerical job in the Park Department office that day. In *Colossus of Maroussi* (New York, 1941), he wrote that he was digging a ditch that day, p. 150. Another summary is given in the *Books in My Life* (New York, [1952]), p. 98. Miller repeatedly calls his life story "autobiographical romance," apparently to indicate that it is not literal autobiography.

2. *Sexus* (Paris, 1960), a double volume first pubilshed in 1949; *Plexus* (Paris, 1959), a double volume first published in 1953; *Nexus,* a single volume so far, was first published in 1960. Some of the fragments that have been published in the U. S. are indicated below; *Sexus,* I understand, cannot at present be legally imported into the U. S.

3. *Tropic of Capricorn* (New York, 1961, actually published 1962) was originally published in Paris in 1939. Further discussion of this book will be found in Chapter IV.

4. Miller has said, in various reported interviews in the past

several years, that there will be one, two, or more, further volumes of *Nexus*. He has also several times announced yet another book dealing with his obsessional self-dramatization of the 1920's, *Draco and the Ecliptic*, which would give the essence or occult significance of the multi-volumed work.

5. In yet another summary of his life, he explains that "rosy crucifixion" means the "transmutation" of suffering into understanding ("My Life As An Echo," *Stand Still Like the Hummingbird* [New York, 1962], p. 81). He also notes that he no longer knows what is true and what is not in his "autobiographical romances." "If I lie a bit now and then it is mainly in the interest of truth," p. 83. When it comes to most of the sexual descriptions (and a number of other episodes as well), I characterize these as fantasies simply because that is the most appropriate literary term for the way they are handled. Whether or not the author had experiences similar to those he adapts for his sexual fantasy scenes seems to me an unimportant question.

6. *Quiet Day in Clichy* (Paris, 1958; original publication 1956), p. 110. *Clichy* seems to have been originally written some years earlier. It is a series of minor but amusing anecdotes of the Paris days after *Cancer*: trip to Luxembourg, Clichy prostitutes, miscellaneous bohemian adventures. It lacks the concentration of *Cancer* and the intense writing, though it sometimes touches the same iconoclastic perceptiveness. Of stolid Luxembourg he notes: "Now I know what makes the world civilized: it's vice, disease, thievery, mendacity, lechery," p. 89.

7. In *Cosmological Eye*, pp. 197-202, she is just called his "wife." The few details (most, of course, are about Miller's responses) are sordid-pathetic rather than mythic. Miller's second wife is identified in various places, by Miller, as June Smith, Edith Smith, and June Mansfield. On internal evidence, there would seem to be little justification for fully indentifying Miller's Mona/Mara figures with any actual person.

8. *Books in My Life*, pp. 96-97. Perhaps some of the mystification in Miller's treatment may be indebted to H. Rider Haggard, to Breton's *Nadja*, and to the heroines of Claude Houghton, among others.

9. *Sunday After the War* (New York, 1944), pp. 291-94. Miller's other pieces on Nin are overdone encomiums, including a letter in the same volume, pp. 276-84, and "Un Etre Etoilique," *The Cosmological Eye* (New York, 1939), pp. 269-91.

10. Miller calls it the "Amarillo Dance Hall"; here, and elsewhere, he may be describing the Roseland Ballroom, Time Square. In an author's copy of *The Winter of Artifice* (Paris, 1939) in the "Special Collections" of the U.C.L.A. library there is a list, "Identification of Characters," apparently in Nin's handwriting. Hans is given as

Miller, Djuna as Anais Nin, Johanna as June Mansfield Miller, André as Perlès and Lilith as sometimes Nin, sometimes Mrs. Miller. In this shapeless and over-fervent book, the main points that come through are the polymorphous sexuality and feelings and Millers overwhelming self-love. A composite figure with Mona/Mara characteristics appears in other Nin works, as does a Miller-like figure called Jay.

11. See his comments about Balzac, who wrote his occultist *Louis Lambert* in his thirty-third year (*The Wisdom of the Heart* [New York, 1941], pp. 211-12).

12. For a sexual fillip Miller casually sketches in an orgy with two other women friends (*Sexus*, p. 523). A scholarly student informs me that the protagonist of Miller's "autobiographical romances" has a distinguished sexual record which includes five women in one day, nine orgasms in one night, and other sterling performances.

13. I know of no detailed literary commentary on the role of the destructive-desirable Jewish Dark Lady in literature, though the iconography runs at least from the Renaissance through Iris Murdoch's witty novel, *A Severed Head* (1961).

14. This occult woman seems much indebted to a similar figure, Iris, in Alfred Perlès, *The Renegade* (London, 1941).

15. Wallace Fowlie notes, in an otherwise weak essay, that Miller's fear of domineering women encourages him to reduce them to prostitutes ("Shadow of Doom: An Essay on Henry Miller," *Of-By-and-About Henry Miller* [Yonkers, 1947], p. 23).

16. I do not recall any sexual scene in the first 400 pages of *Plexus*, and even the friendly "orgy" started then is soon permanently disrupted by a discussion of the esthetics of Gottfried Benn (it seems unlikely that Miller would have read Benn until some years later). The absence of sex in *Plexus*, in marked contrast to *Sexus*, may have been partly in response to the criticisms of Lawrence Durrell, discussed later.

17. See also *Colossus of Maroussi* (New York, 1941), p. 71. "I have always felt that the art of telling a story consists in so stimulating the listener's imagination that he drowns himself in his own reveries long before the end. The best stories I have heard were pointless. . . ." This is a hopeless esthetic.

18. The lesbianism is first brought out as a minor motif in several of the dream fantasies (*Plexus*, pp. 272-95). Miller quite aptly makes clear a general common-sensical attitude towards homosexuality (*Nexus*, p. 19). Yet the dramatization indicates a contrary fearful masculinity in which his wife's preference for a woman points to some inadequacy in him.

19. The lesbian friend, Anastasia, appears to be identical with the Thelma of a Brooklyn Heights basement, a devotee of Rimbaud

who died in an insane asylum, as described by Miller in *The Time of the Assassins* (New York, 1956), p. 3.

20. A considerable part of the Osmanli and of the following episode has been reprinted in *Sunday After the War*, pp. 161-88.

21. Claude Mauriac, voicing the common argument of Miller admirers that Miller's work cannot be criticized because of its unique fusion of good and bad, seems to claim the volumes of *The Rosy Crucifixion* to be a major work simply because it is big work (*The New Literature*, trans. S. F. Stone [New York, 1959], p. 59).

22. There has been much less personal recollection by those who knew Miller in the Brooklyn period than in the Paris period. Emil Schnellock wrote a genial personal reminiscence, "Just a Brooklyn Boy," *The Happy Rock* (Berkeley, 1945), pp. 7-24. He does note that Miller's portraits of his friends show "viciousness" and "monstrous cruelty."

23. There are, of course, quite a number of other Brooklyn portraits, but MacGregor seems the most significant. I have not discussed the repeated stories of Miller's early loves—such as his first "mistress," a pathetic older woman—or the mawkish descriptions of a teen-age infatuation. The latter story is retold in "First Love," *Stand Still Like the Hummingbird* (New York, 1962), pp. 46-49.

24. A rather bland antiquarian friend of Miller's amusingly notes in a weak essay, "I've never known women such as Miller describes." Miller, he says "sounds like a high school boy boasting of his amatory exploits" (Herbert Faulkner West, "The Strange Case of Henry Miller," *The Mind on the Wing* [New York, 1947], p. 126).

25. The argument has been made that Miller is searching for the absolute by way of sex. See, for example, Pierre Fauchey, *"Un Epopée du Sexe," Of-By-and-About Henry Miller*, p. 41. While the argument can be applied to D. H. Lawrence, Wilhelm Reich, and even, at times, to Norman Mailer, as well as to certain ancient religious movements, I can find no evidence for it in Miller. In a rather miscellaneous discussion of sex and related matters in Miller and in general, George Villa properly notes Miller's primarily masculine emphasis and his inadequate comprehension of women (*Miller et L'Amour* [Paris, 1947], p. 115).

26. Much more could be said about sex and obscenity in Miller's work. Miller himself has had much to say about sex in the writings of Miller. *The World of Sex* (New York, 1940; rev. ed., Paris, 1957) partly discusses the subject, and makes some odd and suggestive points, amidst some absurd anecdotes and a wild range of ruminations. But we should note that Miller's arguments about

what sex means, frequently of an ecstatic religious cast (indebted to D. H. Lawrence), run antithetical not only to most of his sexual descriptions in his other books, but even to the personal details and anecdotes he gives in this book. Miller, certainly, is not clear about his own sexual sensibility or about the cast of his writings, and has no over-all coherent response to sex. The same must be said for Miller on the issue of censorship. His main essay on the subject, "Obscenity and the Law of Reflection," *Remember to Remember* (New York, 1947), pp. 274-91, makes some suggestive (and some badly garbled) points; but it does not confront the issue of sex in the writings of Henry Miller. He is generally even less relevant in his later writing on the subject, as in the letter to the Norwegian Supreme Court, *Henry Miller Reader* pp. 372-79, and in the trite invective of "I Defy You," *Playboy* (January, 1962).

27. Sexual fascination with the Jewish woman appears in other scenes in the book, as in his lavish praise of Rebecca (wife of Arthur Raymond) as superior to all ordinary American women (*Sexus,* pp. 431ff. and 490ff.). A Jew is also given a speech explaining that Jewish women develop a passion for a "lost gentile" (*Sexus,* p. 532). There are also several gross sexual fantasy episodes concerning hyper-passionate Jewish girls.

28. In a note to the republication of this piece, Miller writes that the ghetto was his favorite part of the city, an inspiration, and the only place to meet an "interesting character" (*Miller Reader,* p. 72). He sentimentally fails to see the horror of the ghetto.

29. Another aspect of Miller as imaginary Jew comes out in his identification with the prophetic role and Old Testament rhetoric; see *Plexus,* pp. 31ff. For Miller's ecstatic account of the effects of some Yiddish literature upon him, see *Books in My Life,* pp. 260ff. See also Miller's lavish praise of two Jewish friends in *Big Sur and the Oranges of Hieronymous Bosch* (New York, 1957), pp. 196 and 203-4. For some rather odd praise of Jewish religiosity, see his comments in *Hamlet* (New York, 1941), I, 263. Fraenkel, in turn, acutely points out the hostility in Miller's notions about the Jewish heritage. That Miller's family and his own early feelings were anti-Semitic becomes cumulatively emphatic in the episodes from his early days scattered throughout *The Rosy Crucifixion.* The evidence is not altogether clear, but I would guess that a long Germanic obsession with Jewishness, made knowledgable by his Paris associations, becomes an increasingly mythic identification after his return to the United States, and culminates in the re-creation of his past as an imaginary Jew.

30. Part of the Kronski material has been reprinted in *Sunday After the War,* pp. 212-31.

31. That Miller is telling the literal "truth" in the volumes of "autobiographical romance" seems to be rather touchingly assumed by Henk van Gelre, *The International Henry Miller Letter* (Netherlands), II (December, 1961), 13-22.

32. Very few of the readers of the later works find them better than the early books. A minor exception, amusingly enough, is Samuel Roth, well-known publisher of marginal erotic literature, who apparently did not like the early Miller but found *Plexus* wonderful ("An Open Letter to Henry Miller," *American Aphrodite*, IV [1954], 3-4).

33. There has been little significant discussion of *The Rosy Crucifixion*. Perhaps the most curious is that one in Lawrence Durrell's correspondence with Miller. Though a long-time admirer and friend, Durrell wrote (September 5, 1949) violently attacking *Sexus* as "moral vulgarity" and a "childish explosion of obscenity." More important, he judged it a "puerile narrative" with "little real feeling." Miller's defense (September 28, 1949) weakly discussed the great time he had devoted to it, his sincerity, and his truthfulness. (I draw upon the manuscript of the forthcoming Miller-Durrell letters, generously made available to me by Professor George Wickes.)

34. In another letter to Durrell, Miller wrote (October 3, 1959) that he so desperately wanted to be a writer that he "sinned" against everything, and denied reality, even his religious purposes. Miller makes a somewhat more restricted admission in *Art and Outrage*, "A Correspondence about Henry Miller between Alfred Perlès and Lawrence Durrell (With an Intermission by Henry Miller)," (London, 1959), pp. 56ff.

35. In his two letters in *Art and Outrage* Miller in effect grants most of the criticisms of his defective art but justifies himself in terms of his spiritual "break-through" into new being (pp. 28 and 60-61). On a purely individual level, there can be no argument, for no doubt the strangest actions can have therapeutic effects in individual cases. However, Miller is on dangerous ground when he goes on to justify himself because his readers have been "unanimous in writing of the therapeutic value of my work" (p. 29). As the social scientists put it, those who wrote were not a proper sample. And as the literate say, such quantitative and valueless standards can, with just a little imagination, be turned upside down. How weigh the bored readers against the inspired letter writers?—Outraged Durrell against some admiring adolescent in Detroit? But let us grant that Miller may have been a therapist, with all the dangerous ambiguities that implies, for a certain audience neither open to some other nostrums nor to some of the best literature. Therapy, of course, can also be used destructively.

Chapter Four

1. *Sunday After the War* (New York, 1944), pp. 63-106. I know of nothing other than passing comments on this sketch, though most of them seem to be favorable. Herbert Read, for example, calls it a "masterpiece" in *Of-By-and-About Henry Miller* (Yonkers, N. Y., 1947), p. 14. See also, Read, *The Tenth Muse* (London, 1957), pp. 250-55.

2. This episode, repeated in *The Rosy Crucifixion,* would seem to be crucial to Miller's overstated hostility between America and the artist. Annette Kar Baxter summarizes some other points on the artist in America in *Henry Miller, Expatriate* (Pittsburgh, 1961), Chapter IV.

3. *Tropic of Capricorn* (New York, 1961 [1962]) has almost invariably been discussed as a continuation or parallel of *Cancer.* See the Critics in Chapter I. Herbert J. Muller briefly finds Miller's attacks on America in *Capricorn,* as well as his "romantic nonsense" and "yea-saying," distinctively American ("The World of Henry Miller," *Kenyon Review,* II [Summer, 1940], 313-18). The shapelessness of *Capricorn* and the considerable bad writing in the main episodes (Cosmodemonic, the Dark Lady, the conclusion), make the book difficult to discuss and evaluate.

4. In his suggestive but cranky essay on Miller, Kenneth Rexroth over-praises the Cosmodemonic section because he agrees with its view of our "insane and evil society" with "its orgy of human self-alienation." His view is a common one. Perhaps tricked by memory, Rexroth claims Valeska as "Beatrice" and "one of the most real women in fiction," though she is hardly developed by Miller ("Introduction," Henry Miller, *Nights of Love and Laughter* [New York, 1955], p. 16).

5. Miller, in adapting surrealist dogma, has repeatedly stressed the involuntary nature of parts of his writing, especially the "Interlude" section of *Capricorn.* He amusingly, and probably ingenuously, describes the "Voice" of unconscious dictation working against his will in this section of *Capricorn,* in *Big Sur and the Oranges of Hieronymous Bosch* (New York, 1957), pp. 126-30.

6. This may either be the characteristic failure of Miller's writing or the characteristic falsification of his life; that trip, he repeatedly notes elsewhere, became a "turning point" in his life because of his meeting Emma Goldman, hearing her lecture, and buying Nietzsche from her consort (Ben Reitman) in San Diego in 1913. See the *Henry Miller Reader* (New York, 1959), p. 384, and *Books in My Life* (New York, [1952]), p. 306. The lectures may have been those given in her book, *The Social Significance of Modern Drama* (Boston, 1914) since it seems doubtful that Miller

could have heard them in San Diego. According to Richard Drinnon and the sources he cites in his life of Goldman, *Rebel in Paradise* (Chicago, 1961), p. 136, Emma Goldman went from the railroad station to the police station, and then was escorted out of San Diego in 1913. She did briefly lecture in San Diego in 1915, but Reitman was not with her; and, according to all of his accounts, Miller was back in New York from 1914 on. No doubt Miller saw announcements of the lectures planned but not given in 1913. Given this evidence, and the usual self-romanticizing inaccuracies of Miller's autobiographical material, the influence of Goldman and this trip must remain doubtful. Very little of Miller's autobiography should be taken literally.

7. Miller several times refers to the impact made on him by Otto Rank's *Art and Artist.* See, for example, *Stand Still Like the Hummingbird* (New York, 1962), p. 84. While he does not cite other Rank works, their effect seems highly probable, considering the portentous and permanent influence some of Rank's German-romantic views of the artist had on Miller. Miller's use of psychoanalytic imagery and notions is usually fantastic rather than analytic. See his laudatory essay on an inspirational analyst, E. Graham Howe, in the entitling essay of *Wisdom of the Heart* (New York, 1941), pp. 31-46, and his dithyrambic use of womb imagery in "The Enormous Womb" and "Uterine Hunger" in that volume.

8. Just when and to what degree the occult influences become crucial is debatable. In "Autobiographical Note"—one of his better self-sketches in *Cosmological Eye* (New York, 1939)—he emphasizes his early reading was mostly religious and philosophical. *Books in My Life* does not altogether confirm this. The *Hamlet* letters show him quite involved in Oriental religious notions in 1936. The importance of occult religiosity increases with each book in the 1930's.

9. To indicate the parts of *Capricorn* retold or modified in *The Rosy Crucifixion* volumes and elsewhere would be a lengthy process. Many shifts in tone and focus indicate that Miller was anything but clear on where he was headed with the autobiographical materials.

10. *Cosomological Eye,* pp. 337-45. Other comments by Miller on America may be found in his account of part of a visit in *Aller Retour New York* (New York, 1945), a letter-essay to Perlès which has a Celine-like violence and disgust. Miller is weirdly full of resentment at being "a neglected American author" (44); he burlesques subways and the Empire State building and inordinately praises France. In the more disinterested stance of his earlier outcast role, America was "dead and Europe moribund" (*Semblance of a Devoted Past* [Berkeley, 1944], p.1). In this letter he also announced, half-humorously, "America must be destroyed" (p. 21). It seems likely that Miller, searching for a role, intentionally cul-

tivated that of the American anti-American. In his high praise of Duhamel's *America the Menace*—one of the most extreme of European attacks on America as the epitome of modern dehumanization —we probably see a major literary source (along with Celine) of Miller's invective.

11. *The Air-Conditioned Nightmare* (New York, 1945; reprint, 1961). A common assumption seems to be that Miller's role as "philosopher on a binge" comes with his return to America. So suggests Phillip Rahv in *Image and Idea* (New York, 1957), p. 160. However, as *Capricorn, Colossus,* and even earlier material indicate, Miller had long been inebriated with his own pronouncements.

12. *Remember to Remember,* "Vol. 2 of the Air-Conditioned Nightmare" (New York, 1947). Three of the essays collected in this volume are discussed in other chapters below.

13. In a note to a reprinting of one of the burlesques from *Nightmare,* Miller says he received "several hundred dollars" advance. Given certain publishing practices of the time, it was more likely near a thousand dollars—a very substantial sum in the early 1940's, when a machine operator in a Midwestern factory, as I can testify, might earn less than three dollars a day. Improvident Miller's frequent and bitter complaints about money should not be taken literally. It is possible that, if the total earnings and gifts for Miller's thirty years of published writing life were averaged out, his income would not only be way above most "average" incomes but above that of the great majority of published writers. This is not to deny that he suffered discomfort, anxiety, and several periods of hardship during the Depression. But, contrary to certain devotees, Miller, for the kind of writer he is, has done exceptionally well both in being widely published and in earning considerable money. He has, of course, "cultivated" editors and other literary "contacts."

14. Though Miller repeatedly cites *Le Grand Meaulness* as a profound child-vision of the world, which is dubious, we can amusingly note that his first published comment on the book called it "feeble" and an illustration of the "inherent weakness of the French character"—soft fantasy (*Wisdom of the Heart,* p. 48). Similarly, Miller's earlier comments on France and French culture are perceptively and bitterly negative, as in his comment on the French "death rhythm" in *Cosmological Eye,* p. 194. There is a direct disproportion between Miller's successful *role* as artist and his effective astringency.

15. *The Wisdom of the Heart,* pp. 103-39.

16. A better portrait of Hilaire Hiler appears in the letters in *Semblance of a Devoted Past,* pp. 25-34. This also appears in

Hilaire Hiler, Henry Miller, and William Saroyan, *Why Abstract?* (London, 1948).

17. Another anecdote from memory in the *Nightmare* is the brief "A Night With Jupiter" where Miller describes falling through a glass door in Paris and is assured by his astrologer, Moricand, that his Jupiter protected him from serious injury.

18. Miller, never bashful about putting everything in print, has also published one of the notebooks of his American trip. See *The Red Notebook* (Highlands, North Carolina, [1958]). Not particularly interesting, it catalogues places to see, exotic words, occultist quotations, his silly predictions about World War II, a recipe for Irish stew, notes on Rimbaud, and ends with his favorite quotation from L.-F. Celine: "I piss on it all from a considerable height." Miller's trip was touristic, and he showed little interest in ordinary life.

19. A more adequate analysis of Miller's humor would require elaboration of its background; one part of his Hollywood burlesques might be related to that sub-genre. See my "The Hollywood Image," *Coastlines Literary Magazine* No. 17, V (1961), pp. 17-35.

20. Karl Shapiro calls *Tropic of Cancer the* "Horatio Alger story with a vengeance," but this seems to me more ironically applicable to the later Miller (*In Defense of Ignorance* [New York, 1960], p. 317).

21. There are numerous chatty descriptions of Miller at Big Sur by his friends. See Lawrence Clark Powell, "The Miller of Big Sur," *Books in My Baggage* (New York, 1960), pp. 148-53; Raymond Bruckberger, *One Sky to Share* (New York, 1952), pp. 136-40; Harold Maine [Walker Winslow], "Henry Miller—Bigotry's Whipping Boy," *Arizona Quarterly*, VII (Autumn, 1951), 197-208; Alfred Perlès, *Reunion in Big Sur* (Northwood, England, 1959). A hostile discussion is Mildred Edie Brady, "The New Cult of Sex and Anarchy," *Harpers*, 194 (April, 1947), 312-32. In her general discussion of central California bohemianism, she mistakenly lumps the influence of Wilhelm Reich with that of Henry Miller. Like most "slick" magazine discussions of Miller (*Time, Life,* etc.) this essay is snide without being acute.

22. *Big Sur and the Oranges of Hieronymous Bosch* (New York, 1957). The long Moricand portrait also appeared as *A Devil in Paradise* (New York, 1956). The reviews—the only comment—tended to the negative. The high proportion of bad writing in Miller's later works may have additional causes than the comfortable identity as a Big Sur artist: age and decline in sexuality, lack of intense confrontation with harsh reality, ease with which he could get almost anything published, uncritical praise of many friends, and his occultist emphasis. Miller's defense of his bad writing is that the "slag" is justified as a part of life (*Art and Outrage* [London,

1959], pp. 40-41). Even allowing for it in the personal act of writing, its relevance to publishing bad writing is not at all clear.

23. In a note, Miller voices regret at not having developed his portrait of Jaime de Angulo, apparently a cultivated and wild misanthrope (*The Henry Miller Reader* [New York, 1959], p. 77).

24. M [aurice] M [agnus], *Memoirs of the Foreign Legion,* with Introduction by D. H. Lawence (New York, 1925).

25. See Chapter I, note 17, for a contrasting view.

26. The loosely controlling motif, as Miller points out, comes from Wilhelm Franger's *The Millennium of Hieronymous Bosch* (Chicago, 1951), which many scholars consider an eccentric interpretation. Throughout, Miller shows fragmented admiration for many kinds of utopian and antinomian writing.

27. Miller's discussion of "call girls" is neither very relevant nor witty. For general information on the subject, see Harold Greenwald, *The Call Girl* (New York, 1958). For a confession of a prostiute which shows up the traditional masculine sentimentality which blinds Miller on that subject, see the poignantly insightful anonymous *Streetwalker* (New York, 1961).

28. William Barrett emphatically criticizes Miller's late work and his "tiresome tirades on the obvious" ("Henry Miller: His Exuberant Reflections," *Saturday Review of Literature,* XL [August 3, 1957], 7).

29. Charles I. Glicksburg, "Henry Miller, Individualism in Extremis," *Southwest Review,* XXXIII (Summer, 1948), 289-95, emphasizes Miller as an egotistical, intellectually confused, sexually obsessed rebel.

30. *Stand Still Like the Hummingbird* (New York, 1962)—all but one piece previously published in periodicals and books.

31. Miller has a number of minor pieces belligerently praising Europe and attacking America. When something is bad in Europe, it is because it is like America. See, for example, "Impressions of Bruges," *The Colorado Review,* I (Winter, 1956-57), 35-37. Kenneth Rexroth shrewdly labels this role of Miller's as that of the "amateur European." "Introduction," *Nights of Love and Laughter* (New York, 1955), p. 12. Even more essential, I think, is to recognize that Miller makes these gestures because of his commitment to the role of renegade.

Chapter Five

1. Almost every work of Miller contains discussions of his reading and writing. Thus in summarizing I am drawing generally on his work and not just on the account given in *Books in My Life* (New York, [1952]). For reasons of space, I am ignoring some

obvious contradictions and resisting commentary on the peculiar ways Miller read many books.

2. *Wisdom of the Heart* (New York, 1941), pp. 1-12. I am partly assuming in my discussion the view of Lawrence which I have developed in detail in my *The Art of Perversity: D. H. Lawrence* (Seattle, 1962).

3. Such ideas are probably greatly indebted to Michael Fraenkel, whose influence on Miller's best writing seems considerable, and inadequately acknowledged. Besides the two volumes of *Hamlet* letters, other writings of Fraenkel's such as *Death Is Not Enough* (London, 1939), would be relevant here.

4. "Reflections on 'Extasy'," *Cosmological Eye* (New York, 1939), pp. 63-74.

5. *Southwest Review*, XXXI (Summer, 1946), 254-56. Reprinted in *Sunday After the War* (New York, 1944).

6. "Into the Future," *Wisdom of the Heart*, pp. 159-72.

7. *Sunday After the War*, pp. 232-75.

8. *Cosmological Eye*, pp. 107-34. Rahv calls it a "truly inspired piece of criticism" (*Image and Idea* [New York, 1957], p. 166).

9. "Seraphita remains the high peak of my experience in the world of books" (*World of Sex* [New York, 1940], p. 7,). His long friendship with Moricand seems also to have depended on the latter's having brought him *Seraphita*. See *Devil in Paradise*.

10. *Wisdom of the Heart*, pp. 208-50.

11. *Ibid.*, pp. 192-207.

12. The most charming and suggestive discussion of occultism in literature that I know is John Senior, *The Way Down and Out: The Occult in Symbolist Literature* (Ithaca, New York, 1959). His view could be used as a partial antidote to the one I present.

13. *The Time of the Assassins* (New York, 1956). In my contrary comments I am drawing, as does Miller, not just on Rimbaud's work but on Enid Starkie's biography. Miller's two Rimbaud essays were originally written and published in the mid 1940's. One of the few to praise highly the Rimbaud book is Karl Shapiro, *In Defense of Ignorance* (New York, 1960), p. 334.

14. *Books in My Life*, p. 113.

15. He discusses Gutkind in "The Absolute Collective," *Wisdom of the Heart*, pp. 78-93; "The Hour of Man," *Stand Still Like the Hummingbird* (New York, 1962), pp. 6ff.; *Books in My Life*, pp. 231-32. *The Absolute Collective* is a minor theological rhapsody with marked similarities to the ideas of Martin Buber in its emphasis on religious communion with immediate, concrete, and fully physical life. Miller may have been much taken—his remarks do not make clear—with Gutkind's thou-saying to the world while denying its institutions and moralities and civilized forms. A better anarchistic

theologian, Berdyaev, may also have appealed to Miller, but not until much later.

16. *Stand Still Like the Hummingbird* (New York, 1962).

17. *Books in My Life,* pp. 287-316.

18. See his preface to Haniel Long, *The Power Within Us* (New York, 1944), which is a selective summary of Cabeza de Vaca's *Relacion.* See also Miller's comments in *Books in My Life,* p. 171. The reader may conveniently evaluate Miller's view by examining the recent translation, Cabeza de Vaca, *Adventures in the Unknown Interior of America,* trans. and ed. Cyclone Covey (New York, 1961).

19. Miller's fullest discussion of Whitman is in *Books in My Life,* pp. 221-43. He also has a weak essay on him in *Stand Still Like the Hummingbird,* pp. 107-10.

20. *Books in My Life,* pp. 264-86. For some of the differences between the early and late Miller, one might also contrast the remarks on painting, sex and God—they also show much the same changes.

21. *Wisdom of the Heart,* pp. 19-30. Similar statements are scattered all through. See, for example, the citations in Chapter III.

22. "I would one day give up writing altogether, give it up voluntarily—in the moment when I would feel myself in possession of the greatest power and mastery" (*Colossus of Maroussi* [New York, 1941], p. 205). There are many similar statements which indicate that Miller wanted art to lead him to a power beyond art, but, somewhat pathetically, writing itself became the pyrrhic power which he has never shown much sign of giving up.

23. Besides many similar statements, Miller also points more slyly at times to his deification. For example, he often praises Claude Houghton [Oldfield] who wrote bland occultist allegories in which the artist figure turns out to have protean salvational powers. See his *I Am Jonathan Scrivner* (New York, 1935). Miller says that Houghton's *Hudson Joins the Herd* (London, 1947) reveals the secret story of Miller's own life (*Books in My Life,* p. 46). The main motif of *Hudson* is a sensitivity too great for this world. Other elements that no doubt appealed to Miller include a schizophrenic and nymphomaniacal heroine who commits crimes for the artist-hero, the view of the artist as unique savior, and the emphasis on childhood dream obsessions.

24. "I don't care particularly anymore whether I am a saint or not" (*Wisdom of the Heart,* p. 147). Miller has quite a number of other comments on his own saintliness—frequently denials which are a bit elusive in tone. An example of the gross cultism around Miller may be found in Robert Fink's calling Miller a "saint" and a "nearly perfect man" in *The International Henry Miller Letter,* I (June, 1961), 3. The point was made more vivaciously by Karl

Shapiro who called Miller "Ghandi with a penis." Other admirers, such as Durrell and Perlès, also use the saint label now and again.

25. *Wisdom of the Heart*, pp. 94-103.

26. *Ibid.*, pp. 187-91.

27. *Cosmological Eye*, pp. 1-7. Miller's early work, but not his later writing, can be closely related to many surrealist dictums. For example, see the conclusion to André Breton's *Nadja* (Paris, 1928), p. 215: "*Le beauté sera convulsive ou ne sera pas.*"

28. *Books in My Life*, p. 95.

29. *Remember to Remember* (New York, 1947), pp. 407-24.

30. *Wisdom of the Heart*, pp. 157 and 184. A good summary of his anti-art position appears at the end of one of his best autobiographical summaries, *Cosmological Eye*, pp. 357-71. Related material on the American artist may be found in Miller's pamphlet, *The Plight of the Creative Artist in the United States of America* (Berkeley, 1944). This reprints several open letters from Miller in which the main points are that any commercialization of art is "prostitution," that "creative spirits" are unique and have no responsibility but to themselves, and that the world somehow owes all artists a living. With rather more perception, Miller argues elsewhere that the true artist needs few material goods, though he does need understanding, appreciation, and engagement to his own "insanity" in our world (*To Paint Is to Love Again* [Alhambra, California, 1960], p. 44).

31. *Cosmological Eye*, pp. 151-96.

32. *Cosmological Eye*, p. 367. See also his refusal of any and all war, "The Situation in American Writing," *Partisan Review*, VI (Summer, 1939), 50-51. Miller apparently avoided the draft in World War I and was over-age in World War II.

33. *Remember to Remember*, pp. 126-216.

34. *Maurizius Forever* (San Francisco, 1946) is a rambling, didactic monograph on Jacob Wasserman's *Maurizius Case*. Miller doesn't discuss the book as the novel it is but as "propaganda" for "a new vision of things" in which love apocalyptically supersedes justice, evil, and the murderer in every man. As with so many novels that seem to have a magical effect on Miller, there is a destructive witch-woman (Anna Jahn), some violent views of America, etc. While sometimes interesting work, it will hardly bear Miller's didactic load. Here, as with much of Miller's response to books, his reactions were fortuitious and idiosyncratic.

35. Don Kleine expresses the point well of why it is hard for the reader, and perhaps for Miller, to take Miller's occultism seriously: his is "mysticism declaimed by a writer with an essentially positivistic sensibility" ("Innocence Forbidden: Henry Miller in the Tropics," *Prairie Schooner*, XXXIII [Summer, 1959], 128).

36. In his published notes from the Clichy period, he advises himself to exploit both psychoanalysis and astrology for satire, which he does (*Henry Miller Miscellanea* [Berkeley, 1945], p. 24).

37. Miller's fullest comment on astrology originally appeared as "A Great Writer Talks About Astrology," 1958 *Guidebook to Astrology*. ed. Sydney Omarr (Los Angeles, 1958), pp. 116-27, from which my citations are taken. It has been reprinted as the foreword to Sydney Omarr, *Henry Miller: His World of Urania* (London, 1960). Omarr's uninformative book is flat praise, quotation, and paraphrase of obvious Miller passages using astrology. There would seem to be no other commentary on the subject.

38. Several years later he also argues characteristically that writers cannot change the world ("Jesus did not write a line"), only the saints can. See *Last Chance*, "11 Questions on Issues Determining Our Destiny: Answered by 26 Leaders of Thought in 14 Nations," ed. Clara Urquhart (Boston, 1948), pp. 42-44.

39. Even bosom companion Perlès dismisses Miller's religion, philosophy, and exotic literary interests (*My Friend, Henry Miller* [New York, 1956], pp. 228ff.).

40. *The Smile At the Foot of the Ladder* (New York, 1948). The book has an appreciative introductory essay by Edwin Corle, mostly praise of *Cancer*, and an epilogue by Miller. Some slight comments on the story may be found in Weldon Kees, *et al.*, "To Be or Not; Four Opinions on Henry Miller's *Smile At the Foot of the Ladder*," *The Tiger's Eye*, I (October 20, 1948), 68-72. Miller's playing with traditional forms during this period includes rather heavy and poor burlesques of fairy tales: *Plexus* (Paris, 1959), pp. 454-63; and *Big Sur and the Oranges of Hieronymous Bosch* (New York, 1957), pp. 81ff.

41. Letter from Stewart Millpond to the author (July 17, 1960).

42. Charles Glicksburg takes Miller as representing an apocalyptic school of social rebellion, anti-politics, and individualism running from D. H. Lawrence through Dylan Thomas ("Literature and Society," *The Arizona Quarterly*, VIII [Summer, 1952], 138). Miller's origins are not so Anglo-Saxon as this article would seem to suggest.

43. A rather left-handed praise of Miller by intellectuals is fairly common. Miller at his best, writes Seymour Krim, gives a "vivid experience of what shapeless modern existence could become" ("The Netherworld of Henry Miller," *Commonweal*, LVII [October 24, 1952], 271).

44. Such rhetorical gestures have their own tradition. I recall that in some piece or other written in the 1920's, Maxwell Bodenheim, the archetypal Greenwich Villager and destructive bohemian, spoke of "the Coney Island of the soul."

Strange Artistic Sophistication of America," *Four Quarters,* XI (Nov., 1961).

45. See Miller's preface to Jack Kerouac, *The Subterraneans* (New York, 1959), pp. 5-7. Kerouac, of course, is indebted to Miller in another sense in following out his fractured life-style, including an attempted withdrawal to *Big Sur.* See his 1962 novel of that title.

46. For a discussion of the relevant tradition, see my "The Literary Rebel," *Centennial Review,* VI (Spring, 1962) and "The American Road," *University of Kansas City Review,* XXVI (Summer, 1960).

47. I have, of course, omitted Miller's influence and role outside of America. *The Black Book,* by Miller's best-known protegé, Lawrence Durrell, is a rather self-consciously rococo adapation of *Cancer,* and of low-life confession, rhetorical cadenzas, uterine imagery, and labyrinthine poses. It lacks the defiance and exuberance of Miller's best writing.

48. Miller again attempts a comic literary form in *Just Wild About Harry* (New York, 1963), a somewhat derivative and forced "antidrama." Drawing on Ionesco, Saroyan, Sartre (*No Exit* seems the basis for the final, and most interesting, scene), he also draws heavily on stock Miller material: the golden-hearted whore, the young "innocent" girl, the Brooklyn boy thug-pimp (Harry), and a number of minor vaudville types (a dwarf, a German in long winter underwear, a blindman, a double-talking doctor, etc.). The theme is grossly sentimental, and tough-guy Harry really does love the innocent girl in the end—love is all. There are several nice iconoclastic bits, such as Harry's long (and completely out of character) common-sense polemic against "the bomb" (pp. 122-25). There is an endless amount of stage business—occasionally suggestive but mostly excessive and imposed nostalgic folderol from ancient vaudeville. The play, in the anti-theater tradition, jokes about itself, but not very humorously, and certainly not enough to cover up the embarrassment of its sloppy development, flat dialogue and mawkish "ideas."

Selected Bibliography

This bibliography contains most of the book publications of Miller (complete duplications—including those under different titles—and some pamphlets and letters are not included; many of the collections repeat each other). Only the most recent bibliographies are listed. The two main anthologies about Miller, and a few of the useful books, articles, and introductions are annotated, but not all the works cited in the notes.

PRIMARY SOURCES

(Parenthetical dates refer to year of original publication when later, more convenient, editions are listed. The later reprintings are not given. Arrangement is by date of original book publication.)

Tropic of Cancer. (1934) New York: Grove Press, 1961.
Aller Retour New York. Paris: Obelisk Press, 1936.
Black Spring. (1936) New York: Grove Press, 1963.
The Cosmological Eye. (1938: *Max and White Phagocytes*) New York: New Directions, 1939.
Tropic of Capricorn. (1939) New York: Grove Press, 1962.
The World of Sex. (1940) Rev. Ed. Paris: Olympia Press, 1957.
The Colossus of Maroussi. New York: New Directions, 1941.
The Wisdom of the Heart. New York: New Directions, 1941.
Hamlet (with Michael Fraenkel). Vol. I (first complete edition): New York: Carrefour, 1943; Vol. II: 1941.
Sunday After the War. New York: New Directions, 1944.
The Air-Conditioned Nightmare. New York: New Directions, 1945.
Henry Miller Miscellanea. Berkeley, California: Bern Porter, 1945,
Semblance of a Devoted Past. Berkeley, California: Bern Porter, 1945.
Maurizius Forever. San Francisco: Colt Press, 1946.
Remember to Remember. New York: New Directions, 1947.
The Smile at the Foot of the Ladder. New York: Duell, Sloan & Pearce, 1948.
Sexus (Book One, *The Rosy Cruifixion*). Paris: Olympia Press, 1949.
The Books in My Life. New York: New Directions [1952].
Plexus (Book Two, *The Rosy Crucifixion*). Paris: Olympia Press, 1953.

Quiet Days in Clichy. Paris: Olympia Press, 1956.

The Time of the Assassins. New York: New Directions, 1956.

Big Sur and the Orange of Hieronymous Bosch. New York: New Directions, 1957. (The significant part of this was published separately as *Devil in Paradise.* New York: New American Library, 1956).

Reunion in Barcelona. Northwood, England: Scorpion Press, 1959.

Nexus (Book Three, *The Rosy Crusifixion*). Paris: Obelisk Press, 1960.

To Paint Is to Love Again. Alhambra, California: Cambria Books, 1960.

Henry Miller: "Watercolors, Drawings and His Essay, 'The Angel is My Watermark'." New York: Abrams, 1962.

Stand Still Like the Hummingbird. New York: New Directions, 1962.

Just Wild About Harry. New York: New Directions, 1963.

Lawrence Durrell and Henry Miller, A Private Correspondence, ed. George Wickes. New York: E. P. Dutton, 1963.

SECONDARY SOURCES

Bibliographies

MOORE, THOMAS H., *Bibliography of Henry Miller.* Minneapolis; Henry Miller Literary Society, 1961. To date, the most complete bibliography of Miller's writings, somewhat inconveniently organized and with only a few writings on Miller.

RILEY, ESTA LOU. *Henry Miller, An Informal Bibliography, 1924-1960.* Hays, Kansas: For Hays Kansas State College, 1961. Very conveniently lists a large number of writings about Miller as well as an adequate list of Miller's writings.

RENKEN, MAXINE. "Bibliography of Henry Miller: 1945-1961." *Twentieth Century Literature,* VII (January, 1962), 180-90. Particularly important for a number of writings about Miller which are not in Riley or Moore. (Reprinted in pamphlet form: Denver: Swallow, 1962.)

Anthologies of Writings About Miller

The Happy Rock. Ed. Bern Porter. Berkeley, California: Bern Porter, 1945. An anthology of recollections, responses, and comments on Miller. Most of the contributions are praise by friends, and many are poor; but there is some significant documentation as well as evidence of the peculiar responses Miller has often engendered. The Fraenkel and Weiss essays are suggestive.

Henry Miller and the Critics. Ed. George Wickes. Carbondale, Illinois: University of Southern Illionis Press, 1963. This includes many of the influential or important essays plus some reminiscences and material on the tribulations of *Cancer.*

Other Writings

BAXTER, ANNETTE KAR. *Henry Miller, Expatriate.* Pittsburgh: University of Pittsburgh Press, 1961. This un-critical academic study does not examine any work but draws together some of the motifs and statements relating to Miller's expatriate role.

DURRELL, LAWRENCE, ALFRED, PERLÈS, and HENRY MILLER. *Art and Outrage.* London: Putnam, 1959. Letters by two of Miller's long-time friends, with answers by the subject, discussing in an erratic but sometimes revealing way Miller's literary role.

KLEINE, DON. "Innocence Forbidden: Henry Miller in the Tropics," *Prairie Schooner,* XXXIII (Summer, 1959), 125-30. An unusually intelligent and perceptive criticism of Miller's dual attitude.

MAURIAC, CLAUDE. "Henry Miller," *The New Literature,* trans. S. F. Stone. New York: Braziller, 1959. The chapter on Miller is weak; it shows a cultivated European's response.

MULLER, HERBERT J. "The World of Henry Miller," *Kenyon Review,* II (Summer, 1940), 313-18. There are several suggestive points in this intelligent critic's attempt to admire Miller.

ORWELL, GEORGE. "Inside the Whale," *A Collection of Essays.* New York: Doubleday-Anchor, 1954. Written in 1940, this long and generally laudatory essay on the early Miller (and other subjects), overemphasizes the sociology of Parisian and lower-class life but provides a good introduction for those not acquainted with the more extreme forms of modern literature.

PERLÈS, ALFRED. *My Friend, Henry Miller.* New York: John Day, 1956. A casual biography in which a friend of Miller's gives a firsthand account of the Paris period and hearsay information for other periods. It is pleasant and sometimes perceptive. (New edition: New York: Belmont, 1962—includes an epilogue.)

RAHV, PHILLIP. "Henry Miller," *Image and Idea.* New York: New Directions, 1957. Written in 1942. An intelligent, though somewhat snidely sophisticated, discussion of the early Miller.

REXROTH, KENNETH. "Introduction," *Nights of Love and Laughter.* New York: New American Library, 1955. An idiosyncratic suggestive introduction to a slight anthology.

SHAPIRO, KARL. "The Greatest Living Author," *In Defense of Ignorance.* New York: Random House, 1960. This essay, which serves as introduction to the American edition of *Tropic of Cancer,* is enthusiastic and amusing, but not critically perceptive.

Index

797266 ✓

813.5
Widmer, Kingsley

Henry Miller

797266

813.5
Widmer, Kingsley

Henry Miller

$3.50

DATE DUE	BORROWER'S NAME	ROOM NUMBER
JUN 3 '85	*Carroll Holland 9ᵗʰ*